JAPAN AND BENGAL

JAPAN AND BENGAL

Exchange and Encounter (1893-1938)

PRATYAY BANERJEE

MANOHAR
2023

First published 2023

This edition is for sale in India, Sri Lanka, Nepal, Bangladesh, Afghanistan, Pakistan and Bhutan.

ISBN 978-93-94262-40-9

Published by
Ajay Kumar Jain *for*
Manohar Publishers & Distributors
4753/23 Ansari Road, Daryaganj
New Delhi 110 002

Typeset by
Kohli Print
Delhi 110 051

Printed at
Replika Press Pvt. Ltd.

To
The memory of my father

Contents

Acknowledgements

I would like to express my sincere gratitude to all the Professors of Comparative Literature, Jadavpur University, for encouraging me and providing me valuable suggestions, without which the completion of this book would not have been possible. At the beginning, my ideas were limited to the scope of writing a book on this topic. This occasion gives me the opportunity to thank my teachers of the department, for giving me an opportunity to write a book on the history of Bengal's cultural and political relation with Japan, in the early twentieth century. Words are inadequate to express my gratitude to Dr. Sayantan Dasgupta, my Supervisor, whose feedbacks and suggestions have been extremely helpful to raise my argument, during the course of writing this book. I remain indebted to Professor Kyoko Niwa, my Co-Supervisor, for her valuable suggestions and guidance in preparing this book. I received valuable documents from Professor Parthasarathi Bhaumik, a set of soft copies of Bangla magazines of the early twentieth century. The documents have been extremely helpful in writing my book. I remain thankful to him. I also remain thankful to Dr. Suchetana Chattopadhyay, Department of History, Jadavpur University, for her valuable suggestions. During the period of my research, I visited the Central Library of Jadavpur University, the West Bengal State Archives and the National Archives, Rabindra Bhavana Archives in Santiniketan and many other institutions. I also remain thankful to the staffs of these institutions for their support. I have received encouragement and support from all my fellow researchers of this department, and also from other departments. I sincerely thank them for assistance to complete my book. I owe my thanks to Anindya Kundu and Bipul Krishna Das, Sarmistha De and many others, for the encouragement I received throughout.

To conclude, the book would not have been finished, had I not received support from my family members. I remain thankful to them too.

Kolkata
30 May 2022

PRATYAY BANERJEE

Introduction

The rise of Japan as a modern Asian nation occupies an important part in the history of Asia of the late nineteenth and the early twentieth century. In 1868, Japan ended her long isolation policy of two centuries; also opened her ports to foreign powers of Europe and America. This historical event is known as the Meiji Restoration. It 'signalled the end of feudalism in Japan'.[1] Within a few decades after the Meiji Restoration of 1868, Japan rose as an important power in Asia; Japanese industrialisation made significant progress and Japan underwent rapid internal transformation, which transformed the nation from a feudal state to a capitalist one.[2] It must be remembered that the Meiji Era that brought a renewal of contact with the rest of the world, also restored Japan's association with Bengal and other parts of the British Empire. Since the middle of the nineteenth century, many educated Indians have paid visits to the Land of the Rising Sun. Further, many of them have penned down their experiences in the form of diaries, memoirs, travelogues, etc. Among those who visited Japan from Bengal in the late nineteenth century, Swami Vivekananda's name deserves mention. Vivekananda's interview published in English newspapers, and his letter written from Yokohama, praise the Japanese people for their industrious nature, patriotism, cleanliness and artistic sensibilities.[3] Among the earliest writings on Japan in Bangla language, mention should be made of Madhusudhan Mukhopadhyay's *Jepan,* a translation of Matthew C. Perry's book, *Narrative of the Expedition of an American Squadron to the Chinese Seas and Japan.* Perry is usually credited for having opened Japan to the western world, following the Kanagawa Treaty. Madhushudhan Mukhopadhyay's book seems to be the earliest attempt in introducing Japan to the Bengali reader. It is true that other than Bengal, many other enterprising persons from different parts of Colonial India took the task of visiting Japan. Many of them have written memoirs, travelogues or essays on Japan. For instance, we can mention the name of M. Visvesvaraya, who visited Japan in 1898.[4] Based on his experiences, he authored two books on Japan. *From his Reconstructing India* and his *Memoirs of My Working Life*, we get fascinating accounts of the development of Japan, which he experienced and felt to be exemplary. I have referred to these texts in my chapters. However, on the whole I have tried to restrict my enquiry to the case of Bengal, so far as reception of Japanese culture and politics is concerned. This book is based on my doctoral thesis and in order to narrow down my research work, I have excluded other materials as texts written on Japan by writers from other provinces.

Sushila Narasimhan in her article entitled 'India and Japan: Historical and Cultural Linkages', also, T.R. Sareen in his article entitled, 'India and Japan in Historical Perspectives', and also Brij Tankha in his book entitled, *Narratives of Asia*, have tried to locate how the emergence of Japan as a modern Asian nation, attracted Indian leaders like Vivekananda, Tagore and Aurobindo Ghosh. Also, their enquiry into this critical subject, have referred to a few texts written by notable Indians, which speak of this interaction between Japan and Bengal, and other parts of British India that took a significant turn by the end of nineteenth century. I owe my indebtedness to these articles for helping me to locate the broad area of my book. Also, these articles helped me to select texts, having a close study with reference to my research area, i.e. influence of Japan on Bengal of the late nineteenth and the early twentieth century. Japan's self-reliance, her success in safe-guarding her territorial integrity, and more particularly, Japan's success in defeating a western nation, namely Russia in the Russo-Japanese War enkindled the nationalist aspiration of the intelligentsia of Bengal. This I have discussed in details in my book.

The history of India's relation with Japan can be traced back to the sixth century AD; the time, when Buddhism got transplanted in Japan from India, through China and Korea. Also, Buddhist art and literature were imported into Japan, either by the monks, who visited at that time, or indirectly. One significant fact of this phase of early reception is the arrival of an Indian Buddhist monk named Bodhisena at Nara, the ancient capital of Japan. From Sushila Narasimhan's article entitled 'India and Japan: Historical and

Cultural Linkages', we come to know that Bodhisena reached Japan in AD 736. He lived there for 24 years. Narasimhan has referred to the *Daianji Bodai Denraiki* (Succession Records of the Todajii Temple) to recount this history of the early contact. Regarding this interaction, no documents are available in India.[5]

In contrast to this earlier transportation of Buddhist religion and culture from India to Japan, the historical event of Meiji Restoration, with which Japan turned into a leading power of Asia, caused a new reception of culture and intellectual ideas from Japan to India. Japan's success to safeguard the sovereignty of her nation, had a galvanizing effect upon the colonised nations of Asia like India. Notable Indians like Vivekananda, Jamshetji Tata and M. Visvesvaraya visited Japan during the late nineteenth century. They were impressed by Japan's progress in different fields like education and industry. In the first Chapter, I have tried to locate a few English articles, which were printed in different nineteenth century magazines like the *Indian Magazine* and the *Calcutta Review*. They give an impressive account of the progress in different fields; chiefly in education, which Japan had secured by the end of nineteenth century. Special mention should be made of 'The Education in Japan', an article written by Constance Plumptre. It was included in the *Indian Magazine* of 1886.

With reference to the above-mentioned observations, I would like to mention an anecdote that is narrated by Sarala Devi Chowdhurani, in her autobiography *Jiboner Jhora Pata*. While recounting the visit of the Japanese painters to the residence of Surendranath Tagore, Sarala Devi has narrated this incident in her autobiography. The author to her surprise found that the Japanese visitors were carrying with themselves apart from useful things, a lot of papers, for writing letters to their relatives in Japan. Being asked, why they have done so, one of the Japanese visitors informed her that they were uncertain whether or not paper would be available in India.

Sarala Devi's reaction to this is worth noting: 'Is it not amazing that for poet Hemchandra, Japan is nothing but an uncivilized country! On the contrary, for these Japanese, British India is such an undeveloped country, that there is not even the hope of finding a piece of paper'.[6]

It must be noted that in Sarala Devi's narrative, and also in many other early twentieth century writings from Bengal, Japan has been represented as an emerging nation of the East. The picture of Japan, as we find in these texts, is far from being a remote space, located in the midst of the Pacific Ocean. In contrast to the very few texts on Japan that can be traced as authored and published from Bengal during the nineteenth century, the beginning of twentieth century, gave rise to an increasing interest in Japan's material achievement, and also in her politics. Almost all issues of *Prabasi, Bharati, Bharatbarsa*, and also English magazines published from Bengal as *The Modern Review*, contain at least one article on Japan. The diversity of the articles is no less interesting. From an account of Japan's achievement in trade and commerce to Japanese politics, from Japanese visual art to Japanese Buddhism, they indeed cover a wide range of subjects. What kindled this vigorous interest in Japan, on the part of the literate sections of Bengal? Needless to say, the change in the political scenario, in both these parts of Asia, was the prime factor behind this renewed interest in Japan.

The early twentieth century, during which, a spirit of resistance against the empire was taking a concrete form in Bengal, and in other parts of British India, also witnessed Japan's rise as an empire and as a world power. Japan was playing an important role to determine the future of many colonised countries of Asia. An important historical event that has been acknowledged by historians, as having exercised a significant impact upon the educated sections of Bengal, and other parts of India, is the success of Japanese army against a European nation, namely Russia, in the Russo-Japanese War (1905). Japan's military success over Russia in the Russo-Japanese War (1905) exploded the myth of western supremacy. Professor Sumit Sarkar in his *Modern India* has rightly observed that the news of Japanese victory 'was ecstatically hailed by the Bengal press'.[7] We find reference of this event in many writings on Japan from this time; these we will refer to afterwards. Also, enterprising men from Bengal, and other provinces were going to Japan to gain technical education. Many of them, after returning, played important roles in the development of Swadeshi enterprises that flourished during the first phase of Swadeshi movement

(1905-20). This is also a major reason why I have emphasized on Bengal's cross-cultural association of Japan of that period.

Another important event of the early twentieth century, which acted as a cementing force in strengthening the bond between Japan and undivided Bengal, is the eminent Japanese art critic, Tenshin Okakura's visit to Kolkata (known as Calcutta before 2001) in 1902. Okakura, accompanied by Miss MacLeod[8] and Shitoku Hori, a young Buddhist scholar, who later became the first foreign student of Tagore's ashram, finally reached the Belur Math in Kolkata on 10 January 1902, as mentioned in Dinkar Kowshik's book *Okakura.* Okakura's visit was followed by that of Taikan Yokoyama and Shunsho Hishida to Kolkata; they met Abanindranath Tagore and Gaganendranath Tagore, and exchanged their views on art with them. There are quite a few memoirs recollecting this phase of exchange. Among these, mention should be made of Rabindranath Tagore's addresses, the autobiographies of Abanindranath Tagore (*Jora Sankor Dhare*) and Rathindranath Tagore (*On the Edges of Time*) and many others. Among travelogues written by Bengali writers of the early twentieth century, Tagore's *Japan Jatri,* first comes to our mind. Stephen Hay in his book *Asian Ideas of East and West,* and also Kyoko Niwa in her doctoral thesis, has taken an exhaustive review of the impacts of Tagore's successive visits to Japan and the response it generated in Japan, and in other parts of the world. The long preparation for the bard's maiden visit to Japan, his travel experiences, as it has been rendered in *Japan Jatri,* the speeches Tagore delivered in Japan, which speak of his anxiety in witnessing Japan's acceptance of the ideology of western nations, and finally, the impact of his message among Japanese intellectuals, all these issues have been dealt in details in their writings. However, there are many other travel writings as well, giving us fascinating glimpses of variegated aspects of Japan of that time. In the early twentieth century, we can name three people, who authored travelogues on Japan, prior to Tagore's first visit to Japan in 1916. They are Hariprobha Takeda, Manmatha Nath Ghosh and Sureshchandra Bandyopadhyay. Manmatha Nath Ghosh went to Japan in 1906 to take industrial training. His exposure to the industrial world of Kobe and Tokyo in Japan, finds a vivid narration in his travelogue *Japan Probash*. It was published in 1910. Ghosh, also authored two other books on Japan, based on his travel experiences. They are entitled *Nabyo Japan* and *Supto Japan*. Both the books were published in the year 1922. Sureshchandra Bandyopadhyay, another traveller, also visited Japan in 1906, and authored a book entitled *Japan*. Sureshchandra Bandyopadhyay's travelogue, with its recounting of various issues, such as the social life of Japanese people of that period, education and politics of Japan, which the travel writer witnessed during his time, is another primary source of studying this cross-cultural reception on the part of Bengali visitors to Japan. Hariprobha Takeda, the first Bengali woman to visit Japan, left for Japan on 3 November 1912, accompanied by her husband, Uemon Takeda. During her stay at the ancestral house of Takeda, located in the countryside of Japan, she got the opportunity to encounter the rural Japanese society; and this experience has been brilliantly narrated in her travelogue entitled *Bongo Mahilar Japan Jatra*. As noted earlier, Bangla magazines of this period like *Prabasi, Bharati, and Bharatbarsa* have printed many travelogues on Japan and essays written on Japan, based on the writer's exposure to Japanese society. As a researcher, I am fascinated to undertake a comparative study of these texts in order to locate certain key aspects of Japanese society. Do we come across a similar kind of image of Japan in these narratives, or do they incorporate dissimilar and even contrasting tropes also? Needless to say, this book will try to enquire into these aspects in the following sections.

During the British period, the presence of Japanese nationals in British India always underwent a careful surveillance on the part of the colonial administration. For instance, even the news of a visit of two Japanese employees of the South Manchurian Railway Company to India, came under the scrutiny of the Intelligence Branch of the British Government.[9] Successive visits to the West Bengal State Archives, and the National Archives in New Delhi, gave me the opportunity to come across many significant documents relevant for my work.

Thus, this book aims at a close study of texts of a myriad nature, such as travelogues, autobiographies, letters, essays and archival sources, which shed light upon the history of cultural and intellectual exchange between Japan and pre-Independent Bengal of the late nineteenth century and the early twentieth century. In order to avoid being amorphous, I have tried to restrict my search to a span of 45 years, viz., from 1893 to 1938. It is a well-known fact that Swami Vivekananda went to Japan in 1893.[10] On 7 July 1937, the Japanese army made a sudden aggression on China.[11] It was Japanese aggression on China in 1937, which led to an epistolary debate between Tagore and Yonejiro Noguchi, a Japanese poet, who had been earlier known as an admirer of Tagore. In the following chapters, we will see how during the 1930s, recurrent news of Japanese aggressive foreign policies created a strong reaction among many Indian leaders. The news of Japanese aggression on China became known to all, as it was making headlines of newspapers published from Bengal. For instance, *The Statesman* of 11 January 1936, published news titled 'Japanese Demands: Stronger Garrison in North China'. In this news, was mentioned that following a conference of the high Japanese officers, a decision was taken to increase garrison in North China, to be prepared to face turbulence caused by Chinese troops in that region.

It must also be remembered that many other important historical events, such as the history of the formation of the Indian National Army (INA), remain outside this time span. We will try to locate some documents dealing with Rash Behari Bose's and Subhash Bose's role in the creation of the INA. However, on the whole, we opt to restrict ourselves to this span (1893-38).

Leaving aside this issue of time span of the book work, the more relevant question that needs asking is what image of cross-cultural interaction, do we come across in the writings that have been mentioned above. Delving deep into these texts, we can attempt to locate certain key motifs, representing the Bengali writer's response to the culture and political scenario of Japan, of the late nineteenth and the early twentieth century. Needless to say, the chapters division is based upon these motifs that I will try to explore in this book.

The first Chapter entitled 'Representation of Japan in the Writings of Bengal', tries to look at the issue of representation, i.e. how impressions of Japanese culture, such as those of social customs, could differ from one traveller to another, according to their ideological positions. The travellers coming from undivided Bengal, which was then a part of the British Empire, have tried to describe Japan according to their world view derived from their experiences of their past; where they differ, needs to be mentioned, and are attractive issues to be noted. It is commonly known that in the texts of the colonial period dealing with the Orient, we find stereotyped representation of the 'Other'. How has Japan been depicted by Bengali writers of this period? Do we come across texts, in which Japan has been represented according to a western perspective?

The rise of Japan as a modern state following the Meiji Restoration of 1868 also marks the rise of Japan as a world power, to determine the fate of many colonised races of Asia.[12] Japan was then keen on exercising her power upon the neighbouring nations.[13] Thus, the ideology of Pan-Asianism, which solicited the clustering of Asian nations under the leadership of Japan, is also closely related to Japanese expansionist policy of that period. Pan-Asianism, the subject of our enquiry, is far from being a single homogenous discourse.

The second Chapter entitled 'Pan-Asianism and Bengal' aims at finding out how Indian writers, chiefly from Bengal of that time, have reacted to this discourse of Pan-Asianism.

The contact between these two cultural zones of Asia, Japan and Bengal of the early twentieth century, initiated a vibrant exchange of aesthetic ideals and cultural practices. We have earlier mentioned Tenshin Okakura's association with the intelligentsia of Bengal of that period. Okakura's visit was followed by the successive visits of Japanese painters, who came to Bengal, and this led to a sustained interaction and exchange among the artists of Bengal and Japan, during the first three decades of the twentieth century. In 1903, two Japanese artists, Taikan Yokohama and Shunshu Hishida, came to Kolkata and spent a considerable time working at Abanindranath Tagore's studio. Also, Shaokin Katsuta, another Japanese painter, visited Kolkata in 1905.[14] This led to a new age of exchange in the arena of visual art in Bengal. It must be remembered that during the time, the Japanese artists were paying visit to Jorasanko in Kolkata, a new movement in Indian art was taking shape under the guidance of Abanindranath Tagore and Gaganendranath Tagore; a movement, in which the artists strove to seek indigenous modes of artistic expressions, rather than showing adherence to European techniques of art. Abanindranath reminiscences in Rani Chanda's *Ghorowa*, how under the spell of the Swadeshi age, the artist sought indigenous expressions of art:

> I was determined to look for indigenous modes of artistic expression. Ravi Verma has also drawn paintings based on Indian mythological subjects. However, he could not free himself from western influence. Thus, Ravi Verma's Sita resembles Venus. I started discarding western portraits and looked for the works of the Bengal pots.[15]

Thus, a close reading of texts, relating to the interaction between painters of Bengal and Japan, can throw light upon certain significant aspects of this exchange in the world of visual art of this period. How the reception of Japanese aesthetics on the part of artists, like the Tagore brothers (Abanindranath and Gaganendranath), and also of their students, led to a new movement in visual art, which strove to make a synthesis of aesthetics, belonging to different cultural zones, is one significant aspect to be noted. How each individual artist has responded to the aesthetics of Japan, according to his individual taste, is another important aspect to be noted.

Painting and sculpture were not only the areas enriched by this cross-cultural experience. Bengal in the first two decades of the twentieth century, also showed receptivity to many other cultural items associated with Japan, such as *Jujutsu* (Japanese martial art), Japanese tea-ceremony and flower-arrangements, etc.[16]

There are quite a few texts that give an account of Tagore 's role in recreating various Japanese cultural activities in Santiniketan.

I have tried to refer to these books in the following chapters. Among them, mention should be made of *Bharatsilpi Nandalal* by Panchanan Mandal, *Makers of a Mission* by Supriya Roy, etc.

It is widely known that Tagore invited educators from all over the world to provide his students an exposure to the new ideas that flourished in various corners of the world. Interestingly, many Japanese teachers and students also visited Santiniketan, during the first few decades of the twentieth century. Their participation in the making of Visva-Bharati, deserves mention in this context. Tagore, a great admirer of traditional Japanese culture, was also an ardent admirer of *Jujutsu*. In 1905, Jinnosuke Sano came to Santiniketan and started teaching the skills of *jujutsu* to the students of the ashram.[17] Also, Makiko Hoshi, the sister-in-law of Rash Behari Bose, came to Santiniketan and started teaching Japanese flower-arrangement and the art of tea-ceremony to the students. From Nandalal Bose's recollection, narrated by Panchanan Mandal, we come across a lively recounting of organizing the Japanese tea-ceremonies in Santiniketan. From Nandalal Bose's recollection, and also from that of Amita Sen, we learn about Kintaro Kasahara, and his art of carpentry and horticulture. We must remember that Tagore's receptivity to Japanese culture did not lead to the encouragement of all cultural practices associated with Japan. Only certain cultural practices of Japan attracted him. Tagore took the pain to transplant these cultural practices in his school, under the guidance of Japanese experts. Do we not notice a synthesis of cultures, belonging to different cultural zones of Asia, as far as Tagore's endeavour to transplant these practices in Santiniketan is concerned? This section of the third Chapter aims at exploring such critical issues.

We have earlier referred to Madhusudhan Mukhopadhyay's *Jepan*, a translation of Matthew C. Perry's book, *Narrative of the Expedition of an American Squadron to the Chinese Seas and Japan.* Apart from this particular text, some other translations of Japanese writings, belonging to this period, can also be traced. These include Priyambada Devi's translation of Okakura's English work *The Book of Tea*, Hemlata Devi's translation of Ekai Kawaguchi's travelogue *Three Years in Tibet*, which was serially published in the Bengali magazine *Prabasi*, under the title 'Tibbot Rajye Tinbochor', and also Tagore's translation of *Haiku*, a Japanese poetic genre of three lines, consisting of 5-7-5 syllabic pattern. What critical approaches of translation do we notice in these works? Have the target language texts been regarded as a specimen of 'higher culture', to which the translators have tried to remain faithful? Or, can we trace a liberty on the part of the translator, in dealing with subject of his translation?

The renewal of contact between Bengal and Japan from the late nineteenth century also caused a series of visits of Japanese Buddhist scholars to India, in search of studying Buddhism. Buddhism is one of the most important cultural threads, which integrates India with China and Japan. Though initiated by Japanese scholars like Ekai Kawaguchi or Ryukan Kimura, their interest in Buddhist studies, received encouragement from the educated sections of Bengal. Thus, this rekindling of interest in Buddhism should also be acknowledged as a result of this interaction between Bengal and Japan of this period, and this too, deserves addressing in this book.

In short, a study of these texts can help us to trace Bengal's response to the culture of Japan that is full of diversity, depending upon individual receptor's choice, taste and ideological position.

With the exception of a few translated texts, all other translations from Bangla to English have been prepared by the author. In case of those texts for which English translations are available, the English translations done by some other writers, have been cited with due care and respect.

NOTES

1. Amit Bhattacharya, *Transformation of Japan 1600-1945* (Kolkata: Setu Prakashani, 2009), p. 116.
2. Ibid., pp. 109-15.
3. Swami Vivekananda 'Conversations and Dialogues', in *Epistles, Complete Works*, 4th edn. vol. 5 (Kolkata: Advaita Ashrama, 1936), pp. 244-322.
4. Rajaram Panda and Yoo Fukazawa, *India and Japan: In Search of Global Roles* (New Delhi: Promilla & Co., 2007), p. 346.
5. Ibid., p. 331.
6. Sarala Devi, *Jiboner Jhora Pata* (Kolkata: Deys Publishers, 1975), p. 318.
7. Sumit Sarkar, *Modern India 1885-1947* (New Delhi: Macmillan India, 1983), p. 109.
8. Dinkar Kowshik, *Okakura* (Kolkata: Patralekha, 2011), pp. 56-8.
9. Govt. of West Bengal, I.B. Records of the State Archives, *Visit of Two Japanese*

Employees of the South Manchurian Railway Company to India,. F.N. 137/ 1923.

10. Swami Vivekananda, 'Letter from Yokohama', *Epistles, Complete Works*, pp. 3-9.
11. Bhattacharya, *Transformation of Japan*, p. 200.
12. Marlene. J. Mayo, 'Introduction', *The Emergence of Imperial Japan* (Massachusetts: D.C. Health and Co., 1970), pp. vii-xiv.
13. Bhattacharya, *Transformation of Japan*, pp. 146-76.
14. Panchanan Mandal, *Bharatsilpi Nandalal* (Santiniketan: Rar-Gabeshona Parshod, 1982), vol. 1, p. 137.
15. Rani Chanda, *Ghorowa* (Kolkata: Visva-Bharati, 2007), p. 32.
16. There are quite a few texts that give an account of Tagore's role in recreating various Japanese cultural activities in Santiniketan. I have tried to refer to these books in the following chapters. Among them, mentioned should be made of *Bharatsilpi Nandalal* by Panchanan Mandal, *Makers of a Mission* by Supriya Roy etc.
17. Kazuo Azuma, *Japan O Rabindranath: Satoborsher Binimoy* (Kolkata: N.E Publishers, 2004), p. 130.

CHAPTER 1

Representation of Japan in the Writings of Bengal

James Clifford, the editor of the book *Writing Culture: The Poetics and Politics of Ethnography*, has viewed ethnography as 'situated between powerful systems of meaning'. According to the writer, ethnography as subject, is intrinsically related to issues such as civilization, culture, class, race and gender.[1] With reference to Clifford's observation on culture as essentially a political subject that makes an inclusion of 'contested codes and representations', it would be worth paying attention to the different writings on Japanese life and culture that were penned by people, who visited Japan during the late nineteenth and the early twentieth century. In the introductory Chapter, I have already referred to different narratives on Japan, as sources to study this cross-cultural exchange between Japan and Bengal during the colonial period.

Japan, which remained isolated from the rest of the world for two centuries, underwent rapid modernization according to the western standard, during the late nineteenth and the early twentieth century.[2] The emergence of Japan as a powerful Asian nation attracted the Bengali intelligentsia of the early twentieth century, as it attracted people of other parts of the globe during that time. In the Introduction, I have referred to Madhusudhan Mukhopadhyay's *Jepan*, which seems to be one of the earliest writings on Japan in Bangla language. Mukhopadhyay's *Jepan*, which is a translation of a renowned travelogue of Matthew C. Perry, seems to be a depiction of Japanese life and society, according to the perspective of the West. The later part of this chapter, will have a detailed study of this text. If in Mukhopadhyay's *Jepan*, we find an acceptance of the hegemony of the West in representing Japan, we can also locate some essays published at the end of the nineteenth century, where we find a shift of paradigm in viewing Japan. This chapter, will try to refer to some English essays that were published in English magazines from Bengal during the later part of nineteenth century. These writings no longer view Japan as an inferior Asian race. Rather, they talk of the emergence of a new Japan, a cultural space, subjected to the process of a fast socio-political transformation. One of the early travellers, Manmatha Nath Ghosh, who visited Japan during the first decade of twentieth century, authored a text titled, *Nabyo Japan*, that was first published in the year 1915. The title of his text, which translates as 'the New Japan', can be taken as a key motif, which we can locate in the texts, dealing with these cross-cultural exchanges between Japan and Bengal of this period. This chapter, will refer to texts such as travelogues, essays published both in vernacular and in English magazines of the late nineteenth century and the early twentieth century. A detailed study reveals the acceptance of Japan as the leader of the East, and also how advancement achieved in different aspects in Japan, served as a contrast to that of the colonial Bengal of that period.

Travel writers, who visited Japan during the early twentieth century, have tried to negotiate with different cultural practices of Japan in accordance with their 'structure of feeling',[3] i.e. their world view, based on their lived experience of their past. The difference that we notice in interpreting and representing different cultural issues of Japan of that time is no less an attractive subject. Thus, it would be wrong to suppose that travelogues on Japan of this period represent a similar kind of image of Japanese life and society. Rather, people who visited Japan during this phase came from different backgrounds and class positions. This difference in perceiving and representing the same object, on the part of the traveller, can be traced even before they landed on the shore of Japanese islands. The long sea voyage to Japan depicted in the travelogues, bear instances to hammer home this point. The ship that sailed to Japan on the route had to pass by the Andaman Islands, which at that time, was chiefly used as a place of deportation, by the British government. Rash Behari Bose's *Atmokatha*, the only Bengali writing of Bose, which was published in a vernacular magazine named *Probortok*, and later on suppressed by the British government, contains a description of seeing the light of the Andaman Islands from the captain's room at night. Bose in an emotional manner, has described his comradely feeling for those, who were imprisoned there, a fate, which he himself narrowly escaped: 'There was seen a light afar. The captain said, 'That's the Andamans'. I startled after hearing these words; and thought of many patriots was rotting there, for their service to their nation. Gariboldi and Washington had performed the similar task for their countries'.[4]

The same sight of the light, coming from the top of the island, perhaps from the Cellular Jail, was seen from the ship by another traveller, Sureshchandra Bandyopadhyay, who reached Japan in 1906. Later, he authored a book entitled *Japan*. However, we note how differently the same incident has been presented. In Sureshchandra's narration, the writer's attitude to those hapless prisoners is more of pity than anything else:

> On the fourth day of our journey, around 9.30 in the morning, we could spot the Andaman islands. Further, another two hours journey led the ship very close to the island. I saw trees and hills of that island. However, despite many atttempts, I was not able to spot a single person on that island. The place seems to be heavy with the sighs of many hapless souls; men, who might have taken a drastic act in their lives, and now are marooned in this island, far away from their dear ones.[5]

The travellers having different ideological positions have generated different responses towards Japanese life and culture, which they encountered during the time of their visit. Their background, their lived experiences in different part of India, as well as their exposure to Japanese society and culture, differ from each other. How representation of Japan varies from one text to another is an important aspect to be studied. For instance, in the following sections, we will try to locate how travel writers' accounts of indigenous Japanese culture vary from one another. The travellers coming from undivided Bengal, which was then a part of the British Empire, have represented Japan according to their 'structure of feeling'; where they differ, needs mention. It is commonly known that in the texts of the colonial period dealing with the Orient, we find stereotyped representation of the 'Other'. How has Japan been depicted by Bengali writers of this period? Do we notice anywhere an unconscious yielding to the ideology of the Empire in representing Japanese culture? Needless to say, these are the questions, we need to address in this section of the book. To begin with, I would deal with the different themes, which recurrently appear in the texts on Japan, during a particular period of time, i.e. 1893-1938.

WRITING THE SELF IN THE LIGHT OF THE 'OTHER'

The travel writer, notes Casey Blanton[6], engages himself in the act of 'mediating between things foreign and things familiar' and helps us to 'understand that world which is other to us'.[7]

In the three travel writings mentioned above, and also in other travelogues on Japan, one recurrent motif that we come across is how cultural exposure to another land acts as a tool to redefine and reassess our homeland and the socio-cultural phenomena, which are an intrinsic part of our homeland. Wherever the traveller goes, or whatever he views or experiences, the idea of 'home' is never absent in his mind. What we come across is testing and assessing one's own culture, religion, society, and political system, in the light of the new experiences gathered in a distant land. It must be noted that the travellers who reached Japan during this period, were certainly not of a homogeneous type; their tenure of stay, as well as their exposure to Japanese life and culture, varied from each other. For instance, Manmatha Nath Ghosh, the author of the text *Japan Probash*, went to Japan and during his stay acquired industrial training. His voyage began on 1 April 1906. In Japan he first arrived in Tokyo; from there, he went to Kobe and Osaka. There, the writer took industrial training in celluloid and in button making; Ghosh's text includes a plethora of Japanese vocabulary, even common conversational Japanese expressions, which is a unique feature of the book. While working as an apprentice at a button-making factory in Kobe, he participated in the funeral of his employer's daughter. The poise, with which the employer and his wife faced their daughter's death, reminded him how Indians become restless and scream on the occasion of their loved one's demise. Ghosh's observation is worth remembering: 'When someone dies in our country, relatives start crying loudly. Some say that this helps in purging off the excessive emotion. There may be a grain of truth in it. However, it must be acknowledged that such practices are crude and unsophisticated.'[8]

In the above-mentioned passage, we get a constant reference to India, which comes to the mind of the writer. The narrator's own past, his lived experiences in his homeland serve as a yardstick, against which all experiences regarding the 'other' are to be judged. In all the other travelogues on Japan, as well as in other writings, containing ingredients of travel writings, this trope of assimilating alterity with familiar terms, can be traced. The texts however, differ in form as letters written by Mukul Dey from Japan, or prose writings as M. Visvesvaraya's book *Reconstructing India.* The diversity in form, within the genre of travelogue, is no less an attractive issue.

Japan, which remained cut-off from the rest of the world, underwent rapid modernization in the late nineteenth century and the early twentieth century. Following the end of the Tokugawa Period in 1867 and the beginning of a new era, known as the Meiji Period, the new government took rapid reforms to bridge the country's difference with the West. These included administrative reforms, educational reforms after the French and German education system, rapid armament, in order to meet the challenge of western aggression and many others. From Kenneth Scott Latourette's book entitled *The History of Japan*, and also from similar books on Japanese history, we come to know how Japan underwent a phase of drastic internal reform following the historical event of Meiji Restoration. For instance, Kenneth Scott Latourette has referred to the reorganization of the Japanese currency that took place during this period. Further, a commissioner from Japan was sent to the United States to study its finances. Kenneth Scott has also mentioned that the decimal system was introduced in Japan, during this period. Other financial measures introduced in Japan, as mentioned in Kenneth Scott's book, include the introduction of a new coinage, the planning of national banks and the adoption of paper currency.[9]

With reference to this historian's account of internal transformation that followed after the Meiji Restoration of 1868, it would be worth paying attention to some of the essays on Japan that were published in different vernacular magazines of Bengal, of the early twentieth century. Interestingly, the accounts of transformation of Japan, as we come across in these essays, correspond with that of historians like Kenneth Scott and others. A particular essay that needs citing in this context is *Japan*, by Girindrachandra Mukhopadhyay, an article that was published in successive serials in the Bangla magazine *Bharatbarsa.* The essayist too has given a detailed account of how during this period, enterprising Japanese students started visiting the West, and brought back the gifts of the new world, which eventually developed and empowered Japan of their time. Following is a passage from *Japan* by Girindrachandra Mukhopadhyay that was published in *Bharatbarsa* (1937):

> Taka Hama, an affluent Japanese young man, went to Japan and started working in ship building factories as an ordinary labourer. Japanese young men excelled in mastering the technology of manufacturing firearms in no time. Thus, Major Salluci succeeded in manufacturing a modern rifle and marvelled the Europeans.[10]

It has earlier been mentioned that the exposure to the development of Japan on the part of the Bengali intelligentsia of that time, was always a sad reminder of the lack of progress in Bengal, and in other parts of British India of their time. Girindrachandra Mukhopadhyay has also lamented that many Bengali youths of their time, visited England, however, their first-hand experience of a developed society, left almost no contribution to the Indian society: 'Many educated Indians have also visited European countries. Even now, learned youths go to European countries for further study. However, their knowledge has left no contribution for the betterment of their countrymen.'[11]

Thus, a close study of travelogues written by Bengali writers visiting Japan, during the early twentieth century, and also of articles published in different magazines, reveal certain important aspects. First, we come across a picture of the development of a society, which is systematic, disciplined, and more like the West. In all the three travelogues mentioned above, we come across the depiction of a society, in which the administration is extremely cooperative, and is far removed from that of colonial India. On every crossing of the city, notes Manmatha Nath Ghosh in his travelogue *Japan Probash,* there stands traffic assistance booth, it is gifted with a map of the vicinity, and an armed police officer stands in charge of the station; it provides immense help to foreigners. The writer, while recollecting how he received assistance there has made a remark, worth noting here: 'The Japanese police officer accompanied me for almost half-a-mile. I could not but compare their behaviors, with those of our Indian policemen. I felt that the administration of Japan was yet to be introduced in India.'[12]

The friendly and cooperative role of the police system of Japan, which is in sharp contrast to the repressive police system that existed in British India, has also been pointed out in other writings on Japan. In an essay entitled 'Japaner Rajniti', written by Sri Jadunath Sarkar and published in the Bangla magazine *Bharati* (1313 BS), we find a similar image of Japanese police system that the travel writer witnessed during the period he had stayed. For both the writers, the humane face of the police system, they witnessed in Japan, was sharply in contrast to the colonial police administration that existed in British India, which was more a system of repression than an institution, serving the people:

> Japan has never wasted money in setting up Police Commissions. Instead, they have compared the police administration of Japan with those of other countries. After accomplishing this, they have come to the conclusion that their own system is the best. In India, the colonial police system evokes terror in the mind of our countrymen. It is believed that the police system has been introduced in the colonial administration as an instrument of exploitation.[13]

Sureshchandra Bandhyopadhyay, another traveller, reached Nagasaki on 1 January 1906. The first thing that drew his attention on his maiden visit to Japan's capital Tokyo, was the complete absence of destitutes on streets. A passage from his travelogue *Japan* may be referred to in this context: 'Barefooted destitutes, wearing tattered clothes can hardly be spotted in Japan. Begging in Japan is considered to be ignominious.'[14]

The above-mentioned passage from Sureshchandra's travelogue clearly shows how the writer's memory of destitues in his homeland, was in contrast to his travel experiences in Japan. The trope of the 'hard working Japanese', we come across in this passage, can also be located in several other travelogues on Japan, of the same period.

In other writings as well, we notice such frequent references to the condition of Bengal and other parts of India, under the colonial rule, which serves as a contrast to the travellers' experiences in Japan. These, we will note in the later part of this chapter, with reference to the travellers' depiction of the Japanese society, which achieved remarkable progress in fields such as trade and commerce, education and industry and in others, during the late nineteenth and the early twentieth century.

NARRATIVES OF THE MAKING OF MODERN JAPAN

The year 1868 has been regarded by historians as a landmark in the history of modern Japan. It was in this year that Japan underwent a drastic change that ended the Shogunate regime, which had been continuing for the previous two centuries. The emperor took the control of the state. The new era, named after the emperor, is known as the Meiji Period. This historical event, also known as the Meiji Restoration, restored Japan's relation with the rest of the world, as Japan had been cut-off from all contact with Europe, and other parts of the globe since the Edo period (seventeenth century).

The outcome of this historical incident was that it led to the establishment of a highly centralized government; feudalism in Japan came to an end, and rapid administrative and social changes took place to ensure capitalist development. This transformation of a society from a feudal to a capitalist one was achieved within a period of about 50 years. For instance, the new government ordered all feudal lords to hand over their landed properties to the emperor. Thus, a kind of a restructuring of Japanese society had been done by the 1870s. Japan, which had faced the danger of foreign aggression, established a powerful army and navy to meet this challenge. Educational development, progress in agriculture, industry and trade, took place very rapidly from the time of Meiji Restoration in 1868. Thus, the whole world witnessed the emergence of a new Japan by the end of the nineteenth century. Dr. Amit Bhattacharya in his book *Transformation of Japan 1600-1945*, has referred to another Japanese scholar, Kamekichi Takahashi, and has rightly pointed out that though in Europe, the abolition of feudalism took almost 200 years, in case of Japan, it had been 'accomplished in 8 or 9 years only after the MR'.[15]

This astounding success of Japan drew the attention of the world, and it is no wonder that by the end of the nineteenth century, news and reviews of Japan reached the reading public of Bengal in printed form. We have earlier referred to the translation of Matthew Perry's travelogue by Madhusudhan Mukhopadhyay. It was published in the year 1863. Mukhopadhyay's text *Jepan* seems to be the first Bangla writing dealing with the life of Japan and her people. The book recounts many adventures of the western navigators to this island, and finally how Commodore Perry became successful in compelling the Japanese emperor to negotiate with the West. Needless to say, the rendition is from the western point of view and contains even frightful description of atrocities meted out to shipwrecked American sailors: 'Sixteen American mariners were sailing eastward in a vessel. Their ship met with a violent storm and they finally landed on a Japanese shore. They were imprisoned by the Japanese and underwent tortures. They were threatened to be executed, if they refused to kick the Holy Cross.'[16]

Such descriptions of hostile attitude of Japanese towards foreigners abound in the text. It is interesting to note how western dress and manner play an important part in imposing the domination over Japanese people, as mentioned in the book. Thus, as narrated in this translated text, we also come across a description of how American sailors putting on impressive attire, and the soldiers with their aggressive attitude, scared the Japanese ruler. With reference to the representation of Japanese people as barbaric and uncivilized, as we find in this translated travelogue on Japan, it would be worth paying attention to Susan Bassnett's study of travel writing as intrinsically related to the colonial discourse. Thus, Bassnett has rightly pointed out that 'travel writing relies heavily on stereotypes'.[17] Stereotypes occur in representing the 'Other' and Basnett in her essay entitled, 'The Empire Travel Writing and British Studies', has justly pointed out how in the travel writings of the colonial period, frequent stereotyped representation of the 'Other', on the part of Insider, can be traced. Similarly, in Madhusudhan Mukhopadhyay's translated travelogue entitled *Jepan,* we can notice recurrent stereotyping of the indigenous customs and cultures of the Japanese people. Thus, Sumo wrestling, which Commodore Perry and his men saw in Japan, has been depicted in the translated travelogue as a barbaric practice: 'After having seen the barbaric wrestling match (Sumo), the Americans went to examine the achievements of the Japanese people in setting up railway and telegraph system.'[18]

It is surprising that the existence of different forms of physical cuture in Bengal, and also in other parts of India, must not have been unknown to the translator. Yet, in this translated book, Japanese Sumo wrestling has been represented according to western perception.

The translated text narrates how after repeated persuasion, the Japanese government agreed to open Hokkaido for the American. The book describes how the treaty was celebrated on the Japanese fleet. Feasting on the deck was organized by Commodore Perry. Finally, a treaty written in four languages was signed on 17 September 1855, by both the parties.[19]

Mukhopadhyay's *Jepan,* a translated text, remains true to the original text; thus the representation we find of Japan in this text is from the point of view of the West. It is nothing but viewing Japan according to the perspective of the West. The translator could have inserted his own view point by using footnotes in the text, which he did not. Still the book is pioneering in introducing the Bangla reader to the life of Japan. Only at the end of this text, it has mentioned the fact that Japan had made considerable progress since the time of Commodore Perry.

Another attractive article on Japan, which was published in the *Calcutta Review* (no. 95-6, 1869) is entitled 'The East India Company in Japan'. 'Japan was a sealed country until the expedition of the United States Navy in 1854', begins the anonymous writer, and the writer in this essay, has described in details the history of successive voyages to the islands of Japan, and also how Japan gradually opened herself to the West. The process of western contact following Perry's visit to Japan, and the treaty that took place between the Japanese authority and Americans, have been described in details. However, this initial treaty provided the Americans no more than obtaining shelter for vessels in distress, and hospitable reception of ship wrecked mariners. We also learn that in the same year, Admiral Sterling 'obtained the same meager terms for the British'.[20] It is fascinating to note that in this article, Japan has been depicted as a territory full of possibilities, which the European and American navigators need to explore as a means of incorporating it within the map of the empire. In comparison to these earlier writings on Japan, a few more writings, which were published in the *Indian Magazine*, may be referred to as providing a balanced presentation of Japan.[21] These are 'Progress in Japan', an article published in the *Indian Magazine* (1886), and another text, entitled 'The Education in Japan' (1886), authored by the same writer, i.e. Constance Plumptere, as mentioned in the texts. The writer, like many of his contemporaries, goes on pondering over the idea of a binary opposition between the civilized West and the untutored East. Thus, the writer differentiates between Japan and other Asian and Eurasian communities, and he comes to the conclusion that in terms of 'cleanliness' and 'education', the Japanese civilization surpasses those of Irish or Russian agrarian communities. However, the significance of these texts lies in providing an account of the progress Japan achieved in the nineteenth century. The chief developments that had been ensured by the Japanese authority, as mentioned by the writer, are judicial reformation relating to the severe laws of criminal punishment, the introduction of cheap postage, improvements relating to money system in accordance with the European standard, such as the establishment of a mint, and also the introduction of paper notes. The other article entitled 'Progress in Japan', has described in details the measures taken by the Japanese government to ensure educational development. We must remember that without these measures, Japan's emergence as an important nation could not have been possible. The main achievements in the field of education in the nineteenth century Japan, as mentioned by the author, are in short, the establishment of the educational department in Japan, which brought into control the education of all the prefectures (Ken) in Japan, the introduction of Roman script (Roma ji) for the purpose of learning, bringing out good text with proper care, establishment of libraries and educational museums, providing opportunity to Japanese learners to study in western academics, etc.[22]

An Indian who visited Japan in the nineteenth century is Sampatro Gaikawad. The year of publication of his travelogue on Japan in the *Indian Magazine* is August 1894. Probably, he had visited Japan prior to Swami Vivekananda's short stay in Yokohama, on his voyage to Chicago in 1893. The travelogue titled, 'A Glimpse of Japan', does not mention any year of visiting Japan; however, it is evident that the writer must have reached there not many decades after the Meiji Restoration. This is evident as we have been told by the writer that foreigners were not allowed to go beyond the limit of 25 miles from one 'Treaty port without a passport granted by the Japanese government'.[23] Japan maintained an isolation policy for centuries. The isolation policy came to an end in 1867. However, foreigners were not permitted to get down at any port. This shows a double attitude towards acceptance of foreign elements. Following the Meiji Restoration, western influence began increasing in Japanese society. Still, there was another opposite point of view that emphasized on maintaining their national culture. In Japanese vocabulary there exists a word—'gaishokujin', meaning foreigner. There exists a script named 'katakana' that is solely used to write borrowed words. Thus, the restriction on foreigners in travelling to Japan, as we learn from Sampatro Gaikawad's travelogue, is in harmony with the process through which Japan was initiating a dialogue with the rest of the world.

This travelogue also gives us a picture of Japan of a by-gone era. We find descriptions of men and women travelling in 'Jin-rickshaw', descriptions of kimonos worn by men and women, the writer's first experience of having a bath in a traditional Japanese bath and many such fascinating accounts.

Swami Vivekananda, on his way to the 'World Congress of Religion' in 1893, came to Yokohama in Japan and stayed a few days. His letter written from Yokohama, dated, 10 July 1893, as well as his interview given to the correspondent of *The Hindu*, dated, February 1897, bring out his admiration for the Japanese people. Among Indians, Vivekananda was a pioneer in urging young Indians to visit Japan and to learn the success they had accomplished during the Meiji Period. A portion of his letter written from Yokohama, which is included in the 5th part of his *Collected Works*, may be referred to with reference to his appreciation of the progress he witnessed in Japan:

> The Japanese seem now to have fully awakened themselves to the necessity of the present times. They have now a thoroughly organized army equipped with guns which one of their own officers has invented and which is said to be second to none. Then, they are continually increasing their navy. I have seen a tunnel nearly a mile long, bored by a Japanese engineer.[24]

From the letter, we further learn that he had the opportunity to visit matchbox factories, which he found to be worth visiting. The letter also mentions his visit to Japanese temples where to his astonishment, he found old Sanskrit mantras being carved in old Bengali scripts. Vivekananda wanted that young Indians should visit Japan and see the development the Japanese people had achieved by that time. The other text that records Vivekananda's reflections on Japan, is an interview given to the correspondent of *The Hindu*. 'The world has never seen such a patriotic and artistic race as the Japanese', observed Vivekananda, while giving reply to the correspondent's questions. Almost all writings on Japan during this phase have tried to address the one question—'What is the key to Japan's sudden greatness?', to this question asked by the correspondent of *Hindu*, Vivekananda's reply was that it was simply the faith of the Japanese in themselves, and their love for their country.[25]

Vivekananda has greatly praised the Japanese people for their patriotism. In this context, it must be said that though in case of Japan, the development process almost overlaps with a rise of militant nationalism, and the Sino-Japanese War (1894-5) took place just a year after Vivekananda, visited Japan, still at that time, the cause of this nationalism was yet to be visible. In later writings on Japan by others in twentieth century, we will notice how this reaction against Japan's militarism has been reflected in Indian writings. In the following chapters, referring to the writings of Tagore, and also to articles published in different magazines, we will try to locate how the advent of militarism in Japan did not escape the notice of the intelligentsia of Bengal and caused a sharp reaction against it.

Among Vivekananda's contemporaries, J.R.D. Tata, who was his fellow passenger in their voyage from Japan to the West Coast of America,[26] was also extremely influenced by the instance of Japan. He came to Japan with the intention of meeting Shibusawa Eiichi (1838-1931), the highest official of the Shipping Company, Nippon Yusen Kaisha. His objective was to start a shipping business with the help of the Japanese.[27] From the biographical details provided by R.M. Lala in his book *For the Love of India,* the biography of Jamsetji Tata, we come to know that in Japan, both Vivekananda and Tata stayed in the same hotel, in an overlapping period and finally boarded the same ship. On board, they indulged in exchanging their ideas and it is said that Vivekananda suggested to Tata that he should manufacture matchboxes in India, which at that time were being imported from Japan. The fact that the meeting had an impact upon Jamsetji, is evident from the letter he wrote to Vivekananda informing him of his decision to open a research institute for India. This letter, which Tata wrote to Vivekananda on 23 November 1898, has also been included in the biography. It has been learnt that Vivekananda did receive another invitation to visit Japan, an invitation which came from Tenshin Okakura to which his response was at first positive; however, he failed to keep this promise owing to his ill health. From Yasuko

Horioka's essay entitled 'Okakura and Swami Vivekananda',[28] published in the journal *Prabuddha Bharata* (January 1975), and also from the letter of Vivekananda to Miss MacLeod, dated 18 June 1901, referred to by Horioka in the same essay, we learn that he accepted a cheque from Okakura and his invitation. However, he finally withdrew from his decision due to his ill health. His letter to Mary Hale dated 5 July 1901, speaks of his change of plan due to his ill health. This letter has also been included in the journal *Probuddha Bharata*[29]; and this letter also brings out his love and admiration for Japan.

In the introduction to this chapter, we have discussed how the beginning of the twentieth century, with its change in the political scenario in Bengal, as well as in Japan, fostered a feeling of solidarity among Asians. Needless to say, it had its impact upon the reading public in Bengal. We have earlier noted that the different magazines published from Bengal in Bangla, and in English, such as *Prabasi, Bharati, Bharatbarsa* and *The Modern Review*, have printed many appealing travelogues and essays on Japan. In these articles, we come across the history of the making of Modern Japan. In the magazine *Bharati,* quite a few erudite articles have been printed on Japan, the author's name as mentioned, is Sri Jadunath Sarkar. It is evident from the essays that the writer stayed in Japan for a period of time. The essays also give an account of his travel within Japan that he undertook during his stay. Further, we also get to know that he learnt Japanese language while staying there. This person should not be confused with the eminent historian, Sir Jadunath Sarkar, as we learn from the biographers of Sir Jadunath Sarkar that the latter never went out of India.[30] Leaving aside this confusion about the identity of the author, it must be said that the essays on Japan give us a comprehensive idea about the making of new Japan, its different aspects, like administrative changes to ensure development, reconstruction of the Japanese army and navy in accordance with the European standard, development in trade and commerce, and finally, educational development in Japan, and opportunities, which Indians could avail from Japan at that time. In an article entitled, 'Japaner Sikha O Banijyo' (*Bharati*, Joistho, 1321 BS), Sri Jadunath Sarkar has dealt in details how Japan managed to achieve an immense progress in industry in a relatively shorter span of time than many countries. Referring to an exhibition that was hosted in Chicago in 1803, Sarkar has pointed out that at that time, Japanese products such as cotton and silk garments, pottery and handicrafts of bamboo, and of cane, could only be displayed. Whereas, by 1854, Americans found that Japan's industrial growth was so much that the market of United States were flodded with Japanese products. How could they master such development? Sarkar has come forward with the answer—for him the Japanese have proved themselves to be diligent and industrious in learning new skills from the West; very few people could be found idle in Japan. A portion from this text ('Japaner Sikha O Banijyo') may be cited with reference to this topic:

> Judiciously considering the achievements of European countries in trade and industry, Japan has introduced those industrial items, which could be produced at a lower cost. This has enabled the Japanese people to compete with the rest of the world in trade and commerce . . . People, who are not engaged in any work, can hardly be spotted in Japan.[31]

The above-mentioned passage from 'Japaner Sikha O Banijyo' reminds us of Sureshchandra Bandyopadhyay's *Japan*, and its account of the absence of destitutes on the streets of Japan he visited. Bandyopadhyay has also emphatically pointed out that in Japan, during the time he visited, begging was considered to be ignominious.[32] In many other travelogues, this trope of the 'industrious japanese' can also be located.

Sri Jadunath Sarkar has observed that the Japanese government provided loans to entrepreneurs. This testifies to the fact that the Japanese government took the responsibility of boosting industrial growth in Japan. The same idea has also been cited by another traveller, M. Visvesvaraya, whose experiences in Japan have been described in his book *Reconstructing India.* M. Visvesvaraya reached Japan in March 1898.[33] He stayed there for three months, his exposure to the development process in Japan, which he witnessed there, has been noted in his books *Memoirs of my Working Life* and *Reconstructing India.* His reviews on Japan also deserve mention for the richness of their contents.

According to Visvesvaraya, Japan could offer India the most 'valuable lessons in material advancement and reconstruction'.[34] The writer refers to the case of Japan, where a direct relation exists between the Government and industry. He has referred to the instance of the shipping industry in Japan which obtained direct assistance from the government as subsidies. In the essay 'Japaner Sikha O Banijyo', Sarkar has given a long account of technological development that followed since the late nineteenth century. These include the development of railway, which was first introduced in 1872 from Tokyo to Yokohama, also, Japan's success in shipping industry and also increase in foreign export.[35] According to the writer, for Indian students aiming to obtain industrial training, Japan was the best place. As noted earlier, the writer's exposure to industrial growth in Japan is always a reminder of the lack of it in his motherland. The writer has emphatically pointed out how gloomy was the scenario of industrial development during that time in British India. This gloomy condition of indusrial development in British India, the author has emphasized, was sharply in contrast to the development in industry and in trade that Japan had secured by that time:

> In Bengal, and in other parts of British India, traditional cottage industries that existed at different places, have now come to an extinct. Now, we can only mention certain sweetmeat producing areas as Bardwan for *Sitabhog,* Bagbazar for *Rasgollas,* Bhimnag for *Sandesh,* Joyhori for *Kulpi*, Fatullah for *Chira* and Bikrampur for curd.[36]

With reference to this account of industrial expansion, it must be noted that by the end of First World War, Japan succeeded in capturing a great part of the Indian market, a fact we have mentioned earlier. An important document that can be cited is a secret report that was sent to the Secretary of State for India (name not found). Later, this document was included in the Home Political section of State Archives, West Bengal. The report states that Japan succeeded in seizing the opportunity offered by the war and by referring to statistics, the report points out that both import and export between Japan and British India, actually multiplied during the period of war. Not only that, the number of Japanese vessels entering the Indian ports increased in the period 1918-19.[37] Further, many Japanese merchants established branches in India to handle their business. This sudden expansion of Japanese trade in British India has been looked upon as 'a menace to Indian and British production'.[38]

Japan faced the menace of western aggression when Commodore Perry with his fleet of ships, reached Japan in 1853. The period following the Meiji Restoration (1868) in Japan, witnessed drastic steps on the part of the Japanese government to reconstruct her army and navy in accordance with the western standard. Among essays dealing with this history mention should be made of 'Japaner Sena O NauBahini' by Jadunath Sarkar, an article, published in *Bharati* (Falgun, 1318 BS), and *Japan,* a travelogue written by Girindrachandra Mukhopadhyay, published in the magazine *Bharatbarsa* (Ashin, 1344 BS). One important measure was to send young Japanese learners to foreign countries to master their technology. Thus, from Mukhopadhyay's essay 'Japan', we learn that the treaty that followed between the Americans and the Japanese government, allowed Japan to buy arms from America, but instead of remaining content with that, Japanese young men went to European countries, and there, they worked as labourers in factories in order to master technology. By the year 1880, Japan became successful in manufacturing rifles in their country.[39] According to Mukhopadhyay, the self-sacrificing nature of Japanese people and their devotion to their motherland could ensure such success. So, we come to know how both in the naval industry and in rapid armament, Japan achieved astonishing progress. From 'Japaner Sena O NauBahini', an article we have earlier referred to, we learn that apart from technological borrowings, the whole army in the post-Meiji era was reconstructed according to western standard: 'In 1884, Marshal Oyama and General Kawakami and also General Count Katsura visited some European nations and studied their military system. After having returned to Japan, they reconstructed the Japanese army according to the standards of the military system of Prussia.'[40]

The article also throws light upon how rapidly Japan excelled in manufacturing cargo ships and warships in their country. The writer has also described how during his stay in Japan, he got an opportunity to visit a Japanese naval station and flagship. In another essay entitled 'Japaner Rail O Tram', published in the magazine *Bharati* (Falgun, 1319 BS), Sarkar has described the history of the establishment of modern transport system in Japan, a development which played no lesser impact.[41] We have earlier mentioned that the transformation of Japan, from a feudal state to a capitalist one, was achieved in a peaceful way, and also in a relatively shorter period than the West. The administrative reforms which ensured this transformation have been dealt in two essays, by the same author. These are entitled 'Japaner Rajniti' (*Bharati*, 1313 BS) and 'Mikado' (*Bharati*, Ashin1319 BS). With reference to Vivekananda's writings on Japan, we tried to find out how all essays of the period try to address one question—the secret of Japan's sudden development. According to Jadunath Sarkar, Mikado the emperor, who ascended the throne in 1868, i.e. the year of Meiji Restoration, took certain positive measures which augmented this transformation. Referring to a western historian, whose name has not been mentioned, the writer in his essay 'Japaner Rajniti' has pointed out that the constitution was the 'voluntary gift of the Mikado'. The Japanese emperor's positive attitude towards administrative reforms, the writer has pointed out, differs and in most cases is in contrast with the European experiences, where such changes were mostly brought out by force.[42] The writer has further pointed out that it was the leadership of Mikado that brought out administrative changes such as the establishment of Senate in 1875, and the establishment of the Parliament of Japan in 1881, and the reconstruction of it in 1885. The other reason, cited by both Sarkar and Mukhopadhyay is, judicious borrowing from the West. From the essay entitled, 'Japaner Rajiniti', we come to learn that like the French people Japanese administrators of that period, divided the whole country in prefectures, with each prefecture having its governor. It is widely known that following the historical event of Meiji Restoration in 1868, Japanese society underwent rapid westernization, not only in terms of imitating western culture, but also in terms of introducing western administration.[43] However, both Mukhopadhyay and Sarkar have found nothing to disagree with these changes that Japan of that time, was undergoing. For both Mukhopadhyay and Sarkar, Japan of the early twentieth century, can be taken as an instance of how western props can be introduced in Asian nations, retaining their indigenous racial characteristics. It is a known fact that the feudal Japan was agriculture based, with the advent of an industrial society, rapid social reforms were taken to bring changes in the lives of people, engaged in agriculture. From M. Visvesvaraya's book entitled *Reconstructing India,* where the writer has time and again referred to his travel experiences in Japan in the year 1898, we come across accounts of such measures. According to the writer, a comprehensive programme was under taken on the part of the government to ensure this change. According to the author, the average standard of earning in Japan was four times of what it was at that time in India.[44] The writer has also credited the role of agricultural societies in Japan in bringing changes in the existing social structure.[45] Eminent Buddhist scholar Rahul Sankrityayan, who visited Japan in 1936, also witnessed this reconstruction of agrarian economy in Japan during that time. According to Rahul Sankrityayan, though feudal class divisions still persisted in the rural societies of Japan of his time, it is the use of new technology, which yielded more crops, in comparison to the condition of Indian peasants during that time. To conclude this section, a portion from the translation of the second volume of Rahul Sankrityayana's autobiography entitled, *Meri Jeevan Yatra,* may be cited:

> As in our country, Japanese feudal lords are also extremely powerful. The Japanese emperor may well be considered to be the most powerful of them. Japanese farmers are compelled to offer a lion's share of their produce to these lords. However, in Japan, farmers receive many helps from their government. Japanese agricultural schools do not end up in making government servants, rather, they create skilled farmers.[46]

REVIEWS OF JAPANESE EDUCATIONAL SYSTEM IN THE CONTEXT OF COLONIAL EDUCATION SYSTEM IN UNDIVIDED BENGAL

To begin with, I would like to refer to an article entitled 'Japane Bharatiyo Chatro', which was published in the Poush issue of the

Bangla magazine *Bharati* (Poush, 1309 BS). According to the writer, it was about the time of Sino-Japanese War in the late nineteenth century, when Japan became an attractive destination for Indian students aspiring to learn technical education abroad. The writer has named the early learners, who went to Japan and studied science and technology there.[47] Many of these visitors, who went to Japan to undertake technical training, witnessed the advent of a developed education system there. Their writings on Japan, as well as their travelogues, contain reviews of salient features of the Japanese education system, which they felt to be exemplary, particularly in the context of poor educational standard that existed at that time all over India. Considering its relevance in the Indian context, these new ideas about Japanese education, which were written and published at that time, deserves a detailed study.

It was primarily lack of educational opportunities, which induced many enterprising Bengali youth to visit Japan for undertaking technical education. The Bangla magazines of this time contain quite a few articles on educational opportunities in Japan. The editors had taken the task of dishing out all necessary information, which an Indian student needed to know, before embarking upon a voyage to Japan. A portion of an essay entitled, 'Bharotbashir Japane Shilposhikha', published in the magazine *Bharati* (Bhadro, 1309 BS), may be cited in this context: 'The education system in Europe is extremely costly. Moreover, Europeans are far from being willing to provide technical education to Indians. Thus, so far obtaining technical education can be, Japan is the most suitable place.'[48]

No doubt, the Pan-Asian ideology that created a strong influence at that time in Bengal, also accounted for this reliance on Japan, as we find in the above-mentioned lines. The anonymous writer has given a list of branches of technical education, which could be mastered in Japan. These include subjects as, Mining, Pottery, Porcelain, Oil-Refining, etc.

It is a well-known fact that the rise of the Swadeshi Movement in Bengal following Lord Curzon's decision of implementing the partition of Bengal, also gave rise to a spirit of self-reliance. Many Swadeshi enterprises were founded at that time. For learning new technology, Japan became the chosen destination for many. The Dawn Society, founded by Satish Chandra Chatterjee, made some ennobling efforts to promote national education. It must be noted that the Dawn Society was founded in 1902; a time, much earlier than the rise of the Swadeshi Movement in Bengal. It is true that from the end of the nineteenth century, a section of Bengali intellectuals became skeptic about the role of the British government in providing training in science and technology. All these contributed in popularizing Japan as a place of learning new technology. It is said that two of the teachers of the Dawn Society, Ramakanta Roy and Kunjabehari Sen, were trained in Japan, in electrical and textile engineering, respectively.[49]

The article 'Japane Bharatiyo Chatro' (*Bharati*, Poush, 1309 BS), which has already been cited earlier in this section, has given a fair picture of Ramakanta Roy's academic career in Japan: 'Ramakanta Roy was the third Indian student to obtain technical training in Japan. After completing his diploma degree, he started working in the Matsui Coal Mines, and learnt industrial skills there.'[50]

Further, it must be noted that many of the Swadeshi enterprises that were established in the first decade of the twentieth century, had either technicians trained in Japan, or in some cases Japanese technicians assisting the production. From Dr. Amit Bhattacharya's book entitled, *Swadeshi Enterprise in Bengal,* we get a list of certain indigenous enterprises, which received this kind of support from Japan. These include 'The Boolbool Soap Factory', which was founded in Dhaka in 1903, and had an expert trained from Japan. Also, the Bengal Soap Factory, which according to the writer, was the oldest soap industry in Bengal. 'The Boolbool Soap Factory' had as an expert, who had returned from Japan having gained knowledge in Chemical industry.[51] The book also refers to cerain enterprises, which had no foreign expert, either western or Japanese, and were relying on their resources alone.

We have earlier referred to Manmatha Nath Ghosh's travelogue *Japan Probash.* Manmatha Nath Ghosh reached Japan on 30 April 1906. During the period he stayed in Japan, he first took training in a commercial school in making buttons. Later, he went to Osaka and learnt the technology of Celluloid there. His experiences as an apprentice in Celluloid making have been wonderfully narrated in the travelogue. It is interesting to note that the brief travelogue contains quite a few pages dedicated to this subject, i.e. technical education in Japan. A separate chapter has also been included. The chapter is entitled 'Japane Shilpo Sikha'. A portion from *Japan Probash*, demands mention with reference to this context: 'Almost all cities of Japan have commercial museums. Unfortunately, there is not even one in our Capital. Nothing can be regrettable than this. In Japanese commercial museums, learners are taught to differentiate between the uses of foreign and indigenously manufactured commodities.'[52]

Rash Behari Bose escaped from India and reached Kobe on 31 May 1915. During the period of his political asylum in Japan, Rash Behari Bose was helpful to Indian students, who visited there for the purpose of further study. Rash Behari Bose's 'Notes from Japan', published in the magazine *Standard Bearer*, contain an essay, in which he has described in detail the prospects of various streams, which could be mastered in Japan. Also, necessary qualifications for the enrolment, and fees required to learn such subjects, have also been described. With reference to Bose's encouraging attitude towards Indian students, who visited Japan during that period, Nandalal Bose's remembrance, penned down by Panchanan Mandal in *Bharatsilpli Nandalal,* needs mention: 'Rash Behari said, "Please send some of your students to Japan". Noticing my doubtful look, he further said, "Let them see an independent nation. More than learning anything let them see, how an independent nation performs."'[53]

From *Bharatsilpli Nandalal* by Dr. Mandal, we further come to know that following Nandalal Bose's visit to Japan, a few students from the Kala Bhavana, Santiniketan, got the opportunity to go to Japan. Biswarup Bose, Nandalal Bose's son, was among them.[54]

The editors of different magazines published from Bengal during the early twentieth century, also published news items relating to the overseas studentship in Japan. A short essay entitled, 'Japane Bharatiyo Chatrer Koto Bay Hoy', by Anathbandhu Sarkar was published in the magazine *Prabasi.*[55] Also, news of successful students, who received training from Japan, was also posted for encouragement. Following is one such news-item, included in the miscellaneous section of that particular issue: Three Indian students have returned after completing their industrial training in Japan.

Dinesh Chandra Majumder has learnt Ceramics in Japan. Nanibal Dutta has taken training in Sugar industry and Rashik Ranjan Ghosh has learnt the techniques of making silk.[56]

With reference to this issue of popularization of Japan as a place of learning new technology, mention should also be made of Nagendra Mohan Gupta, an enterprising Bengali gentleman, who went to Japan in 1904. He studied in the University of Tokyo in the Pharmaceutical Department. From a handwritten biodata of Nagendra Mohan Gupta, which is one among the private documents that has been handed down to the posteritry of Nagendra Mohan Gupta, we further learn that he stayed in Japan from 1904 to 1907; during this period, he learnt subjects like Inorganic Chemistry and Organic Chemistry, Pharmaceutical Chemistry, Forensic Chemistry and Bactereology. Further, as mentioned in the said document, he undertook practical training in factories in Osaka during his long vacations. From the correspondences of family members of Nagendra Mohan Gupta, we further learn that his indomitable aspiration for knowledge, and for new experiences, led him to take a risky decision of boarding a cargo ship bound for Japan as an illegal immigrant from East Bengal (presently Bangladesh). He was facing a starving conding in Tokyo, until he met an Austrian countess, who at that time was teaching in a university in Japan. It has been mentioned in the biodata of Nagendra Mohan Gupta that he left Japan in 1907. He then went to Vienna, from where he obtained his doctoral degree in Chemistry.[57] The development of technical education, which Japan achieved within the first decade of twentieth century, is an integral part of the overall progress in general education, without which the advent of an industrial society could not have been possible. Many of the travelogues on Japan, written and published during this time, contain comments and observations on the Japanese education system, which according to the writers was far better than the education system of India at that time. We have earlier referred to the writings of M. Visvesvaraya, who visited Japan in 1898. Visvesvaraya later took charge of the office of the Dewan of the princely state of Mysore. While contemplating on the lack of economic growth in the state of Mysore, he has given emphasis on educational development as necessary criteria for economic progress. His travel experiences in Japan, and in the western countries, made him realize this. Visvesvaraya's observations in this regard, included in his *Memoirs of My Working Life*, should be quoted:

> I was convinced that the unsatisfactory economic condition in Mysore was due chiefly to neglect of education. My travels in Japan towards the closing years of the nineteenth century had created a deep impression on me in this respect. The Japanese leaders had found that education was the basis of all progress.[58]

As in Visvesvaraya's recounting of his travel experiences in Japan, travelogues of others, such as those of Sureshchandra Bandyopadhyay, Manmatha Nath Ghosh, to which we have earlier referred to, represent the same picture of fast progress in education in Japan, which seemed to be contrasting with the poor educational opportunities in Bengal, and also in other parts of British India. Sureshchandra Bandyopadhyay's travelogue entitled *Japan* includes a chapter, in which he has given an account of the education system he witnessed there. The chapter mentioned above begins: 'The Japanese Emperor earnestly wished and took steps to ensure complete literacy in Japan. Not even in rural areas one can locate a family, where there are illiterate people.'[59]

The role of the Japanese emperor, in accelerating the educational growth in Japan, has also been mentioned elsewhere. We come across the reference of the 'Code of Education', declared in the express command of Mikado, the emperor of Japan at that time, in M. Visvesvaraya's memoir mentioned earlier. Japan was also indebted to many countries in respect of this educational development that followed during the post Meiji era. According to Sureshchandra Bandyopadhyay, Japan followed the education system that existed in the United States at that time.[60]

Around the late nineteenth century, the Japanese government took many important measures to ensure universal education. One such was the establishment of the education department known as the *Mombusho*. An essay entitled, 'Japaner Sikha', written by Ganapati Roy and published in the Bengali magazine *Bharati* (Bhadro, 1317 BS), has taken into account of the steps taken by the Japanese government for this purpose. According to Ganapati Roy, the establishment of the *Mombusho* (Education Department) in 1868, and the Education Code of 1872, to which we have earlier referred, played an important part in spreading education. As mentioned by the writer, other significant measures adopted by the Japanese government in this regard, were to import foreign teachers, and to send learned Japanese men and women to western countries, to be trained in contemporary branches of learning. Also, a special emphasis was given on girls' education.[61] Hariprobha Takeda, the first Bengali woman to visit Japan, during her first visit to Japan in 1912, had the opportunity of visiting a girls' school in Japan. Her travelogue *Bango Mahilar Japan Jatra* narrates her first-hand exposure to Japanese school system:

> On 16 January, I visited a girls' school. I met a lady teacher, whom I found to be fluent in English. She had taken her education in England and was well-educated. The school curriculum includes a variety of subjects as Chemistry, Botany, Geology, Human Physiology, Home Science, Gardening, Visual Art, etc.[62]

From the travelogue of Takeda, we come to know that Japan by that time had been successful to eradicate illiteracy. The government's endeavor ensured free and compulsory education for all children. The popularization of print media, and daily newspapers in Japan, also played a significant part in general education and mass awareness. Another of Jadunath Sarkar's essay entitled, 'Japaner Songbadpotro' (Magh, *Bharati*, 1317 BS), has also described the role newspapers and magazines played in Japan, in fostering the development process of this period.

Common people in Japan are educated and to quench their thirst for knowledge they read newspapers regularly. Even daily wage earners also take newspapers regularly.[63]

The Bangla press was extremely receptive to any news relating to Japanese education system and we can across quite a few writings on Japanese education, published in different magazines from Bengal during this period. These include a long list; among these mention should be made of writings, such as 'Japaner Sikhaniti' by Sri Gourchandra Nath[64], also, 'Japan O Bharaotborsh' (*Prabasi*, Chaitro 1310 BS), 'Japane Stri Sikha' by Sri Brojosundor Sanyal, published in the magazine *Prabasi* (Agrahan, 1315 BS), 'Education in Japan', by Lajpat Rai, published in the *The Modern Review* (September 1910)[65] and many others. In these essays, the writers have dealt in detail, various aspects of Japanese education system, which they felt to be admirable and worthy to be followed, in the context of the colonial education system that existed in our country at that time. These are as follows:

- Direct involvement of the Japanese government in educational matter.
- Introduction of kindergarten system below the elementary level.
- Existence of different types of schools according to the age of the pupil as Elementary, Junior, etc.
- Provision of technical education and agricultural training.
- Emphasis on girls' education.
- Mother tongue as the medium of instruction.

As noted earlier, this exposure to the educational condition of another country is a sad reminder of the lack of opportunities in education that existed in India at that time. A single passage from an essay entitled, 'Japane Sikhar Obostha', written by an anonymous author, that was included in the miscellaneous section of *Prabasi* (Agrahon, 1343 BS), is good enough to bring home this contrasting picture of education, existing in two Asian countries of the same period:

> 99 per cent of students, belonging to the primary school going age-group, have been enrolled in schools in Japan. How about comparing this with that of India? Even during the beginning of the Company period, when the government had not taken the task of educating people, the rate of education was higher than that of the present. We come to know about this fact from the Adam's Report, that was created a century before. Why then the present government cannot ensure spreading of mass education, if it has taken the task of performing this duty?[66]

WESTERNIZATION OF JAPANESE SOCIETY AS WITNESSED BY THE TRAVELLERS

The historical significance of Meiji Restoration in 1868, in which Japan entered a new phase of negotiation with the western powers, has already been discussed in the previous chapters of this book. Though historically, the need to establish business and diplomatic relation with colonial powers had dawned by the end of the Tokugawa period.[67] When Commodore Perry reached Japan, with his fleet of warships, compelling the Japanese authority to open Japan's ports in July 1853, a section of the Tokugawa regime tried to stick to the isolation policy and to uphold the policy of repelling the barbarians. However, a more pragmatic view of establishing business ties with America, and other foreign nations, gained force. Also, the predicament of many colonized Asian nations and the degradation of neighbouring China had taught Japan that she must escape the situation, which many other Asian nations could not. Finally, the treaty of Kanagawa, to which we have earlier referred, was signed in 1854. Following this treaty, Japan agreed to open her ports.

During the period, which followed the Meiji Restoration (1868) Japan made astounding progress.[68] The Meiji Restoration also marks the beginning of westernization of Japanese society. A text of this period, which has been cited by several writers as a seminal one, showing this change of attitude towards West, also towards other Asian nations, is Yukichi Fukuzawa's essay 'Transcending Asia'.[69] The argument that Yukichi Fukuzawa raised in this essay was that Japan needed to transcend Asia, which for him, represented the old order, and should join the western world to accentuate her modernization process. The change in the political and administrative world in accordance with European nations that followed with the Meiji Restoration had subsequent impact on Japanese society. And it is no wonder that travel writings on Japan, written by Bengali writers, show their reaction towards the westernization of Japanese society, which they witnessed during their stay in Japan.

One important facet of this westernization of Japanese society, which drew the attention of travellers, is popularization of English language, and a craze to master the foreigner's tongue. We have earlier referred to Sureshchandra Bandyopadhyay's travelogue *Japan*, which was first published in 1910 (1317 BS). Sureshchandra's travelogue recounts quite hilarious situations, which show how far this craze for English became common among young Japanese in the urban areas. One such incident described in the book may be cited here:

> While walking down the lane, we were conversing in our mother tongue (Bangla).
> Suddenly we noticed that a student was following us. He waved his cap and asked:
>
> 'Do you know Mr. Rao? He is my best friend.'
> I replied that he was not known to me. I asked him how he became familiar with Rao.
> 'I came by him in the tram.'
> 'Then?', I asked.
> 'I have never seen him since then'.
>
> I realized that the boy has picked up the word 'best friend' very recently. So, he did not hesitate to coin the word, even though using in an improper fashion.[70]

Sureshchandra Bandyopadhyay reached Japan on 1 January 1906. The city Tokyo which he saw, and which has been described in his travelogue, is very much different from Tokyo of our time. Surechchandra has commented that the 'Tokyo is much smaller than a city, it looks like a cluster of villages'.[71] Nevertheless, the Tokyo he encountered, had stores of western commodities. Some of these stores displayed signboards written in faulty English, with too many misspelt words: 'Most of the signboards are written in English. However, they are written in erroneous language. For instance, "Rugs and Bugs" will be "Rugs and Bags"; "Mirik Hore" is the misspelt use of the word "Milk Hall", and "Europe of Confectionery" will be "European Confectionary".'[72]

Like English language, western clothing also gained popularity among Japanese during this phase, i.e. the first decade of twentieth century. The Japanese word 'Yofuku', which literally translates as western clothing, can signify the impact it had on a society that was first changing. *Japan,* Sureshchandra Bandyopadhyay's travelogue, also has given an account of how this process of westernization led to the overwhelming acceptance of certain western clothing as, the frock-coat.: 'Almost every Japanese male possesses a frockcoat. This he puts on on Sundays, and also during festivals. It is believed that by wearing such a coat, one can counterfeit western manners.'[73]

The sarcasm in describing the mimicry of West, so very evident in this travelogue, may not be witnessed elsewhere. Yet, in other travel writings also, we find recurrence of the same issue. Manmatha Nath Ghosh, whose writings on Japan have already been referred to, has also noted how westernization became quite fashionable in Japanese society, during that time. From Manmatha Nath Ghosh's narrative, we come to know that Japanese males were more influenced by western culture than their female counterpart. Also, among educated Japanese of that time, westernization became quite fashionable:

> Most of the educated Japanese people have discarded their national dress in favour of western attire. In offices, they prefer to use tables and chairs instead of Japanese style of sitting arrangements. I have also heard that they have also shown preference for western cuisines. This change, due to European impact, is most visible among men. However, Japanese women are yet to have undergone this change. They retain their native customs and practices.[74]

Ghosh's observation seems to be justified. The fact was that women in Japan, during the feudal rule of the Shogunates, occupied an unimportant position, and led a life of subjugation. With the Meiji Restoration, new ideas from the West were pouring, and society was fast changing. Still, women even at the beginning of the twentieth century were less exposed to western culture than men. We come across a similar kind commentary in Tagore's *Japan Jatri.* Tagore expressed his dislike for the advent of a world, where the office uniform of hat-coat rules:

> Nevertheless, on the face of the cities of Japan there is no sign of Japan. She has even taken leave of her individuality of dress! That is Japan has taken off her home dress and put on her office dress. . . . It is for this reason that what attracts the eye most strongly on the streets of the cities of Japan are the women of Japan. I feel that they, atleast represents the home of Japan—they do not belong to the office.[75]

Tagore has praised Japanese women wearing traditional kimono, instead of western attire. However, in our times, women wear kimono only on certain ceremonies such as marriage or on the occasion of *Hatachi*, (ceremony of attaing adulthood).

It would be another oversimplification to derive that westernization in Japan during this phase, only led to the mimicry of western items. It also developed religious tolerence, and paved the way for the advent of a secular Japanese society. It is a known fact that during the seventeenth century, persecution of Christians had taken place in Japan.[76] This development of religious tolerance, which came after the Meiji Restoraion, in accordance with the flood of new ideas from outside, should be viewed as a positive influence of this cultural contact. Travel writers of this period, have also significantly commented on this change, which they noticed during their stay in Japan: 'Very few Japanese are found to be blindly following any religious creed. A few of people may be located among uneducated masses. However, with the change of time, their numbers are decreasing drastically.'[77]

The flood of new ideas from the West brought this sea change within a very short span of time. This has led some writers to conclude that modern Japan is a fine instance of a fusion, of western and eastern values. This has been observed by Dhirendra Mukhopadhyay in his article *Japan*: 'This aspect, can hardly be noticed in India. Western influence has made us incongruous. . . . However, the Japanese people have become successful to make a happy synthesis of borrowed customs and their intrinsic merits.'[78]

We come across a similar argument, in another essay, which was written by Shitoku Hori, the first international student of Santi niketan. This artitcle entitled, 'Japaner Sanaton Adorsho', was published in the Bangla magazine *Bharuti*. As mentioned in the editorial note, it was translated from English, in which it was written by the author. Hori also, begins with the same question that were addressed by other authors, as we have seen earlier—how could Japan achieve so surprising a progress, within so short a period of time?

According to the author, it would be wrong to suppose that western education only, accounted for such progress. For Shitoku

Hori, it is love for one's nation, and a faith in the traditional ideals of Japan, which is the source of her[79] strength.

Japan underwent a process of westernization within a short span. In spite of many positive endowments, the fact that westernization of Japan, also led to an unquestionable acceptance of imported cultural items, is something that cannot be ruled out completely. In this context, a passage from Yukio Mishima's novel *Haru no Yuki (Spring Snow)* may be quoted. In *Spring's Snow*, the novelists mention a list of western food items to be served on the occasion of traditional Japanese festival *Hanami* (Cherry Blossom viewing Festival):

The Evening Banquet of the Cherry Blossom Festival 6 April 1913
The Second Year of the Taisho Era Soup
Turtle Soup Finely Chopped Turtle meat floating in Broth
Chicken Soup Broth with Thin Slices of Chicken Entrees
Poached Trout Prepared in White Wine and Milk
Roast Fillet of Beef Prepared with Steamed Mushrooms
Roast Quail Stuffed with Mushrooms
Boiled Fillet of Muttons Garnished with Celery
Pate de Foie Gras Served with Assortment of Cold Fowl
And Sliced Pineapple in Iced Wine
Roast Gamecock Stuffed with Mushrooms
Individual Salads
Vegetables
Asparagus Green Beans
Prepared with Cheese
Desserts
French Custard Petis Fours
Ice Cream A Choice of Flavour[80]

In this menu, there is no mention of traditional Japanese food like Sushi or Sashimi. Such was the hegemonic influence of the West among the educated people of the Taisho Era! Thus, Dhirendra Mukhopadhyay's eulogy of post-Meiji Japan, being a harmonious unity of eastern and western values, seems to be oversimplistic.

The process of westernization of Japan began with the Meiji Era in 1868. It also brought a change of attitude towards India and other Asian countries. Historically, India had been revered by

Japanese people as 'Tenjiku' (heavenly kingdom); Brij Tankha, in his book *Narratives of Asia from India, Japan and China*, has rightly pointed out that the changes that were taking place during the Meiji period, included a distancing from the 'Tenjiku'.[81] This is due to the fact that a section of Japanese intelligentsia started considering India, or 'Tenjiku' to be a less developed place. The knowledge about the successive conquests, and finally the colonization of whole India, was not unknown to the Japanese people.[82] Brij Tankha's opinion about this process of Japan's distancing from 'Tenjiku', which had earlier been the cradle of Japan's culture and religion, can also be testified, by referring to some Bangla travelogues on Japan, of the early twentieth century. Among these writings, one that deserves mentioning is 'Japaner sohit Bharater Sombondho', an essay written by Jadunath Sarkar. It was published in the Bangla magazine *Bharati* (Jaistho, 1319 BS). According to Sarkar, as early as the time of Russo-Japan War, this change of attitude of Japanese people towards India could be witnessed. However, the writer has also admitted that, though occasionally Indians received humiliating remarks from young Japanese in the streets of Japan, India even then occupied a respectable position in the minds of educated people of Japan.[83] Contrary to this view, many travelogues as Hariprobha Takeda's travelogue entitled *Bango Mahilar Japan Jatra O Onnano Rochona*, tells us about this bond of friendship, among Japanese people and Indians, which she witnessed in Japan:

> I was overwhelmed to find the compassionate and considerate attitude of the Japanese people towards foreigners. Once, an Indian family was facing a tough time in Japan. They were not having any maid at home. In that wintry climate, they were facing difficulties in accomplishing the household jobs, along with looking after their little child. Considering their problem, a Japanese girl of a well-to-do family rendered help to them.[84]

The considerate attitude of the Japanese towards a foreigner, is quite overwhelming. Hariprobha Takeda in the same writing has recollected how caring her Japanese mother-in-law and other relatives in Japan were. They tried their best to relieve her from experiencing any hardship in a foreign land. To conclude this section, I would like to refer to an argument, raised by Sushila Narasimhan in her essay, 'India and Japan: Historical and Cultural

Linkages', included in the collection of articles entitled *India and Japan: In Search of Global Roles.* The writer has rightly pointed that not all Japanese of the Meiji period, were in favour of dissociating from Asia, as the only means of attaining modernization like the West. As mentioned earlier, this was suggested by eminent Japanese educator of the late nineteenth century Japan, Yukichi Fukuzawa (1835-1901). There were some Asian minded Japanese, and they spoke of forging solidarity among Asian countries.[85] The two opposed views and attitudes towards Indians, as recorded in these travelogues, should be viewed from this incongruity of Japan's attitude towards India, China and the rest of Asia, of the early twentieth century.

With reference to this discourse of western influence upon the post-Meiji Japan, it would be worthwhile to go through Tagore's appreciation, as well as his judicious criticism of modern Japan, which we come across in his travelogue, also in his speeches that he delivered in Japan.

From my young days, my thoughts have been constantly twined to Japan.[86]

This is how the bard has expressed his fondness for Japan and her people, in a speech entitled, 'India and Japan', which he delivered during his maiden visit to Japan in 1916. Hay in his book *Asian Ideas of East and West* has given a detailed description of Tagore's preparations for his voyage to Japan. His letters to Rothenstein and to Andrews, prior to his visit to Japan in 1916, which Hay has quoted in his book, well illustrate the restlessness and yearning of Tagore to move towards Far East.[87] Tagore had the firm belief that the greatness of Japanese civilization was rooted in her spiritual nature, and in this sense was in contrast with the spirit of western civilization. Tagore was an admirer of traditional Japan, in which the poet discovered a sensitive attitude towards the beauty of nature. For Tagore, this aesthetic value is an integral part of Japanese civilization, and this idea, Tagore has reiterated in many a works as in 'The Spirit of Japan', a lecture, which he delivered for the students of a private college of Tokyo, and for the members of the Indo-Japanese Association, at the Keio Gaijiuku University in 1916.

> The genius of Japan has given you the vision of beauty in nature and the power of realizing it in your life. And, because of this fact, the power of organization has come so easily to your help when you needed it. For, the rhythm of beauty is the inner spirit, whose outer body is organization.[88]

Also, we can recall a passage from his celebrated travelogue *Japan Jatri,* which describes his admiration for *Ikebana,* a traditional Japanese art of flower-arrangement: 'Yesterday, two Japanese ladies came to the house and displayed their skill in arranging flowers. How much preparation, how much thought and how much skill this takes! Their attention has to be attuned to each leaf and each twig.'[89]

The civilization of Japan, for Tagore, is in harmony with her natural world. Tagore's chosen word for representing this uniqueness of Japan is 'maitri', a term he coined in his lecture 'The Spirit of Japan': 'The ideal of 'maitri' is at the bottom of your culture,—'maitri' with men and 'maitri' with Nature.'[90]

And this is the cause of his apprehension; it must be noted how Tagore conceives this 'overwhelming' influence of the materialistic civilization as a menacing one:

> And this has made me all the more apprehensive of the change, which threatens Japanese civilization, as something like a menace to one's own person. For the huge heterogeneity of the modern age, whose only common bond is usefulness is nowhere so pitifully exposed against the dignity and hidden power of reticent beauty, as in Japan.[91]

Tagore too had misgivings that he would not been able to come across the true spirit of Japanese civilization. His maiden visit to the city of Kobe, was one of disillusionment, so poetically narrated in his travelogue *Japan Jatri*: 'I looked out of my window and viewed the cityscape of Kobe. It gave me an impression of Japan that lacked the warmth of humanity. It was lifeless and stony. The cityscape reminded me of some horrifying Chinese paintings of dragons.'[92]

Also, in another of his speeches, 'India and Japan', which he delivered in Osaka, and was later printed in *The Osaka Mainichi,* Tagore has expressed his doubts:

> The whirlwinds of modern civilization has caught Japan as it has caught the rest of the world , and a stranger like myself cannot help feeling on landing in your country that I see before me is the temple of the modern age. . . . But this is not Japan. Its features are the same as they are in London, in Paris in Berlin or in the manufacturing centers of America.[93]

However, his heart's desire of meeting the real face of Japan was fulfilled; the tea-ceremony, which he attended at Tomito Hara's residence, and which he has described in *Japan Jatri,* his exposure to Haiku (Japanese verse containing three lines), Japanese floral decoration called *Ikebana,* which he saw during his stay in Japan, and above all, a sensitive attitude towards beauty, he found among common men and women of Japan, enabled him to view the aura of a diminishing world threatened by the 'whirlwinds of modern civilization'.

It is worth noting how Tagore's appreciation, as well as his judicious criticism differs from many of his contemporaries. With reference to Japan's prosperity according to western standard, which was a cause of surprise to many, Tagore seems to be reticent in his writings. In 'The Message from India to Japan', a speech Tagore delivered in Japan, on 11 June 1916, the poet acknowledges this fact: 'Japan has taught us that we must learn the watchword of the age, in which we live, and answer has to be given to the sentinel of time, if we must escape annihilation.'[94]

But, Tagore does not stop here, in a more emphatic tone Tagore, he pointed out the redemptive role, Japan ought to play as the leader of the East: 'You must apply your Eastern mind, your spiritual strength, your love of simplicity, your recognition of social obligation, in order to cut a new path for this great unwieldy car of progress.'[95]

Going through these rhetorical statements of Tagore, we can point out certain conclusions. Firstly for Tagore, the strength of modern Japan can never be taken as a consequence of the imitation of the West, a point that he emphasizes in his 'Message from India to Japan'. Rather, it is a spiritual power, a quality of the civilization of the East. The other point to be noted is the discrimination Tagore puts forward, in his argument between imitation of the outwardly features of West, such as food habit or western dress, and a complete acceptance of the ideology of the materialistic civilization of the West. This has been most emphatically voiced in 'The Spirit of Japan', the other speech; we have already referred to:

> What is still more dangerous for Japan is, not this imitation of the outer features of the West, but the acceptance of the motive force of the Western civilization as her own. Her social ideals are already showing signs of defeat at the hands of politics, and her modern tendency seems to incline towards political gambling in which the players stake their souls to win their game.[96]

We agree with Rustom Bharucha[97] that Tagore conceives the predatory role of the political structure of the western civilization. All his arguments are directed against the 'political civilization' of Europe, a phrase he coins in *The Message from India to Japan*: 'The political civilization which has sprung up from the soil of Europe and in overrunning the whole world like some prolific weed is based upon exclusiveness. . . It is carnivorous and cannibalistic in its tendencies; it feeds upon the resources of other peoples and tries to swallow their whole future.'[98]

Thus, we notice that Tagore's arguments are directed against this 'political civilization' of the West, and its possible reproduction and proliferation in Asian countries, rather than superfluous borrowings of western society. In this regard, we can see how Tagore's criticism of Japan, surpasses that of many of his contemporaries. In the following section, dealing with the pastoral life in Japan, by travellers from Bengal of this period, we will also see how Tagore's evaluation of indigenous customs of Japan, differs from those of his contemporaries.

DEPICTION OF THE INDIGENOUS CULTURE OF JAPAN

We have noted how following the end of the Tokugawa Period in 1867, and the beginning of a new era, known as the Meiji Period, the new government took rapid reforms to bridge up the country's difference with the West. However, it would be wrong to suppose that within the first part of the twentieth century, this transformation of a feudal Japan to a capitalist one was ensured. On the other hand, the travelogues give us an interest-ing picture of a society in transition; a society that was feudal and patriarchal, was trying to get along with borrowed world views from the West. This is apparent, when we delve deep into Bangla writings of the period on the pastoral Japan. The perpetuation of the old order could be witnessed in rural areas of Japan. The numerous essays published in Bangla journals, such as *Prabasi, Bharati* and *Bharatbarsa,* give us a fascinating picture of the traditional life of Japan in the early twentieth century, a life, which was then also in harmony with nature, fostered by her physical environment, endangered by the process of capitalist changes, that were taking place. Though not strictly restricting to issues of ecological concern, these variegated writings on rural Japan of the early twentieth century, can well be read from the perspective of Ecocriticism. They emphasize how closely Japanese life and culture was entwined with her physical environment. The physical environment was an integral part of the lives of Japanese men and women, residing in the rural areas of the country. Nature used to exercises a great deal of influence upon the lives of these people. Also, nature shaped their lives, customs and rituals.

To begin with, I would like to refer to a few articles on Japan, which were published in the Bangla magazine *Bharati* of the last century. A passage from an essay entitled 'Japaner Jhorna' (The fountains of Japan), well represents how closely connected was traditional Japanese society with her physical environment.

> The *Shirohito* fountains look like one family. They flow down the foothills of the Mt. Fuji and are close to the Shoji Lake. Truly, they belong to one family. The two main fountains are like the husband and wife of a family.[99]

Since the ancient times, people in Japan have been worshipping natural forces. Thus, in Japan, one can come across many mythological narratives based on the fountains of Japan. The fountains of Japan have added to the beauty of the Japanese landscape.[100]

Manilal Gangopadhyay, the writer, in essay entitled, 'Japaner Jhorna', has described how different myths have been created, based on these fountains. Where there are a cluster of fountains, they have been named according to the Japanese numbers, such as—

Ich, Ni, Sanno Taki (1st, 2nd and 3rd waterfalls), elsewhere, they have been considered as belonging to one big family.

Fountains, being one of the few sources of fresh water in the islands of Japan, had been the source of sustenance for the people since earlier times. The essay narrates how each fountain was worshipped as a deity and the respective myths, which were created for each of these fountains. It must be noted that all these fountains have human names. Further, they have been imagined as family members, a fact, we have already stated in the above-mentioned quotation.

Moreover, the travelogues have described in details, different customs and rituals of Japan, which have also been handed down from generation to generation. They represent the close association of Japan with nature. Manmatha Nath Ghosh's travel writing on Japan has already been referred to in this writing. One of his books entitled, *Supto Japan*, has described many such customs, which the travel writer witnessed. One important aspect, in representing this closeness with nature, lies in worshiping animals and objects of nature, as described by Ghosh in his writing:

> In Japan, the practice of worshipping the turtle is quite in vogue. However, the deity of turtle differs from an ordinary turtle. It has a tail. . . . Many other animals are considered to be ominous and are worshipped in Japan. They include animals like cats and vixen, etc. It is believed that these animals have the power to take human form.[101]

Like these religious practices, Japanese rituals of marriage, as narrated in Manmatha Nath Ghosh's other book *Nabya Japan*, can demonstrate their close tie with the natural settings of this island country: 'After the settlement of the marriage proposal, gifts from the bride's home are prepared. These include dry fishes and seaweed chiefly. In most cases, Rohu fishes are offered as a gift.'[102]

Another traveller, Sureshchandra Bandyopadhyay, in his travelogue *Japan*, has also described the marriage rituals of Japanese people. According to the writer, in case of Japanese marriage, drinking sake (ricewine) in company with others, constitutes the prime part of the ceremony.

During the time of the marriage, hardly any oath is taken.

Neither, is there any arrangement for sacred rites. The Japanese bride and groom drink three cups of Sake. The Japanese marriage ceremony ends up with this ceremonial drinking.[103]

Like these simple rituals of marriage, which testify the closeness of Japanese people with her natural surroundings, their festivals have also been described in the travelogues of this period. One such essay that needs mention is 'Japaner Naboborsho', written by Sri Surechchandra Bandyopadhyay. It was published in the magazine *Bharati* (Boishak 1320 BS). According to the writer, earlier the new-year celebration used to take place during the month of February. It was then the harbinger of the spring. The change of the time of celebration took place, according to the writer, from 1873. No doubt, it was in accordance with the custom of the West to mark 1 January as the beginning of the year. Nevertheless, the customs and rituals of the new-year's celebration are far removed from any western influence. They bear resemblance with many of the practices of our rural areas that are still in vogue:

> The Japanese cousine, which serves as an indispensible part of the new year ceremony, is *Nanakusa.* The Japanese word *Nana* connotes seven and *kusa* means weed or grass. Seven types of weed are taken with rice, to commemorate the beginning of a year. This festival is celebrated on 7 January, every year. This custom of Japanese new year's celebration may well be compared to our practice of eating fourteen 'Shaks' (Bangla word for palatable weed or grass) during the festival of Diwali in Bengal.[104]

With reference to the above mentioned passages from different travelogues on Japan of the early twentieth century, it would be worth paying attention to the kind of depiction of pastoral life of Japan, we find in these writings, and also to see, the point of similarity that can be traced with the indigenous customs of Bengal. Travel accounts are far from from being objective renditions of places and people, which the travellers visit. We can agree with Sachindra Mohanty that travelogues simultaneously accomodates and critiques in its mode 'various social, cultural and ethnographic discourses that lend it a richly textured significance'.[105] Thus, travelogues also include censorship, judgement, prejudice or assimilation with the culture of the space, which the travel writer has visited.

We have earlier mentioned colonial travel narratives, in which stereotyped representation of the people, belonging to the colonized world, can be frequently traced. If in colonial travel narratives, the culture of the colonized world is frequently represented as being in binary opposition to that of the West, in the travel writings written by authors from Bengal, we come across a different motif. The depiction of the rural customs of celebrating the new year's ceremony, as mentioned above, or the reference to marriage rituals, described in Manmatha Nath Ghosh's travelogue entitled *Nabyo Japan*, emphasize upon the commonality of Asian culture, which the writers witnessed in rural areas of Japan of their time. To conclude, it can be said that the represention of the pastoral life of Japan, witnessed by the Bengali travellers, testifies the perpetuation of many residual cultural practices, inspite of capitalist changes, which were taking place during that period. Further, these cultural items bear similarity with many equivalent cultural practices of Bengal of that period.

The travel accounts also make a faithful rendition of the uniqueness of the different cultural practices, that can hardly be related to any equivalent one, either Indian or that of the West. The Japanese word for festival is *Omatsuri*; the use of prefix 'O', as an honorific in verbal usage, can itself denote the importance, and almost religiosity associated with these festivals. A unique festival of Japan, *Hinamatsuri*, or the day for girl-children, has been well described by Sureshchandra Bandyopadhyay in his travelogue, *Japan*.[106]

In the previous chapter, we have referred to Tagore's appreciation of 'Ikebana', a traditional Japanese art of flower-arrangement. Both Tagore and Mukul Dey, during their stay in Japan, had the pleasure of attending a tea ceremony, a traditional ceremony of Japan, where guests are served green tea. The preparation of this ritual undergoes a highly structured method. Artist Mukul Dey, in his letter from Kobe, dated 3 June 1916, has described in details the tea ceremony which they attended in Japan. According to Mukul Dey, it is the quality of self restraint, which can be found in the elaborate rituals of the tea ceremony. The letter has been included in the book *Mukulchandra Dey: Japan Theke Jorasanko*.[107] A similar kind of impression, we get from the description of this traditional ceremony in Tagore's *Japan Jatri*: 'The other day, a wealthy Japanese invited me to his house to attend a tea ceremony—the ceremony that is described by Okakura in the *Book of Tea*. On seeing this ceremony, it became clear that for the Japanese this is a religious ritual; it is one of their highest national achievements.'[106]

Okakura's *The Book of Tea*, was first published in the year 1906. It is evident from Tagore's writing that Tagore had read the book. Both Mukul Dey and Tagore's appreciation remind us of Okakura's appreciation of tea ceremony, as a typical oriental custom:

> Teaism is a cult founded on the adoration of the beautiful among the sordid facts of everyday existence. It inculcates purity and harmony. . . . It represents the true spirit of Eastern democracy by making all its votaries aristocrats in taste.[109]

Many of these festivals, rituals and practices depicted in the writings on Japan, by Bengali writers, have survived and are even celebrated today. Similarly, the courteousness of the Japanese, a mark of their indigenous culture, did not escape the attention of the writers. Japanese people are known for their elaborate custom of greetings expressed in different occasions (*aisatsu* in Japanese language). Manmatha Nath Ghosh, in his travelogue *Japan Probash*, has described these greetings elaborately. The author's narration shows his association with Japanese language and culture.[110] Another aspect of this courteousness of Japanese people, as mentioned in another essay, also needs mention. This has been pointed out by Sri Jadunath Sarkar, whose writings on variegated aspects of Japan and her people have already been referred to. For Sarkar, class distinction in Japanese society, has not yet spoilt the courteous nature of Japanese people. They remain thankful to even the humblest folk in everyday life. To bring home this point of view, I would like to quote a passage from an essay entitled, 'Japani Akriti Prokriti'. It was published in the Bangla journal *Bharati* (Boishak 1318 BS).

When a Japanese visits a house, he greets the host by adressing 'Gomennasai'. The word connotes excuse. Similarly, the landlady also bows down, and sits on the floor to greet the guest. I have visited Japanese professors' houses and have seen their wives, greeting in this fashion.[111]

With reference to these depictions of traditional Japanese culture, another of Jadunath Sarkar's article, which can be referred to, is 'Daidokoro'. It was also published in the Bangla magazine *Bharati* (Magh 1320 BS). This is an article on Japanese kitchen (*Daidokoro* in Japanese, translates as kitchen). The picture of Japanese society of the early twentieth century, we get from Sarkar's writing, is marked by its simplicity. Japanese kitchen, as the writer found during his time, irrespective of the owner's class position, was simple and equipped with certain traditional tools, which have been used for generations. Their choice of food and cooking style, also show a life fostered by its natural surroundings. No doubt, the depiction of the food habit and cooking that prevailed during that time, have been replaced by highly sophisticated kitchen wares of our time, as it has happened elsewhere also. A passage from the text entitled 'Daidokoro' cited below:

> The utensils and furnitures of a Japanese kitchen, whether, it is of the rich or the poor, are of same kind. They include an earthen stove, utensils for preparing rice; a few wooden buckets . . . since ancient times, Japanese people have been using coal instead of wood. It is surprising that proper technical arrangements for the excreation of smoke through chimney, has been suited to their kitchens, since long ago.[112]

As noted earlier, the traveller's exposure to the conditions in Japan is always a reminder of his lived experiences in his own motherland. In this short article, the writer has pointed out the similarity that exists between our food habit and those of the Japanese people. The preference for rice, as the main diet is this point of similarity. Another salient feature of their food habit is their fondness for fishes of various kinds. These have added different dishes in the Japanese menu, including dishes of raw fish. Sarkar's observation in his article entitled, 'Daidokoro', points out how the food habit of Japanese people show their close tie with their habitat: 'One can get fish of various kinds in Japan. The rivers and streams of Japan also abound in fish. We disliked seafish. Japanese people are fond of a sea-fish cousine. For the preparation of this, strips of rawfish are cut like small pieces of cakes. The name of this preparation is "Sashimi"'.[113]

Japanese food items, particularly dishes of raw fishes, have generated diverse response among the receptors. This is in contrast to other experiences, where familiarity with his cultural space has been over and again recalled and emphasized. Thus, Manmatha Nath Ghosh in his book *Japan Probash* has recalled the Japanese food served at the boarding house in Osaka, which he found to be extremely unpalatable: 'During my tenure at the boarding house in Osaka, I started taking Japanese food regularly. Being unaccustomed, the experience was far from being enjoyable . . . the rice that was served at the boarding was dry, the vegetable curry was stale and the fishes were half-baked or half-steamed.'[114]

However, Mukul Dey's description of Japanese food, as we find in his letters written to his mother, gives us a more tolerant impression about the traveller:

> Raw fish finds an important place in Japanese cousine. The raw fish, which is used in Japanese dishes, are soft, but palatable. However, when I think of eating raw fish, it creates nauseating feeling. The Japanese also take salads made of raw vegetables, which are available in Japan, like cucumber, ginger and bringle.[115]

Dey's choice of diction, in describing an alien foodhabit, shows the preparedness on the part of a cultural traveller, to experience a cultural practice of Japan, which is different from that of his own nativeland. On the other hand, a lack of preparedness on the part of other travel writers, have led them to be prejudiced, and jujdgemental about the indigenous culture of Japan. The difference in representing indigenous culture of Japan by travellers is an attractive issue to be noted and will be described later. The various descriptions of traditional culture that were in vogue, when these writers visited Japan, shows a society in harmony with her natural surroundings, a point already mentioned at the beginning. This oneness with nature, according to Tagore, is the intrinsic merit of Japanese culture. This, he has praised in the most rhetorical way in his seminal text *Nationalism*:

What has impressed me most in this country is the conviction that you have realized nature's secrets, not by methods of analytical knowledge, but by sympathy. You have known her language of lines, and music of colours, the symmetry in her irregularities, and the cadence in her freedom of movement.[116]

For Tagore, this has induced an aesthetic quality to be found among common Japanese, a rare gift which has provided them a 'vision of beauty in nature and the power of realizing' it in their life.[117]

This sensitive attitude towards beauty, a trait of traditional Japanese culture, has also been emphasized in many other writings of the period. Among these, worth-mentioning is an essay entitled 'Some Characteristics of Modern Japanese Life and Character'. It was published in the English magazine *Dawn* in May 1903. The names of the writers, as mentioned in the magazine are, Lafcadio Hearn and Basil Hall. According to them, what makes Japanese civilization different from the Occident, is this sensitivity towards beauty, which can be found in all corners of Japan, and among everyone, irrespective of their class positions: 'Those who think of beauty only with costliness, with stability, with "Firm reality" should never look for it in this land of Japan—well called the Land of Sunrise.'[118]

According to the joint writers of this article, Japanese architecture remains entwined with their natural surroundings. The construction of cities of that time, also shows their sensitive attitude towards the beauty of nature:

A Japanese city is more than wilderness of wooden sheds. But interiorly a very large number of the frail wooden buildings of any Japanese city are works of art. Exteriorly, a Japanese street may appear little better than a show of wooden barns or stables, but the interior of any dwelling in it may be a wonder of beauty.[119]

We come across a similar kind of depiction of Japanese architecture, in the travel account of Professor Binoy Sarkar, who visited Japan, during the first two decades of the twentieth century. There also, we also get a picture of Japanese houses, constructed in accordance with her natural beauty. The essay was published under the title 'Japaner Dilli' in the Bangla magazine *Bharatbarsa* (Jaistho 1317 BS).

Japanese houses have been built in accordance with the natural setting of Japanese islands. This is the characteristics of Japanese houses. In every village, human habitat seems to be compatible with its natural surroundings.[120]

Tagore in his lecture entitled 'To The Indian Community in Japan', a lecture, which he delivered in Japan, in April 1925, has recollected his experience of watching how the working men in Tomito Hara's beautiful garden, at the end of the day's work, would indulge themselves to sit under the shade of a pine forest, and watch the beauty of nature. For Tagore also, this is a rare gift to be found among ordinary Japanese men and women, which can hardly be found among the plebian multitudes of other countries:

> These people belonged to the working classes. In other countries , we know what is the foundation of the enjoyment of such people, . . . But here, their holiday time seemed to me like the perfect flower of the lotus opened to the pure light of the sky, to which they came open like a joyous swarm bees to sip the hidden honey insilence. This meant great in the people and it won my heart. . . . It is this profound feeling for beauty, this calm sense of perfection ,that is expressed in their daily conduct.[121]

Tagore had misgivings that this bond with nature and forms might be impared under the impact of 'ugly spirit of the market'[122] a phrase, he coins in the same text. Tagore's first impression in the city of Kobe, during his maiden voyage to Japan, was one of disillusionment. Tagore felt that the acceptance of the culture of the metropolis would be harmful for Japan, would blur and efface, the indigenous traits of the Japanese society:

> One main impediment of our time is that, all educated societies of the world, are dressed in the same fashion. They are losing their intrinsic merits, and are becoming a replica of each other. I look out of my window at the cityscape of Kobe. The cityscape of Kobe seemed to me stony and heartless, lacking the warmth of humanity.[123]

So far, we have been discussing the commonalities among the travelogues, in describing the indigenous culture of Japan. The difference in portraying Japanese customs, by these writers, is no less attractive. For me, the idea of representation involves two things; in some cases, as we have already hinted, representation is from the point of view of the West, and the reaction on the part of the traveller, is one of discovering a culture phenomenon, which had been existing for quite a long time, and was not unknown to the natives of the country. On the other hand, if traveller's account of a cultural aspect is done from their perspective, it shows a preparedness to experience the culture of the 'Other'; on the part of the traveller. To bring home this point, it would be worth noticing how the Japanese communal bathing system has been portrayed by the travellers. *Sentou* or the Japanese Public Bath is a cultural practice, which has survived through ages. According to an entry in the website http://www.japan-101.com/travel/sento.htm, the origin of Japanese *Sentou*, could be traced to the Buddhist temples in India, around eighth century AD. It was introduced in the Nara prefecture in Japan. At the end of the Edo period (1603-1867), the Tokugawa Shogunate (1603-1867), took initiative to prohibit the practice of mixed bathing. The compulsion came from outside, when Commodore Perry visited Japan in 1853 and 1854; he questioned the morality of this practice of mixed bathing. Subsequently, separate bathing houses for both the sexes were created at the end of Tokugawa period.[124] It is interesting to note that in some travelogues as in Manmatha Nath Ghosh's *Japan Pobash*, *Sentou* has been described according to the European standard. Manmatha Nath Ghosh's depiction of this practice, is caustic, and shows influence of Western hegemony:

> The Japanese system of public-bathing may well be criticized.[125]

Sharply in contrast to Manmatha Nath Ghosh's reaction, Tagore's appreciation of Japanese culture shows his preparedness to experience the cultural practices of another Asian nation. We note, how differently the same custom has been described in Tagore's *Japan Jatri*:

> . . . Part of the reason for this the Public baths where it is customary for men and women to bathe together naked, without any implication of shame or 'sin' attached. (Even the closest relatives feel no embarrassment at bathing together.) . . . Unfortunately the practice of public bathing is dying out in the cities now, due to the influence of impure sight and wicked thoughts of the people in other countries; but in the villages it still prevails.[126]

The obvious question, that needs asking, is what accounts for the lack of preparedness to assess other culture in the preceding text, and the presence of it in Tagore's *Japan Jatri.*

As noted earlier, we should once again this attribute to their different value structures, which have accounted for the difference in perceiving the same cultural practice. The memory of their homeland always plays a pertinent role in generating different responses in a foreign land. Dealing with the representation of the condition of Japanese women, as narrated by the writers from Bengal, we will also notice, how this representation, varies according to the ideological positions of the travellers.

REPRESENTATION OF JAPANESE WOMEN OF THE EARLY TWENTIETH CENTURY

The Meiji Period (1868-1912) and the following Taisho Period (1912-26) in Japan, witnessed industrial growth and capitalist development. However, this does not mean that the transformation of a new superstructure came into existence. The travel writings will unravel the truth that many practices and customs, belonging to a residual culture, were quite vivid even to the foreigner's eye. A testimony of this observation can be the existence of depressed classes, as viewed and described by visitors, during the early twentieth century. Modern Japan has eradicated this social evil. However, during the time Rash Behari Bose reached Japan, the problem of outcastes was still prevalent. Rash Behari Bose in his 'Notes from Japan', published in the *Standard Bearer* (vol. II no. 15), has touched upon this issue. For Bose, the problem of outcastes in Japan was a reminder of the existence of the same problem in India, which was quite common. Viewing this from the perspective of the remnants of a feudal system in Japan, as witnessd by Indians in the early twentieth century, it would be worthy to see, how the representation of women in Japanese societies, has been dealt in the travel writings, we have already referred to. This also, bears resemblance with the condition of women in India during that time, and even now.

From Hariprobha Tekeda's article, which is entitled 'Japane

Santan Palon O Nari Sikha', and also from her travelogue, we get an interesting picture of the patriarchal society that she found to be existing at that time. Hariprobha Tekeda left for Japan accompanied by her husband Uemon Takeda, in 1912. While staying at Mr. Takeda's ancestral home in the countryside of Japan, she found the opportunity to see the condition of women in the rural areas of Japan. This has been narrated in her travelogue *Bongo Mahilar Japan Jatra*, and also in another essay, entitled *Japane Santan Palon O Nari Sikha*. According to Hariprobha, the condition of the Japanese women was far better, if compared to that of Indian women, at that time. Universal education for every girl–child had been ensured. Women could assist their husbands in their agricultural activities in rural areas.[127]

Yet, the writer has rightly pointed out that it would be wrong to suppose that gender discrimination and male domination had ceased to exist. Japanese women, Takeda points out, have to act according to the husband's decisions: 'The Japanese wife remains submissive and silently endures all ill-treatment of her husband. In this country, husbands treat their wives like their servants. However, wives have to revere their husbands as their masters.'[128]

Takeda found that Japanese women were supposed to be respectful towards their in-laws, failing which husbands could desert them and remarry, as it was accepted in that society.[129] This hegemonic influence of this feudal society also determined men's attitude towards their counterpart:

> Japanese men are rarely found to be indulging them, in paying attention to their wives. Husbands are rarely found to be showing respect towards their wives. Wives are supposed to attend the household duties. Also, they have to look after their children. . . . Men are engaged in defending their country, and also in earning money. The mother has to bring up her child in a way that in future, he can also earn his living. In some cases, women are also engaged in different jobs.[130]

The demands for Japanese womens' rights were first voiced during the Meiji Era in Japan. Junko Kiguchi in her erudite paper entitled, 'Japanese women's rights at the Miji Era', has referred to eminent educators and intellectuals of the Meiji Era, like Yukichi

Fukuzawa and Mori Arinori, who were pioneers in raising their voices in favour of the equality of sexes. For Kiguchi, this dawning of liberal ideas towards women was facilitated by the influence of western scholars, like John Stuart Mill. The Meiji Period, also witnessed the establishment of many girls' schools and a rapid spread of education among women in Japan. We have already referred to the writings of Takeda; other travel writings as essays on Japan, published during the first half of the twentieth century also, tell us about the spread of womens' education in Japan during this period. An interesting article that needs mention in this regard is, 'Japaner Strisikha' by Brajosundor Sanyal, published in the Bangla magazine *Prabasi* (Agrahon, 1315 BS). According to the writer, Japan succeeded in the spread of primary education throughout the country. The data provided by the author, can show how far Japanese government was successful in ensureing primary education for children of both sexes, by the beginning of twentieth century: 'According to the official statistics, 3,876,495 boys and 3,590,391 girls, in all 7,466,886 students, are regularly attending primary schools of Japanese cities during the academic year 1901-2.'[131]

Other important measures to spread women's education in Japan during the same time, as mentioned by the author, include the setting up of higher school for women, establishment of women's universities, etc. Another interesting fact, that we come across in these writings, is the existence of different originations, solely governed and maintained by women: 'There exists in Japan, organizations, which are solely run by women. The numbers of such organizations are twenty.'[132]

Truly, the Meiji Era with its reformative environment, contributed a great deal for empowering women. Yet, this development process and change of ideas did not result in the upturning of the patriarchal society of Japan that had been in existence for centuries. Rather, the educational policies, adopted during Meiji Period regarding girls' education, were to aim at making 'Goodwife and wise mother'. Thus, home remained the prescribed position for women, even during this period. Viewed from this perspective, the last two lines quoted above from Takeda's essay, aptly describe the position of women, she found during the time of her visit.

Also, this representation of gender politics, we come across in several writings by Bengali travelers, who visited Japan during the early twentieth century. Another traveller, Sureshchandra Bandyopadhyay, whose travelogue *Japan*, we have earlier referred to, has recounted an experience. This narration also suggests the hierarchical position enjoyed by men in Japanese society, during the early twentieth century:

> Japanese wives are often seen to be following their husbands on the streets of Japan. While walking, men do not like to accompany their wives. They also even show resentment in carrying the luggage of their spouses. . . . Nowadays, many Japanese men, who are highly educated, or have returned from foreign countries, are found to be accompaning their wives.[133]

The Japanese word *Kanai*, meaning wife, consists of two characters. *Ka* denotes house and *Nai* denotes inside. This suggests the position of women, determined by the feudal society in Japan that was perpetuated for centuries. Sureshchandra Bandyopadhyay's account of Japanese women also shows that male domination was quite common in Japanese society, at the time he visited. Not only common people, but kings and queens, also were obliged to accept this system of dual status, for both sexes: 'The Japanese emperor and the empress are never seen to be sharing the same car. Far behind the car of the Japanese emperor, the empress rides in a covered car. The Japanese emperor is revered like a god; however, the empress seems to be nothing, other than an ordinary woman.'[134]

The author in the same book entitled *Japan*, has rightly pointed out that though Japan never came under colonial rule, women never enjoyed the same kind of freedom. Women, in Japanese society, during the time of his visit, were supposed to carry out the task of child rearing and were to obey the instructions of their domestic lord.

Male domination exists in Japanese society, as it exists elsewhere. Most of the Japanese men never accept that women can be given other responsibilities, other than, looking after their younger ones. Japanese women are supposed to obey the orders of their husbands.This patriarchal system has been continuing since earlier times.[135]

We have also referred to Junko Kiguchi's paper *Japanese Women's Rights at the Meiji Era,* where she has argued that the Meiji Period, with its many reforms to bring about social changes, also pleaded for the establishment of monogamy system in Japan. In this context, Manmatha Nath Ghosh's description of Japanese society may be recalled. The writer found that during the time he visited Japan, polygamy was commonly practiced in Japanese society. The writer has described the case of an aged woman, and how, after reaching her old age, she willfully allowed her husband to keep a mistress and returned to her own ancestral home, The woman has been referred to in the travelogue as *Obaasan* (The Japanese word for grandmother).

Once, I asked an *Obaasan* (grandmother) the reason, for which she returned to her paternal home from that of her in-laws. Responding to my enquiry, she replied, 'Following my aging, I decided to abstain from my conjugal life. Hence, I gifted my husband a young and fair looking woman, to look after him. I quited the place, and along with my son Taka, returned to my paternal house.'[136]

The author's observation in this context deserves attention: 'Most of the Japanese men spend their leisurely moment with prostitutes and dancing girls (*Geishas*); either taking consent from their wives, or even infront of them. Visitors to Japan, are well aware of this fact.'[137]

In some other travel writings also, we come across similar descriptions of the condition of marginalized women of Japan, including those of barmaids, prostitutes and *Geishas.* According to an entry, published in the britannica.com, a *geisha* is a 'member of a professional class of women in Japan whose traditional occupation is to entertain men'. The *geisha* system, which emerged in the seventeenth century Japan, occupies an important place in Japanese culture. *Geishas,* with their beauty and graceful appearances, have also attracted western audience during the last two centuries. It is interesting to note how during the post-Meiji Period, the sytem of *Geisha* also underwent considerable changes. Sureshchandra Bandyopadhyay in his travelogue *Japan* has mentioned that in the year 1906, in Tokyo city, about 3,526 *geishas* used to reside and the Tokyo municipality of that time, used to receive 1,60,000 Yen as tax. Further, the travelogue also has depicted how a girl child, who came to a *geishi*-house, received rigorous trainings in dancing and playing traditional Japanese musical insruments, and also in nurturing the qualities, they needed in order to be a professional *geisha.*

Another traveller, Manmatha Nath Ghosh, who authored a book entitled, *Nabya Japan,* has likened them to the courtesans of India. It is evident from his writing that mostly girl children were sold by their parents to the *geisha* quarters. They received the training for joining this profession.[138] Thus, for many, the culture of *geisha* is different from prostitution. This has been expressed by Lauren Lockard in his fascinating essay *Geisha: Behind the Painted Smile*: 'To be a geisha requires skill, patience and an undying devotion to continue better oneself until the end, and it is because of this they will always be on a level that a prostitute can never hope to achieve.'[139]

That *geishas* were looked differently, even during the time Manmatha Nath Ghosh visited Japan, as has also been mentioned in his writing: 'In Japan, a teacher and his student, husband and wife, a father and his son, can be seen accompanying each other, to a *Geisha* house. Possibly, in no other country such universal acceptance of barmaids and dancing girls can be seen.'[140]

An appealing article that needs to be mentioned with reference to this topic is one entitled, 'Geishar Swadhitona', published in the Bangla magazine *Bharati* (Poush, 1329 BS). The anonymous author has well described the changes, which were brought in the system of the *geisha*, during the early twentieth century, by amending laws. This short essay, published in the year 1922, shows how this new law empowered a *geisha* even to leave her profession, if desired. The new law empowered the *geishas.* In the past a *geisha* had to sign an agreement with her master. According to this agreement, she was compelled to stick to her profession:

> Mostly, girl children of poor families are sold to the *Geisha* quarters. They receive training in dance and in music, at the *Geisha*-quarter. Once, they become proficient in such arts, they are employed by their buyers to cater the customers. A lion's share of their wages are taken away by their masters. A

Geisha has to sign an agreement with her master and till now this agreement was the main cause of their enslavement. Very recently, with the enactment of a new law in Japan, *Geishas* have been empowered to do away with their past, and to lead a free and normal life.[141]

From the travel writings on Japan by writers from Bengal, we also come across the narration of the condition of women, living in red-light areas of Tokyo city. As mentioned earlier, in this case also, we find how representation differs from one writer to another. Manmatha Nath Ghosh found 'Yoshihara', the main red-light area of Tokyo city, to be considerably clean and according to him, the govermment had employed doctors to administer routine check-up of the prostitutes. However, he has admitted that girl-children, mostly of poor families, were sold by their parents to the owners of the brothels. His overall impression of the place was not one of dislike: 'The red-light area in Japan is quite clean and located beside broad streets. Even temples are located beside brothels. The quarters of the prostitutes are also attractive and spacious.'[142]

It is surprising that the writer has talked about cleanlinesss, or about the goverment's effort to preserve sanitaion in red-light areas. However, the plight of these women residing there finds no reference. Further, he mentions of the co-existence of prostitution and religion, which can be traced in many other countries. The same red-light area of Tokyo city (Yoshiwara), which existed then, has been depicted by Sureshchandra Bandyopadhyay in his travelogue *Japan*. However, we notice how different the representation can be of the same aspect:

> Apart from *Geishas*, many other women are engaged in other undesirable professions (prostitution) in this city. The total numbers of such women in this city are 6379. Almost in all areas, there are brothels. However, 'Yoshiwara', which is located in the outskirts of the city, is famous as a red-light area. . . . Often, fairs are organized in this location. Then the place becomes heavily crowded. Many Japanese gentlemen pay visit to this place, accompanied by their family members. On both sides of the road, these women are found to be waiting in spacious rooms, dressed in colourful attire. The rooms are heavily guarded with iron fencing. From the streets the prostitutes look like caged animals.[143]

The appalling sight of Japanese prostitutes, who were placed in cages, reminds us of a scene in *Yojimbo* (1961), by legendary Japanese director, Akira Kurosawa.[144] There also, we see prostitutes being displayed like caged animals, by one of the lords of a small town, who in the movie, used to run a brothel. Interestingly, the pleasure quarters in Yoshiwara, continued till prostitution was outlawed by the Anti-Prostitution Law, passed by the Diet of Japan in 1956. Today, disguised forms of prostitution, still continues in the area, using a variety of names, such as the 'soaplands'.[145] Considering the subject of representation of women of Japan by travel writers, one aspect can hardly be ignored, i.e. stereotyped presentation of Japanese women, which we sometimes encounter in the travelogues, which have been mentioned earlier. In literary texts, women have often been portrayed from the point of view of a patriarchal society. Needless to say, travelogues on Japan, can also ascertain this fact.

This is evident, when we find that Manmatha Nath Ghosh in his book *Nabyo Japan* ponders over the subject of chastity of women. The author begins the topic entitled, 'Satityer Mulyo' (The value of chastity), by referring to Japanese words like *misao*, which denotes womanly virtues. Interestingly, according to the writer, there is no Japanese equivalent for chastity, as the Japanese word *misao*, is of a less specific coinage, denoting womanly qualities. His concluding observation is in accordance with this derivation:

> However, it would be wrong to suppose that chastity of women is highly esteemed in Japanese society. During the settlement of a marriage, the bride's appearance is given more importance than her chastity. An attractive woman, even if she possesses an unrepute character, finds no difficulty to marry a man of noble birth.[146]

Ironically, in the same book, and just a few pages after, the author has praised Japanese women for not aspiring to attain equal status and opting to play a second fiddle in social life. For the author, this acceptance of the social order, on the part of Japanese women, should be taken as a mark of their feminine qualities. And the author explicitly expresses his preference for a controlled-freedom for women, which would not pose a threat for the patriarchal order of the society:

> In this context, it must be remembered that despite the empowerment of Japanese women, women never aspire to enjoy equal status with men. Like women of other parts of Asia, Japanese women are also found to be following their husbands in every respect. Japanese women show feminine dispositions. They are soft and shy in nature. Those who oppose freedom of women must meet Japanese women of our time. Then they will understand that women, having gained freedom, will never loose their intrinsic feminine traits.[147]

With reference to the above mentioned passages from Manmatha Nath Ghosh's book *Nabyo Japan*, and also remembering his advocacy for a controlled freedom for women, it would not be irrelevant to recall the history of social reforms in colonial Bengal and its impact upon different cross-sections of Bengali communities, as evaluated by Sekhar Bandyopadhyay, in his essay entitled, 'Caste, Widow Remarriage and the Reform of Popular Culture in Colonial Bengal'. Bandyopadhyay in his article has rightly pointed out that 'though the Act of 1856 legalized widow remarriage', yet, it could hardly make it acceptable at that time. Vidyasagar had to rely mainly on social consent. Thus, it was the hegemony of the patriarchal society that posed to be the stumbling block. This failed Vidyasagar's endeavour to see many widow remarriages during his time.[148] Needless to say, this patriarchal society continued to exercise a strong influence also, during the first decades of the twentieth century. The travel writer's unconscious submission to the hegemony of patriarchy, also, his preference for stereotyped representation of Japanese women, may be viewed in the light of the general notion about women's rights, which had been popular at that time.

The other kind of stereotyping, which we come across in the travelogues on Japan, is accepting a dress (*Kimono*) for women, as a construct of their cultural identity. The post-Meiji Era, which showed a tendency of westernization, brought a change in the dress of Japanese men. Many opted for western attire (*Yofuku*) instead of *Kimono*. However, women in general, retained their preference for *kimono* to other western clothing. This we have already mentioned previously. Tagore and other writers have praised Japanese women, for retaining their native custom of putting on *Kimono*. We notice Tagore's rhetorical admiration for Japanese women wearing *Kimono*:

> Nevertheless on the face of the cities of Japan there is no sign of Japan. She has even taken leave of her individuality of dress! That is Japan has taken off her home dress and put on her office dress. . . . It is for this reason that what attracts the eye most strongly on the streets of the cities of Japan are the women of Japan. I feel that they, atleast represents the home of Japan—they do not belong to the office.[149]

How can a person's preference for a dress be taken as his belonging to a particular culture? In this context, I would like to refer to an argument, raised by Olfra Goldstein-Gidoni, in her article entitled 'Kimono and the Construction of Gendered and Cultural Identities'. The Meiji Era, argues Goldstein, with its aim of transforming Japan into a modern nation state, emphasized the role of women as mother and wives, as beneficiary for the nation. Thus, home remained the demarked space for Japanese women; the writer refers to the popular slogan of the Meiji Period—'good wife wise mother', which specified their functional role in the society. According to Goldstein, the preference for *kimono* to western attire on the part of Japanese women was not one of spontaneity. Rather, it was constructed as a symbol of distinction between the sexes, and was related to the image of Japaneseness. The author is correct to conclude that, the representation of the Kimono-clad 'new Japanese women' who gets along with the spirit of the Meiji Period became a symbol of modern Japan.[150] This acceptance of *Kimono* as a mark of feminist, and also, as the cultural identity of Japan, took place during the Meiji Period, in which the state had an important role to play. The writer has also referred to the role of *Kimono* experts and entrepreneurs, who, according to him, played no less part in popularizing *Kimono* as a symbol of traditional Japanese women. It must also be mentioned that in our times, Japanese women wear *Kimono* only on certain ceremonies. Viewed from this historical perspective, Tagore and other writers' praise for

Japanese women, for their preference for native attire, seem to be stereotyped representation, lacking the true picture of the situation, which prevailed during the time they visited Japan.

Japan's emergence as a capitalist nation from a completely feudal state, took place within a relatively shorter span of time than the western world. This fact, we have already discussed in the preceding chapter. Delving into these issues that recurrently come across in the texts, we have referred to the picture of Japanese society and government, which we find in these writings, is one of undergoing rapid transformation. The time frame of my enquiry has also benefited me to view the reception on the part of the travellers, both horizontally and vertically. This is chiefly because, during the time Vivekananda visited Japan (1893), and the time when Tagore visited Japan for the last time (1925), Japan had changed considerably. Similarly, we have also noticed how the reception of Japanese culture and politics on the part the visitors could differ from each other in accordance with their ideological positions which they had imbibed from their homeland. Japan, as we come across in these texts, truly is a space, which is considerably changing and capable to evoke a variety of responses among people of her neighbouring nations. The different sections of this chapter dealing with topics of the modernization of Japan, the impact of the West, as viewed by travel writers from Bengal, the perpetuation of residual culture, the representation of Japanese women by these writers, can probably establish this view. It must also be mentioned that, the same period also, witnessed a rise of a strong nationalist voice in Japan. Following Japan's military success against Russia, a European nation, quite a few articles have been printed in different Bangla magazines, some rejoicing and representing this victory, in the most heroic terms. Also, travelogues of Manmatha Nath Ghosh and Suresh-chandra Bandyopadhyay and others have depicted the rise of a nationalist voice in Japan, during the time they visited Japan. In the following chapter, we will take into account the Indian responses to this discourse of nationalism, and how they have relocated themselves in this discourse.

NOTES

1. James Clifford, *Culture: The Poetics and Politics of Ethnography* (California: University of California, 1986), p. 2.
2. In the year 1868, succumbing to the aggressive demands of the European and American powers, the Tokugawa government was forced to open Japanese ports to the foreign powers. The Tokugawa government came to an end and the power of the emperor was restored. The Meiji Restoration of 1868 also signalled the end of feudalism in Japan. Rapid transformation took place to transform Japan into a capitalist country. For further details, see Amit Bhattacharyya, *Transformation of Japan 1600-1945*, pp. 110-115. As mentioned in Kenneth Scott Latourette's book *The History of Japan*, New York: Macmillan Co., 1968, p. 93, the Meiji era began on 25 January 1868. It ended with Mutsohito's death on 30 July 1912.
3. Raymond Williams in his book *Marxism and Literature*, Oxford University Press, p. 133 has defined 'structures of feeling' as a cultural hypothesis, actually derived from attempts to understand such elements and their connections in a generation, or period, and needing always to be returned, interactively, to such evidence.
4. Rashbehari Bose, Autobiography', trans. Asitava Das, rpt. in *Rash Behari Bose: Collected Works*, ed. Asitava Das (Kolkata: Kisholoy Prakashon, 2006), p. 79.
5. Sureshchandra Bandyopadhyay, *Japan* (Kolkata: Chatterjee & Co., 1910), http://dspace.wbpublibnet.gov.in:8080/jspui/. (Accessed 28 July 2012). p. 9.
6. Casey Blanton Professor of English, Daytona State College and co-editor of *Southern Quarterly*.
7. Casey Blanton, 'Preface', *Travel Writing: The Self and the World* (London: Routledge, 2002), p. 11.
8. Manmatha Nath Ghosh, *Japan Probash* (Dhaka: Dibya Prokash, 2012), p. 49.
9. Kenneth Scott Latourette, *The History of Japan* (New York: Macmillan Co., 1968), p. 93.
10. Girindrachandra Mukhopadhyay, 'Japan', *Bharatbarsa*, Ashin, (1344 BS 1937), p. 612.
11. Ibid.
12. Ghosh, *Japan Probash*, p. 42.
13. Jadunath Sarkar, 'Japaner Rajniti', *Bharati*, Joistho (1313 BS 1906): pp. 205-6.

14. Bandyopadhyay, *Japan*, p. 37.
15. Bhattacharya, *Transformation of Japan*, p. 118.
16. Madhusudhan Mukhopadhyay, *Japan*, (Kolkata: Calcutta School Book and Vernacular Literature Society, 1863), p. 60.
17. Susan Bassnett, 'The Empire Travel Writing and British Studies', in *Travel Writing and the Empire*, ed. Sachindra Mohanty (New Delhi: Katha, 2003), p. 17.
18. Madhusudhan Mukhopadhyay, *Japan*, p. 141.
19. Ibid., p. 137.
20. 'The East India Company in Japan', *Calcutta Review*, (1869), p. 191 (Anonymous writing).
21. The Indian Magazine published by the *The National Indian Association*, was founded by Mary Carpenter in Bristol in the year 1870. The organization is said to have been received assistance from Keshab Chandra Sen. The institution made some progress in encouraging femal education, and the magazine, though published from England, should be taken into consideration for the richness of materials relating to Indian issues.
22. Constance Plumptre, 'The Education in Japan', *Indian Magazine*, 187, (July 1886), p. 345.
23. Sampatro Gaikawad, 'A Glimpse of Japan', *Indian Magazine*, 284, (August 1894), p. 392.
24. Swami Vivekananda, 'Letter from Yokohama', p. 5.
25. Vivekananda, *Collected Works*, 5, p. 140 (See, Vivekananda, 'Conversations and Dialogue' in the Biblio.
26. Refer to Jamsetji's letter to Vivekananda, dated, 23 November 1898. It is included in R.M. Lala's biography, *For the Love of India*, p. 113.
27. T.R. Sareen, 'India and Japan in Historical Perspectives', *India and Japan: in Search of Global Roles*, ed. Rajaram Panda and Yoo Fukazawa (New Delhi: Promilla & Co, 2007), p. 345.
28. Yasuko Horioka, 'Okakura and Swami Vivekananda', *Prabuddha Bharata*, (January1975), p. 31.
29. Ibid., p. 31.
30. Sir Jadunath Sarkar's biography entitled *Life and Letters of Sir Jadunath Sarkar*, ed. H.R. Gupta, records no reference of his travel in foreign countries. Also, in the entry for Sir Jadunath Sarkar, included in the *Dictionary of National Biographies*, ed. S.P. Sen, it has been stated that Professor Sarkar never went out of India.
31. Jadunath Sarkar, 'Japaner Sikha O Banijyo', *Bharati*, Joistho, (1321 BS, 1914), pp. 146-7.
32. Bandyopadhyay, *Japan*, p. 37.

33. M. Visvesvaraya, *Memoirs of My Working Life* (Bombay: G. Claridge & Co., 1951), p. 121.
34. Ibid., p. 128.
35. Sarkar, 'Japaner Sikha O Banijyo', p. 150.
36. Ibid., p. 148.
37. Govt. of West Bengal, Home Political Records of the State Archives, *Trade after the War: Japanese Activities.*, F.N. 36/ 1919, p. 3.
38. Ibid., p. 8.
39. Girindrachandra Mukhopadhyay, 'Japan', *Bharatbarsa*, Ashin, p. 612.
40. Jadunath Sarkar, 'Japaner Sena O Nau Bahini', *Bharati*, Falgun (1318 BS, 1911), p. 1061.
41. Jadunath Sarkar, 'Japaner Rail O Tram' [Japanese Railways & Tramcars'; in Bengali], in *Bharati* (Falgun 1319 BS/1912), pp. 1131-8.
42. Jadunath Sarkar, 'Japaner Rajniti', *Bharati*, Joistho (1313 BS, 1906), p. 199.
43. Kenneth Scott Latourette, *The History of Japan*, pp. 96-118.
44. Visvesvaraya, *Reconstructing India*, London: P.S. King & Son, 1920, p. 3.
45. Ibid., p. 181.
46. Rahul Sankrityayana, *Meri Jiben Yatra* (*Amar Jeevan Jatra*), ed. Satish Mashro and Saikat Rakhit, 2nd vol. (Kolkata: Rahul Sankrityayana Jonmosotoborsho Committee, 1993), p. 288.
47. 'Japane Bharatiyo Chatro', *Bharati*, Poush (1309 BS, 1902), p. 893 (Anonymous writing).
48. 'Bharotbashir Japane Shilposhikha', *Bharati*, Bhadro (1309 BS, 1902), p. 484 (Anonymous writing).
49. Chittabrata Palit and Subrata Pahri, ed., *Satish Chandra Mukherje: The Dawn Society and National Science* (Kolkata: Readers Service, 2002), p. 6.
50. 'Japane Bharatiyo Chatro', p. 898.
51. Amit Bhattacharya, *Swadshi Enterprise in Bengal* (Kolkata: Readers Service, 2008), p. 94.
52. Ghosh, *Japan Probash*, p. 89.
53. Panchanan Mandal, *Bharatsilpi Nandalal*, 2nd vol. (Santiniketan: Rar-Gabeshona Parshod, 1982), p. 211.
54. Ibid., p. 211.
55. Anathbandhu Sarkar, 'Japane Bharatiyo Chatrer Koto Bay Hoy', *Prabasi*, Chaitro, (1315 BS, 1908), pp. 709-10.
56. 'Three Bengali Students in Japan', *Prabasi*, Miscellaneous section, Poush (1316 BS, 1909), p. 759 (Anonymous writing).
57. Family Papers of Dr. Nagendra Mohan Gupta received by the author from Dr. Suchetana Chattopadhyay via gmail, on 20 May 2017 (Anonymous writing).

58. Visvesvaraya, *Memoirs of My Working Life*, p. 55.
59. Bandyopadhyay, *Japan*, p. 157.
60. Ibid., p. 158.
61. Ganapati Roy, 'Japaner Sikha', *Bharati*, Bhadro (1317 BS, 1910), p. 375.
62. Hariprobha Takeda, 'Japane Santan Palon O Nari Sikha', rpt. in *Bongo Mahilar Japan Jatra O Onnano Rachona* (Kolkata: D.M. Library, 2009), pp. 36-7.
63. Sarkar, 'Japaner Songbadpotro', *Bharati*, Magh, (1317 BS, 1912), p. 870.
64. Gourchandra Nath, 'Japaner Sikhaniti' [The Education system in Japan; in Bengali], in *Bharatbarsa* (Srabon 1346 BS, 1939), pp. 258-62.
65. Lajpat Rai, 'Education in Japan', *The Modern Review*, September 1910, pp. 296-305.
66. 'Japane Sikhar Obostha', *Prabasi*, Agrahon (1343 BS, 1936), p. 297 (Anonymous text).
67. Dr. Amit Bhatacharya in his *Transformation of Japan 1600-1945*, p. 98-9, has rightly observed that though 'for the common people of Japan, the advent of Commodore Perry was unexpected; however, for the shogunate it was not. The ruling classes had come to know from the Dutch sources that the Americans had been eyeing Japan for quite some time'.
68. In his book *Transformation of Japan*, Dr. Amit Bhattacharya has rightly pointed out that during the Meiji Era; particular attention was given to set up an industrial structure. The author has referred to the introduction of the postal system in Japan that began in 1871. The author has also referred to the setting up of telegraph, which took place between 1869 and 1880. For further details, refer to the book mentioned above, pp. 122-36.
69. Brij Tankha, *Narratives of Asia from India, Japan and China*, (Kolkata: Sampark, 2005), pp. 48-52.
70. Bandyopadhyay, *Japan*, p. 49.
71. Ibid.
72. Ibid., p. 39.
73. Ibid., p. 88
74. Manmatha Nath Ghosh, *Nabyo Japan* (Kolkata: Sri Devaki Press, 1322 BS, 1915), p. 93.
75. Shakuntala Rao Sastri, trans., *A Visit to Japan by Rabindranath Tagore.* (New York: East West Institute, 1961), p. 68.
76. From the *History of Japan* by Kenneth Scott Latourette, we come to know that in 1614, Iyeyasu, the first ruler of the Shogunates, ordered that all foreign priests be expelled, that all churches be destroyed, and that all Japanese Christians be compelled to give up their faith. For further details, see Latourette, *History of Japan*, pp. 46-51.

77. Ghosh, *Nabyo Japan*, p. 113.
78. Dhirendranath Mukhopadhyay, 'Japan', *Bharatbarsa*, Bhadro (1346 BS, 1939), p. 395.
79. Shitoku Hori, 'Japaner Sanaton Adorsho', *Bharati*, Baishak (1310 BS, 1903), p. 94.
80. Qtd. in Abhijit Mukherjee, 'Tagore's First Visit', in *Tagore and Japan: Dialogue, Exchange and Encounter*, ed. Pratyay Banerjee and Anindya Kundu (New Delhi: Synergy Publishers, 2016), p. 48.
81. The Japanese was *Tenjiku* translates as heavenly kingdom. India being the source of their spirituality, India was revered as a 'Tenjiku' since ancient times.
82. Brij Tankha, *Narratives of Asia from India, Japan and China*, p. 41.
83. Jadunath Sarkar, 'Japaner sohit Bharater Sombondho', *Bharati*, Jaistho (1319 BS, 1912), pp. 125-32.
84. Takeda, *Bongo Mahilar Japan Jatra O Onnano Rachona* (Kolkata: D.M. Library, 2009), p. 50.
85. Sushila Narashimhan, 'India and Japan: Historical and Cultural Linkages', in *India and Japan in Search of Global Roles*, ed. Rajaram Panda and Yoo Fukazawa (New Delhi: Promilla & Co., 2007), pp. 339-40.
86. Rabindranath Tagore, 'India and Japan', rpt. in Japan, *Theke Jorasanko*, ed. Satyasri Ukil (Kolkata: New Age, 2005), p. 262.
87. Stephen Hay, *Asian Ideas of East and West*, (Bombay: Oxford University Press, 1970), pp. 53-4.
88. Rabindranath Tagore,'The Spirit of Japan', http://www.gutenberg.org/ebooks/33131. (Accessed on 18 May 2013), p. 3.
89. Shakuntala Rao Sastri, trans., *A Visit to Japan by Rabindranath Tagore*, (New York: East West Institute, 1961), p. 72.
90. Tagore, 'The Spirit of Japan', p. 4.
91. Ibid., p. 4.
92. Rabindranath Tagore, *Japan Jatri*, (Kolkata: Visva Bharati, 1417 BS, 2000), p. 70.
93. Tagore, 'India and Japan', pp. 263-4.
94. Rabindranath Tagore, 'The Message from India to Japan', rpt. in *Japan Theke Jorasanko*, ed. Satyasri Ukil (Kolkata: New Age, 2005), p. 267.
95. Ibid., p. 269.
96. Tagore, 'The Spirit of Japan', p. 5.
97. Rustom Bharucha, *Another Asia*, (Kolkata: Oxford University Press, 2006), p. 68.
98. Tagore, 'The Message from India to Japan', p. 271.

99. Manilal Gangopadhyay, 'Japaner Jhorna', *Bharati*, Srabon (1320 BS, 1913), p. 420.
100. Ibid., p. 417.
101. Manmatha Nath Ghosh, *Supto Japan* (Kolkata: Sri Devaki Press, 1322 BS, 1915), p. 81.
102. Manmatha Nath Ghosh, *Nabya Japan* (Kolkata: Sri Devaki Press, 1322 BS, 1915), p. 25.
103. Bandyopadhyay, *Japan*, p. 118.
104. Surechchandra Bandyopadhyay, 'Japaner Naboborsho', *Bharati*, Boishak (1320 BS,1913), p. 35
105. Sachindra Mohanty, 'Introduction: Beyond the Imperial Eye', *Trvavel Writing and the Empire*, ed. Sachindra Mohanty (New Delhi: Katha, 2003), p. xi.
106. Bandyopadhyay, *Japan*, p. 128.
107. Mukulchandra Dey, 'Mukulchandrar Lekha Chithi', *Mukulchandra Dey: Japan Theke Jorasanko*, ed. Satyasri Ukil (Kolkata: New Age, 2005), p. 26.
108. Sastri, *A Visit to Japan by Rabindranath Tagore*, p. 72.
109. Kakuzo Okakura, *The Book of Tea* (U.S.A.: Dreamsymth, 1906), https://www.tug.org. (accessed on 12 June 2012), p. 1.
110. Ghosh, *Japan Probash*, p. 68.
111. Jadunath Sarkar, 'Japani Akriti Prokriti', *Bharati*, Boishak (1318 BS, 1911), p. 47.
112. Sarkar, 'Daidokoro', *Bharati*, Magh (1320 BS, 1913), pp. 1065-6.
113. Ibid., pp. 1067
114. *Ghosh, Japan Probash*, p. 65.
115. Dey, *Japan Theke Jorashanko*, p. 35.
116. Rabindranath Tagore, *Nationalism*, rpt. in *Rabindranath Tagore Omnibus III* (New Delhi: Rupa & Co., 2011), p. 16.
117. Ibid., p. 17.
118 . Lafcadio Hearn and Basil Hall, 'Some Characteristics of Modern Japanese Life and Character', *Dawn*, 1903 May, rpt. in *The Dawn*, vol.VI, ed. Madhabendra Nath Mitra (Kolkata: National Council of Education, 2005), p. 284.
119. Ibid., pp. 285-6.
120. Binoy Kumar Sarkar, 'Japaner Dilli', *Bharatbarsa*, Jaistho (1317 BS, 1910); *Sekaler Bangla Samoyikpotre Japan*, ed. Subrata Kumar Das (Dhaka: Nabajuga Prokashoni, 2012), p. 115.
121. Rabindranath Tagore, 'To The Indian Community in Japan', April 1925,

rpt. in *Japan Jatri,* by Rabindranath Tagore (Kolkata: Visva Bharati, 1417 BS, 2007), p. 121.

122. Ibid., p. 125.
123. Tagore, *Japan Jatri,* p. 70.
124. *Sentou* (Japanese Public Bath), http://www.japan-101.com/travel/sento.htm. (Accessed on 12 December 2012).
125. Ghosh, *Japan Probash,* p. 66.
126. Sastri, *A Visit to Japan by Rabindranath Tagore,* p. 75.
127. Takeda, *Japan Jatra,* p. 45.
128. Ibid., 60.
129. Ibid., 47.
130. Takeda, 'Japane Nari', rpt. in *Bongo Mahilar Japan Jatra O Onnano Rachona,* pp. 59-62 (Kolkata: D.M. Library, 2009), p. 61.
131. Brajosundor Sanyal, 'Japane Stri Sikha', *Prabasi,* Agrahan (1315 BS, 1908), p. 436.
132. Sanyal, 'Japane Stri Sikha', p. 439.
133. Bandyopadhyay, *Japan,* p. 104.
134. Ibid., p. 104.
135. Ibid., p. 82.
136. Ghosh, *Japan Probash,* p. 61.
137. Ibid., p. 61.
138. Ghosh, *Nabya Japan,* p. 110.
139. Ibid., p. 31.
140. Ghosh, *Nabyo Japan,* p. 109.
141. 'Geishar Swadhinota', *Bharati,* Poush (1329 BS, 1922), p. 875.
142. Ghosh, *Nabyo, Japan,* p. 11.
143. Bandyopadhyay, *Japan,* p. 63.
144. *Yojimbo,* Dir. Akira Kurosawa, Perf. Toshiro Mifune, Eijiro Tono, (1961).
145. See, Wikipedia.org/Prostitution in Japan, also, Wikipedia.org/Yoshiwara.
146. Ghosh, *Nabyo Japan,* p. 54.
147. Ibid., p. 55.
148. Sekhar Bandyopadhyay, 'Caste, Widow Remarriage and the Reform of Popular Culture in Colonial Bengal', *Women and Social Reform in Modern India: A Reader,* ed. Sumit Sarkar & Tanika Sarkar (Bloomington, Indiana: Indiana U Press, 2008), pp. 145-6.
149. Sastri, *A Visit to Japan by Rabindranath Tagore,* p. 68.
150. Olfra Gidoni Goldstein, 'Kimono and the Construction of Gendered and Cultural Identities', http://people.socsci.tau.ac.il, 2001, (accessed on 17 July 2013), p. 16.

CHAPTER 2

Pan-Asianism and Bengal

The rise of Japan as a modern Asian state, following the Meiji Restoration of 1868, is a significant event in the history of Asia of the last century. Within a very short span of time, Japan rose as an important power in Asia; Japanese industrialization made significant progress, and a complete transformation from a feudal society to a capitalist one, was secured within a relatively shorter period of time, than in many European nations. It must also be noted that the same period following the Meiji Restoration of 1868, also marks the rise of militarism in Japan. Quoting the words of Marlene J. Mayo, the author of the text *The Emergence of Imperial Japan*, it can be said that 'in the long reign of Meiji emperor (1868-1912), Japan became a modern state, an empire and a world power'. Mayo has cited a succession of military interventions that took place before 1910, the year of annexation of Korea by the Japanese government. These include settling in Hokkaido and incorporation of Ryukyu Islands and the Bonins, extending its jurisdiction over Kuriles, and setting up a colonial administration in Formosa (present Taiwan), and also taking over the southern part of Sakhalin.[1] In my opinion, the ideology of Pan-Asianism should be viewed with reference to this process of modernization of Japan, and also with reference to the advent of Japan as a world power, during the late nineteenth and the early twentieth century. In the previous chapter, we have tried to note how the problem of ensuring national security, was a disturbing issue for the Meiji statesmen. Responding to the threat of losing sovereignty, the Meiji emperor, took significant measures to reconstruct the Japanese army, according to the western standard of that time. As mentioned earlier, Japan witnessed this menace of western aggression in 1853. In 1853, Commodore

Perry reached the Japanese shore, and demanded commercial relations withJapan. This historical event paved the way for the end of the long isolation policy taken during the previous Tokugawa period (1603-1868). Also, the degradation of other parts of Asia, following their subjugation to western powers, was not unknown to the Japanese people. Brij Tankha in his book entitled *Narratives of Asia from India, Japan and China*, has dealt in details, how the pre-Tokugawa Japanese idea about both India and China, underwent a transformation, following Japan's contact with the European nations from the middle of sixteenth century. India had earlier been revered as *Tenjiku* (a heavenly kingdom). Tankha has rightly pointed out that as a result of European contact, India, which was revered as *Tenjiku*, lost its position from its place of privilege'.[2] The author also refers to the account of shipwrecked sailors, who gave the Japanese people the changed image of India. In Sushila Narasimhan's essay entitled, 'India and Japan: Historical and Cultural Linkages', we also get a similar impression how, the awareness about successive foreign rule in India contributed to this changed image of India by the Japanese people. The writer has referred to quite a few early Japanese historical texts, dealing with the Mughal period in India, and also the rise of British rule in India. As in the case of India, Japanese impression of China too underwent significant changes, by the end of the Tokugawa period. A text that has been cited by Brij Tankha in his *Narratives of Asia*, and Matsumoto Kenichi in his essay entitled, 'Okakura Tenshin and the Ideal of Pan-Asianism', in their discussion on Pan-Asianism, is a diary written by Takasugi Shinsaku (1839-67), a member of the delegation, which was sent to China by the Tokugawa Shogunate. The diary of Takasugi documented the degradation of China as a process of colonisation by the western powers.[3] Brij Tankha has pointed out that the 'dominant lesson Takasugi drew was the danger of being colonised'.[4] Brij Tankha and other scholars have justly related this change of perception about the neighbouring nations of Japan, at the beginning of the Meiji Era, to this discourse of Pan-Asianism. Further, from these discussions carried out by scholars like Brij Tankha and Matsumoto Kenichi, we learn about the two opposed intellectual positions taken by the

Japanese leaders of the Meiji Era regarding Asian nations. The first group has been categorized by Brij Tankha as, 'transcend Asia'. This shows the direct influence of the eminent Japanese thinker, Yukichi Fukuzawa, who advocated that Japan needed to transcend the reality, which other Asian countries were facing at that time. The second group has been categorized by Brij Tankha as 'Revive Asia'; as in this discourse the success of Japan was related to the development and survival of China and other neighbouring parts of Asia. For Brij Tankha, and for many other scholars, the difference between these two ideological positions taken by Meiji statesmen was negligible. According to Tankha, both the groups stressed heavily on Japan's superiority among other Asian nations.[5]

Thus, Pan-Asianism as an ideology also incorporated Japanese expansionist policies. Matsumoto Kenichi has pointed out this in his essay 'Okakura Tenshin and the ideal of Pan-Asianism', referring to another text entitled, 'Pan-Asianism in Japan' by Takeuchi Yoshimi.[6] The other significant aspect of this ideology, one voicing for the solidarity of all Asian nation, to form a confederation opposed to the western powers, was also admitted by Matsumoto Kenichi in his essay, referring to another article by Nohara Jiro entitled, 'The Great Asian Doctrine': '. . . It calls upon the various Asian races to unite under the leadership of Japan to protest against invasion by the Great Western Powers into Asia.'[7]

Japan's military success against Russia in the Russo-Japanese War in 1905, drew the attention of the world. With this historical event, Japan turned out to be a role model for the whole East. With reference to this impact of Japan's success on Asian nations, another scholar, Yumiko Iida has noted that Tokyo witnessed an 'unprecedented increase in the number of Asian students eagerly seeking knowledge of modernization', and also, Tokyo during this period became a base for expatriate revolutionaries of different Asian nations.[8] Yumiko Iida has referred to the activities of Sun Yat-sen, who took political asylum in Japan, and established the *Chugoku Kakumei Domekai* (Chinese Revolutionary Association) there. Further, according to Yumiko Iida, the Chinese revolution of 1911, which overthrew the Ch'ing dynasty, gained support from Japanese revolutionary idealists like Miyazaki Toten and Kita Ikki.[9] It would not be irrelevant to mention here that Rash Behari Bose escaped from India and reached Japan in 1915. Japan, which signed the Anglo-Japanese Alliance with Great Britain, was obliged to remain as an ally of the Great Britain during the period of the First World War. Later, The British Embassy came to know that Bose was hiding in Japan, and the Japanese Foreign Embassy complying with the demands of the British government, issued a deportation order. From Rash Behari Bose's biography written by Takeshi Nakajima, entitled *Bose of Nakamura*, we get an arresting description of how Rash Behari Bose was rescued by the members of a nationalist group called *Genyosha*, headed by Michiru Toyoma, a nationalist ideologue of Japan at that time. Takeshi Nakajima has also pointed out that the deportation order of two Indian revolutionary, Rash Behari Bose and H.L. Gupta, received severe criticism; the author has referred to an edition of *Tokyo Asahi Shimbun*, which criticised the Japanese government for complying with the 'British policy of dividing the solidarity of Asian'.[10] Both of them were rescued and skilfully hid at Nakamuraya, a bakery in the Shinjuku area of Tokyo city. Nakajima has also cited a translated portion of the autobiography of Kokko Soma, the owner of the baker, who later became the mother-in-law of Bose. Soma has stated that she was even prepared to go to jail, for providing shelter to these political refugees from India. Nakajima's observation is worth noting: 'Such a mindset is the manifestation of emotional Asianism that a majority of the common people in Japan had at that time.'[11]

A similar kind of argument, we come across in the editorial note given by Marlene. J. Mayo, the editor of the book entitled *The Emergence of Imperial Japan*. Mayo in his introductory note referring to an essay entitled 'Pan-Asianism' by Marius Jansen, has commented that 'many Japanese sincerely wanted to help Asia, in particular to revive China.[12] Marius Jansen's essay has dealt in details with Sun Yat-sen's political asylum in Japan, and how he received cooperation and aid from the nationalists of Japan. I am here tempted to refer to a document, which I found in the State Archives, I.B. West Bengal Government. The C.I.D. file (File no. 350/1925) deals with the proscription and forfeiture of a Bangla book entitled, *Sun Yat-sen* by Sri Narendranth Roy. The file includes a typed copy of the translation of certain passages from the book. The excerpts, referred to in the police file, starts describing the process of colonisation in China that started from the time of the Teiping rebellion in 1864. The decadence of China as a consequence of its subjugation to western powers, and also of other parts of Asia, where a mighty civilization had sprung once, an inseparable part of the Pan-Asian discourse, dealing with the possibility of the revival of Asia, and freeing her from colonial yoke, has also been touched upon in the translated text:

> Asia is the birth place of all civilizations of the world. It is with her thought, language and religion that the western world has become so prosperous today. But in return for all that the western nations are today trampling upon the eastern world and treating her as a slave. The humiliation of Asia touched the noble heart of Sun-Yat Sen. He was trying to revive the lost glory of Asia. So once he exclaimed in grief 'On whichever country of Asia I cast my eye I see one or other nation of Europe or America in possession of some part of it'.[13]

Pan-Asianism, the subject of our enquiry, is far from being a single homogenous discourse. As Eri Hotta, the author of the book *Pan-Asianism and Japan's War (1931-45)* has pointed out that it included three major threads. The first type, according to the author, put emphasis on the Asian commonalities in the vast philosophical dimension of Asia, and this included China and India. The second type, according to the author, called for an alliance among closer nations of East Asia on the basis of racial and cultural affinity. The third one, according to the writer, synchronized and got fused with Japan's expansionist and ultranationalist policies, representing Japan as the leader of the whole East.[14] Hotta has coined the term 'transnational nationalism' to describe the true nature of this ideology. The choice of this term indicates the paradoxical nature of Pan-Asianism, which spoke of solidarity among Asian people, and at the same time, emphasized Japan's superiority over other Asian countries. Thus critics like Yumiko Iida, whose essay *Fleeing the West, Making Asia Home: Transposition of Otherness in Japanese Pan-Asanism*, we have already referred to, have rightly pointed out that the theory of 'racial affinity' among East Asian people, propounded by a Japanese ideologue named Tarui Tokichi, received wide acceptance among Asianists of the 1900s. This theory of political unification of countries, based on cultural similarity, was voiced as a justification of annexation of Korea by Japan in 1910, and similar expansionist policies of the Japanese government, during the first three decades of the last century.[15]

It will not be any more profitable, to try to take into account of the role, Pan-Asianism played during the rise of militarism in Japan, referring to many such books, dealing with the history of Japan of the last century. Truly, the scope of this chapter entitled, 'Pan-Asianism and Bengal', does not require a detailed study of the history of the rise of a strong nationalist voice in Japan. In this chapter, we will try to locate how Indian writers, chiefly from Bengal of that time, have reacted to this discourse, more particularly, have relocated themselves within this discourse.

One important historical event that created an excitement in this part of the empire is Japan's victory over Russia in 1905. This incident exploded the myth of white men's supremacy over Asians. The galvanizing impact it had upon the educated cross section of Bengal, can be traced by referring to a variegated document, such as articles published in the magazines like the *Bharati, Prabasi, The Modern Review*, and also, travelogues and memoirs, written during this period. The other significant event, that has already been referred, is the visit of Tenshin Okakura to Kolkata. Tenshin Okakura, the eminent art critic and curator, came to Kolkata, and his association with Tagore and his generation are an integral part of this discourse. In Bengal, this period, i.e. the early twentieth century, witnessed the rise of the Swadeshi and Boycott movement, and also that of the activities of revolutionary groups like the Anushilan Samiti and the Jugantar group. It must be noted that the Anglo-Japanese Alliance was concluded in 1902[16], and during the period of the First World War, Japan remained a political ally of Great Britain. Thus, officially the scope of attaining support for the cause of Indian freedom struggle was limited at that time. Still, nationalists in Japan were positive towards Indian freedom fighters. Thus, a close study of texts, such as memoirs, biographies, dealing with this period, also, archival sources, reveals the anxiety of revolutionaries of Bengal to seek all kinds of assistance from Japan, as, money, arms and ammunitions and also, moral support. Again, Japan's expansionist policies, exploitation and oppression of the people of Korea and other parts of Asia, did not remain unknown to the people of Bengal. Significantly, in many writings, published during this period, we come across disillusionment with Japan's role as a leading Asian nation. It is interesting to note that, within the span of two years, i.e. from 1915 to 1916, Rash Behari Bose, Tagore and Sarat Chandra Das reached Japan. However, their writings on Japan, as well as, their activities, represent different attitudes towards Japan's political role of this period. Rash Behari Bose's articles in English, entitled, 'Notes From Japan', published in the *Standard Bearer* during the 1920s, the radio broadcasts from Japan, which voiced his messages to his countrymen, also, his Japanese writings, speak of his tireless effort to ensure Japanese support for the cause of Indian freedom struggle. With reference to the issue of Japanese nationalism, it must be noted that Tagore's attitude towards Japan, was one of accord and discord. An admirer of a sensitive attitude towards aesthetics, which he found in Japan, Tagore in his lectures has warned the Japanese people against imitation of Western civilization, especially, western political system that relies upon unrestrained use of power. On the other hand, Tibetologist Sarat Chandra Das came to Japan in 1915 along with Ekai Kawaguchi, a Japanese Buddhist scholar, who visited Tibet during the early twentieth century. Sarat Chandra Das delivered an address at the meeting of Indo-Japanese Association, during his stay in Japan. His lecture has been included in the book *Japan theke Jorasanko*, edited by Satyasri Ukil. It conveys a completely different message than those of Tagore and Rash Behari Bose. Das laid emphasis on a political alliance between Japan and England. Reception of an ideology, can never be only of blind adherence, but also includes multiple responses. To conclude, in this chapter, entitled 'Pan-Asianism and Bengal', I will try to locate, how writers from Bengal, have reacted to the political role Japan played as a leading Asian nation, during the early twentieth century. As noted earlier, the time span chosen, gives us a scope of taking into account of literary materials, belonging to a span of roughly 45 years; beginning in 1893, the year Swami Vivekananda visited Japan, and ending in 1938, the year, in which an epistolary debate issued between Tagore and Noguchi, due to their opposed view on Japan's aggression on China in 1931. This can provide us a scope of assessing our divergent responses to their politics.

ACCEPTANCE OF JAPAN AS THE LEADER OF THE EAST

Kamaladevi Chattopadhdhya in the introduction of her book entitled, *Japan: Its Weakness and Strength*, commenting on the historical significance of the Meiji Restoration of Japan, has rightly pointed that it is from this radical transformation of Japan into a modern state that, Japan turned out to be a role model for all oppressed and colonised races of Asia: 'Japan's turning the corner in 1868, known as the Meiji Restoration, is historically of immense significance to the entire Orient. For Japan stood like an oasis of freedom in the bleak colonial desert of Asia.'[17]

Thus, Japan started attracting the attention of millions of colonial India, and other Asian nations, from the middle of the nineteenth century, and much earlier than Japan's military success against Russia in 1905. Another interesting article that can be referred to in this context, is a Bangla essay entitled, 'Japane Bharatiyo Chatro', which was published in the Poush issue of the Bangla magazine *Bharati* (1309 BS). In the first Chapter of this thesis, I have already referred to this essay. According to the anonymous article that was published in the vernacular magazine *Bharati*, it was about the time of Sino-Japanese War (1894-5), when from Japan became an attractive destination for Indian students aspiring to learn technical education from abroad: 'The Sino-Japanese War took place a few decades back. It was from this time that Japan turned out to be an attractive destination for foreign students. People having political insight, could easily foresee that in near future, Japan would become one of the superpowers of the world.'[18]

With reference to these documents, it may be said that the end of the late nineteenth century in Japan, marks the advent of Japan as a modern nation, and also an important power in Asia to determine the fate of many other subjügated races of Asia. In the first Chapter, we have referred to the writings of Swami Vivekananda and M. Visvesvaraya. Both of them reached during the late nineteenth century.

'The world has never seen such a patriotic and artistic race as the Japanese', observed Vivekananda, while giving reply to the questions asked by the correspondent of *The Hindu,* Madras, February 1897.[19] Vivekananda further stated, replying to the interviewer's question, that he considered the Japanese people's love for their nation, and also self reliance, as the prime factor for their astounding success. We have earlier referred to Vivekananda's letter written from Yokohama, dated, 10 July 1893. His interview given to the correspondent of *The Hindu,* has also been mentioned. Both of these writings speak of Vivekananda's admiration for the patriotism of Japanese people. In this context, it must be said that though in case of Japan, the development process, almost overlaps with the rise of militant nationalism, and the Sino-Japanese War (1894-5) took place just a year after Vivekananda visited Japan, still at that time, the curse of this nationalism was not so prominent. In later writings on Japan, by writers of the twentieth century, we will notice how this reaction against Japan's militarism has been reflected. It is the self-sacrificing nature of the Japanese people, which drew his admiration, and this quality he felt, was missing among his countrymen: 'When you have men who are ready to sacrifice their everything for their country, sincere to the backbone—when such men arise, India will become great in every respect.'[20]

From Vivekananda's conversation with Priya Nath Sinha, narrated by the latter, and included in the 'Conversations and Dialogues' (vol. 5), we further learn that Vivekananda had plans to send graduates to Japan for undertaking technical education: 'In my opinion, if all our rich and educated men once go to Japan, their eyes will be opened.'[21]

Priya Nath Sinha while exchanging his views with Swami Vivekananda expressed his admiration for Japanese art, the source of which, according to him was rooted in Japanese culture, and not was borrowed from the West. To this, Swamiji's ready repartee was: 'Don't you see they are Asiatics. . . . The very soul of Asiatic is interwoven with art.'[22]

In the Introduction of this chapter, we have already tried to locate how this conceptualization of Asia, based on cultural affinity, gained confidence among thinkers of various Asian countries of the late nineteenth and the early twentieth century. Amitava Acharya in his article entitled, 'Asia is Not One', has delved deep into these various constructions of Asia that emerged during this period. One such category has been rightly termed by Acharya as *universalist Asia.*[23] We can agree with Acharya that even before Japanese imperialism could sweep through Asia, there emerged another conception of Asia that may be termed *universalist Asia.* According to Acharya, this conception of 'universalist Asia' is based on a common bond of spiritualism among Asia's people'.[24] Thus, Vivekananda's conception of Asia, as inheriting a common heritage of spiritualism, may be viewed as one such construction of Asia, which finds an important place in the Pan-Asian discourse. The same idea of cultural unity of Asia has been echoed in several writings of Tenshin Okakura. It would not be irrelevant here to recall of how Pearson, having spotted an Indian image in a remote temple in the Japanese mountains, was amazed, and was induced to muse on the unity of Asia, based on 'invisible bonds of spiritual kinship', a phrase, he coins, while recounting his feeling in his article entitled, 'On an Indian Image found in Japan'. Pearson's remark in the concluding part of the article needs citing: 'It speaks of her past when she drew from India and from China her daily life. It speaks also of her future that destiny which is in the hands of the gods when she shall give back that which she has received and realize again that Asia is one and not divided.'[25]

Vivekananda was invited by Okakura to visit Japan and offer a lecture. Though Vivekananda responded positively to this invitation, he finally could not avail it due to his ill health.[26] From Yasuku Horioka's essay entitled, 'Okakura and Swami Vivekananda', published in the magazine *Prabuddha Bharata* (January 1975), we further learn that Miss MacLeod, a disciple of Swamiji, during his stay in Japan in the year 1901, carried out a correspondence with Okakura, regarding their plan to invite Swamiji to deliver a speech at a Japanese version of Parliament of Religions.[27] Vivekananda's letter to Miss MacLeod, dated, 14 June 1901, quoted by Harioka, may also be referred to in this context:

> I am so glad you are enjoying Japan especially Japanese art. You are perfectly correct in saying that we will have to learn many things from Japan. The help that Japan will give us will be with great sympathy and respect, whereas that from the West unsympathetic and destructive. Certainly, it is very desirable to establish a connection between India and Japan.[28]

Vivekananda desired to establish a connection with Japan. This, he believed will be helpful for the advancement of India, though it must be remembered that his admiration for Japan had no political implication.

With the beginning of the twentieth century, Bengal and other parts of India, witnessed the rise of a nationalist movement. The beginning of this turbulent age in Bengal was followed by Lord Curzon's decision to partition Bengal. It is during this Swadeshi age, that Japan turned out to be a subject of scrutiny, for the educated classes of Bengal.

Aurobindo Ghosh, the ideologue of the Swadeshi movement, in his essay entitled, 'India and Mongolian', published in the *Bande Mataram* (Calcutta, 1 April 1908) welcomed this rise of a nationalist spirit in China and Japan. For Aurobindo, this awakening of the Mongols had a definite political role to play. He was hoping that this awakening of Asia would facilitate anti-colonial struggle in India, and eventually, India would gain her freedom from colonial rule:

> The awakening of Asia is the fact of the twentieth century and in that awakening the lead has been given to the Mongolian races of the Far East. In the genius, the patriotic spirit, the quick imitative faculty of Japan; in the grand deliberation the patient thoroughness, the irresistible organizations of China, Providence found the necessary material force which would meet the European with his own weapons and outdo him in that science, strength and ability which are his peculiar pride.[29]

Referring to a lecture of Bipin Chandra Pal, who according to Ghosh, pioneered in welcoming the awakening of Asia, and also expecting the 'possibility of China and Japan overthrowing

European civilization', Ghosh in this article shows conformity with Bipin Pal's view. Also, like many of his contemporaries, he has wholeheartedly welcomed Japan's military success against Russia in the Russo-Japanese War: 'The first blow given by the Mongolian fell upon Russia because she stood across the Asiatic continent barring the westward surge his destiny. The second blow will fall on England because she holds Asia.'[30]

In this article, Ghosh has expressed the view that this sudden awakening of the Mongolian races has filled the European nations with terror and are witnessing a 'Yellow Peril'; 'a palsy has come upon their strength' and 'with blanched lips they watch every movement of the two Asian giants'.[31]

Is it not surprising that the expression, 'Yellow Peril', has also been coined by Okakura in his *Awakening of Japan*? Okakura coined the term to show this hyperbolic reaction of the West regarding the success of Japan: 'We are both the cherished child of modern progress and a dread resurrection of heathendom—the Yellow Peril.'[32]

For Okakura, this 'Yellow Peril' is a creation of the West, which for him, is rooted in racial prejudice. *The Awakening of Japan* was first published in the year1905; three years prior to the publication of Aurobindo's essay. It is difficult to say whether or not Aurobindo Ghosh read Okakura's *Awakening of Japan*. Still, in both these two writings, the trope of 'Awakening of Asia' finds an important place. This fact cannot be easily ignored.

Another significant aspect of Aurobindo's vision of Asia is that it is not Japan alone, which gains the central focus; on the other hand, Aurobindo's Asia encompasses China and the Islamic world of the West Asia. Brij Tankha in his book entitled, *Narratives of Asia*, has rightly pointed out this aspect of Aurobindo's political writings. Referring to Aurobindo's another essay, 'Asiatic Democracy', published in the *Bande Mataram* (16 March 1908), Brij Tankha has also pointed out that for Aurobindo, 'the real strength of Asia, lay in the Islamic ideal of equality and the divine unity of man and spirit, as expressed in the Vedanta'.[33] We must also note, how Aurobindo's vision of China, a mighty civilization of the East, differs from that of Vivekananda. It is quite surprising that though

Vivekananda on different occasions has praised Japan and her people, his letter from Yokohama, dated 10 July 1893, and included in the 5th volume of his collected works, speak of his contemptuous attitude towards Chinese towns that he visited:

> But with all its population, all its activities, it is the dirtiest town I saw, not in the sense in which a town is called dirty in India, for as to that not a speck of filth is allowed by the Chinese to go waste; but because of the Chinaman, who has, it seems, taken a vow never to bathe!. . . . The streets are very very narrow, so that you almost touch the shops on both sides as you pass. At every ten paces you find meat-stalls, and there are shops which sell cat's and dog's meat. Of course, only the poorest classes of Chinamen eat dog or cat.[34]

Aurobindo Ghosh, on the other hand, in his article entitled 'India and the Mongolian', has judiciously taken into account the consequence of colonization, an important factor, which according to him, has lead to the degeneration of a great civilization that once developed in India and in China, of which, we find no mentioning in Vivekananda's writing:

> . . . the palace of the Aryan Emperors is now the hut of a crouching slave, small in ideas, mean in his aspirations, his head sunk, his eyes downcast, so that he cannot see the heavens above him or the magnificent earth around. . . . We hold it to be greatest injury of all that England has done us, that she has thus degraded our soul and dwarfed our imagination.[35]

The idea of 'Asian unity', based on a common heritage, has been voiced by many writers of India of this period. However, it must also be remembered that one can also locate contrasting aspects relating to the construction of Asia, as we find in the writings of these two Indian writers.

The beginning of the twentieth century marked the rise of anti-colonial movements in China also, as it happened in India. An interesting document that I would like mention, is a report on an article published in the *Indian Mirror*, 18 March 1906. It was included in the *Report on the Indian Newspapers and Periodicals in Bengal (January-March 1906)*, Home Political, West Bengal State Archives[36]:

The *Indian Mirror* places among the foremost problems of the day the change which is rapidly coming over the relations between the Occidental and Oriental races. The change is illustrated by the efforts that are being made by the Asiatic races to rival their Western brothers. China is straining every nerve to attain Japan's success.

The report published in the *Indian Mirror* and referred to in the *Report on the Indian Newspapers and Periodical*, has stated that about 10,000 Chinese students at that time, were taking education in Japan, further, there were presence of Japanese military instructors and teachers in China. The report has also taken into account the birth of a nationalist spirit, which led to boycotting of American goods and of resistance towards foreign enterprise in general. According to the report, one significant cause of this rise of an anti-colonial spirit should be attributed to Japan's victory over Russia. However, more than that, it is racial discrimination against Asians that had been perpetuated for a long time, which should be the real cause of this situation:

The correct explanation is to be found in the following words of a progressive Chinese official, addressed to an English gentleman, 'The future contains no yellow peril for Europe or America, but it does contain one for Europeans and Americans unless nation and people learn to treat Asiatics with consideration'.

Now, coming back to our earlier issue, i.e. the early political writings of Aurobindo Ghosh, we can say that, though Aurobindo does not refer to any definite political movement of China of that period, he kept an eye on the changing political scenario of China. In his essay, 'India and the Mongolian', Aurobindo in his own rhetorical manner has welcomed this advent of a nationalist spirit in China, during the first decade of early twentieth century: '. . . or what will happen when China, the Titan of the world, shall have completed her quiet, steady, imperturbable preparation.'[37]

It is in the political writings of Aurobindo Ghosh, that the Pan-Asian ideal of an Asian unity, as opposed to western imperialism, is so unequivocally stated. For Aurobindo, this awakening of Asia will ultimately lead to the end of the British rule in India: 'When the inevitable happens and the Chinese armies knock at the

Himalayan gates of India and Japanese fleets appear before Bombay harbour, by what strength will England oppose this gigantic combination?'[38]

We have already noted that Aurobindo Ghosh in his early political writings published in the *Bande Mataram*, wholeheartedly welcomed Japan's victory against Russia in 1905. In the first Chapter, we have also referred to Sumit Sarkar's view that the news of Japanese victory 'was ecstatically hailed by the Bengal press'.[39] In this context, it should be noted that almost in all the travelogues on Japan, written during this period, also, in many articles that were published in different journals, we come across descriptions or references of this war. These accounts of the Russo-Japanese War (1904-5) serve two purposes; firstly, they give us an idea about the rise of militarism in Japan, also, in most cases, they celebrate Japan's victory.

I have earlier referred to Sureshchandra Bandyopadhyay's travelogue *Japan*. Sureshchandra Bandyopadhyay, who reached Nagasaki on 1 January 1906, has recounted his experience of a mob-unrest in Japan, as an outcome of people's outrageous reaction against the Portsmouth Treaty (September 1905)[40] that was signed by both the combatant countries, Russia and Japan, leading to the end of the war. As mentioned in Sureshchandra's travelogue, the treaty led to public agitation as people considered the treaty to be humiliating for Japan.[41] A similar account of public agitation and of mob-violence, as a consequence of this disagreement regarding the Portsmouth Treaty, we also come across in Jadunath Sarkar's article entitled, 'Mikado', published in the Bangla journal *Bharati* (Ashin, 1319 BS). From this account, we come to know that this state-sponsored jingoism became so overpowering that the Japanese government later found much difficulty to restrain this agitation:

> After the end of the war, a treaty was signed between the two countries (Russia and Japan). Though the Japanese government agreed to the proposal of the treaty, the people of Japan strongly resented to the treaty agreements. Soon, people became furious and incidents of mob-violence and lawlessness started taking place. In one night, around 250 police posts in Tokyo were torched and even newspaper offices and houses of government officials came under attack.[42]

That the treaty of Portsmouth, turned to be dissatisfying for the mass of Japan, is also mentioned in Kenneth Scott Latourette's book *The History of Japan.* According to the author, Japanese people had been expecting a large indemnity and the victory of Japanese army also raised the hope that their expectation would be fulfilled. However, the writer is of the opinion that, during the process of negotiation with Russians at Portsmouth, the demand for indemnity was dropped by the Japanese envoys in lieu of an assurance of control over a larger territory. The common people of Japan failed to recognize the trick played by their government, and this misunderstanding between Japan and her people, according to the author, was the source of the violent agitation, which broke after the end of Russo-Japanese War and had been witnessed by travellers from Bengal who had been there during that period.

In other travelogues of Japan of this period, as in Hariprobha Takeda's *Bango Mahilar Japan Jatra,* and in Sureshchandra Bandyopadhyay's travelogue entitled *Japan,* we find references of this particular war. Takeda has described her visit to a Japanese temple, where she found display of canons and other objects, which were captured from the Russians during the war,[43] A similar picture of exhibition of war trophies, we also come across in Sureshchandra Bandyopadhyay's travelogue *Japan*: 'Rifles, canons were displayed in the lawn of the house, where the display was taking place. I found a huge canon and felt that this gun might have bombarded many Russian fortresses. The gun could be pointed at any direction in no time, and also could be lowered or raised high. It was an automatic canon and it needed no soldier for its use.'[44]

The travel-writer has given an impressive description of display of armaments, which he visited during his stay in Japan. He has also mentioned that the display included an iron bed that had been used by Russian officers, later captured by the Japanese. His depiction expresses his wonder at the progress Japan had achieved in warfare. However, nowhere has he objected to this display of looted properties of enemy countries. The fact that such display of war trophies includes jingoism is not at all raised. On the other hand, we notice how description of the same political scenario, can be different in other writings. Thus, referring to a portion from Tagore's *Nationalism*, Hay in his *Asian Ideas of East and West* has rightly pointed out that Tagore during his stay in Japan must have seen some war trophies being displayed in a Tokyo school. Hay has quoted Tagore's denouncement of parading the victor's pride of its own superiority, a practice, which Tagore felt that Japan had imitated from the West:

> To imbue the minds of a whole people with an abnormal vanity of its own superiority, to teach it to take pride in its moral callousness and ill-begotten wealth, to perpetuate humiliation of defeated nations by exhibiting trophies won from war, and using these in schools in order to breed in children's minds contempt for others, is imitating the West where she has a festering sore, whose swelling is a swelling of disease eating into its vitality.[45]

It is true that Tagore's denouncement of Japanese nationalism is an aspect, we hardly notice in other travelogues of that period. Still, it must also be admitted that, the time when Sureshchandra Bandyopadhyay visited Japan, i.e. just at the end of Russo-Japanese War, a larger section of Bengali intelligentsia were overwhelmed by the news of Japanese victory over a European nation. Rathindranath Tagore in his autobiography, *On the Edges of Time*, has recollected how this victory was celebrated in Santiniketan at that time (1905): 'On the day the Treaty was signed we lit a big bonfire in the middle of our football field and sang songs all night long to celebrate the awakening of Asia.'[46]

We find reference to this particular war in Sarala Devi Chowdhurani's memoir *Jiboner Jhora Pata* also. There, Sarala Devi has recalled how on hearing the news of the Russo-Japanese War, an initiative was taken to create a Swadeshi Red Cross Society, which would serve the wounded Japanese soldiers during the time of war:

> The Russo-Japanese War broke out during this period. This historical event provided me a scope to uphold the humanitarian aspect of our Bengali race. I published an advertisement in the newspaper and declared that I was willing to form a Red Cross Society for serving the wounded Japanese soldiers at the warfront. I sought assistance from interested persons and started raising funds.[47]

From Sarala Devi's recounting, we further learn that the advertisement did secure a positive response; many enlisted their names, also monetary help was found, however, the plan of creating a Bengali Red Cross for the service of Japanese soldiers did not materialize. Sarala Devi, like many other enthusiasts, finally learnt that the Japanese government was not willing to take this help from any other foreign country. Sarala Devi's later disillusionment with Japan, finding Japan's repression on her neighbouring countries, has also been described in detail in her memoir. However, we will refer to that part, later in the chapter.

The fact that the victory of Japanese army over a European nation, boosted the nationalist aspiration of many has also been emphatically stated by Hemchandra Kanungoe, one of the early architects of revolutionary movement in Bengal, in his book entitled, *Banglai Biplab Prachesta*. Following is an extract from that book:

> The proposal to partition Bengal was taken in December 1903. However, the agitation against the partition of Bengal, took its shape by the end of 1904. War between Russia and Japan also broke out on 4 February 1904. The military victory of Japan played an important part in exploding the white men's superiority myth, and reserrected among us, the hope of freeing our country from colonial rule.[48]

Earlier we have tried to locate how the magazines published from Bengal (Bangla and English), were quite receptive to any news of Japan. Some of the essays published in vernacular magazines of this period, have described this victory of Japan in heroic terms. An article of this kind is 'Japani Akhanmala', an interesting collection of war anecdotes, recounting the bravery and self-sacrifice of Japanese soldiers during the Russo-Japanese War. The article has also recounted the instance of Japanese people's solidarity towards their soldiers, during the war time. The article was published in the Bangla magazine *Prabasi*.[49]

Earlier, we have referred to Tenshin Okakura, the eminent art critic and curator, who came to Kolkata (known as Calcutta before 2001). We have also taken into account Okakura's association with Tagore, and his generation. Okakura came to Kolkata with the intention of inviting Swami Vivekananda to his country, an idea, which did not materialize due to Vivekananda's untimely demise. Before delving deep into the study of Okakura's English writings, and their reception among the educated classes of Bengal of that era, I would once again, recall Eri Hotta's definition of Pan-Asianism, as a transnational-nationalism.[50] The two important aspects of Pan-Asianism, which appears from this definition, may be summed up as:

1. Asian unity based on a common cultural heritage of Buddhism that binds Japan with the rest of Asia.
2. Japan's leadership in constructing an alliance among Asian races against Western imperialism.

With reference to this argument, it can be well said that, both these ideas of Asian unity and of Japan's supremacy to lead all other nations of Asia, have been emphasized again and again, in almost all of Okakura's major writings. Thus, Okakura's ideas of 'Asia is one', a phrase, which left an indelible impression among the intelligentsia of Bengal, of the early twentieth century, the wide acceptance he received among the 'bhadrolok samaj' of Kolkata, during his visit to Kolkata in 1902, should be taken as an integral part of this discourse, namely, Pan-Asianism. We have also referred to the two opposed standpoints taken by Meiji intellectuals, following western contact. If Yukichi Fukuzawa, an eminent Meiji figure, whom we have already referred to, emphasized the need of escaping the predicament, which many subjugated Asian races have faced, the other group of Japanese intellectuals of the Meiji Era, spoke of reviving Asia. The sweeping rhetorical passages of Tenshin Okakura's *Ideals of the East*, speaking of one common heritage of Asia, represent this revivalist motif on the surface level. The opening lines of the *Ideals of East*, with its poetic descriptions of Asian landscape and its cultural heritage, represent this motif of reviving Asia:

> Asia is one. The Himalayas divide, only to accentuate, two mighty civilizations, the Chinese with its communism of Confucius, and the Indian civilizations, with its individualism of the Vedas. But not even the snowy barriers can interrupt for one moment that broad expanse of love for the Ultimate and Universal, which is the common thought-inheritance of every Asiatic race,[51]

Okakura's rhetorical expression voicing the 'common thought-inheritance of very Asian race' is overwhelming. Yet, a close study of the book would reveal that for Okakura, Japan occupies a historically assigned position to be the leader of the East. The 'Indo-Tartaric blood' of the Japanese people, for Okakura, symbolizes the whole of Asian consciousness.[52] Further, Japan has the 'unique blessing of unbroken sovereignty, the proud self-reliance of an unconquered race'.[53] For Okakura, Japan turns out to be a museum of Asiatic civilization.[54] It is in Japan alone, where the wealth of Asiatic culture remained preserved. Thus, we agree with Rustom Bharucha, for Okakura, Japan's position as the leader remains unquestionable.[55] Japan is a 'museum of Asiatic civilization', declares Okakura, in *Ideals of the East*, which establishes its supremacy over other parts of Asia, as in India, the attainments of Indian art have been effaced by the successive conquest. From the biographical details, we come across in Dinkar Kowshik's *Okakura,* also, in other texts such as Brij Tankha's essay entitled 'Okakura Tenshin: Writing a Good History upon a Modern Plan 'and from Yasuku Horioka's essay, 'Okakura and Swami Vivekananda', we learn about Okakura's sea voyage to India from Japan that began by the end of 1901. Okakura, accompanied by Miss MacLeod[56] and Shitoku Hori, a young Buddhist scholar, who later became the first foreign student of Tagore's ashram, finally reached the Belur Math, in Kolkata on 10 January 1902. This is mentioned in Dinkar Kowshik's book *Okakura.* It was during their stay in Belur Math, that Okakura was introduced to Sister Nivedita. We have already referred to Okakura's *Ideals of the East* and the advocacy of the uniqueness of Japan, he voices there, in remaining an unconquered race and in being a repository of Asian culture. Nivedita in her introduction to the book also, echoes Okakura's ideas: 'Art can only be developed by nations that are in a state of freedom.'[57]

In this context, we can well agree with Midori Wakakuwa that for Nivedita, 'Okakura's discourse was important to underline the centrality of Indian culture in Asia, and to wake up the sleeping people of India, and to give the colonized people a sense of national pride'.[58] For both Okakura and Nivedita, issues relating to nationalism and aesthetics are overlapping subjects. Enquiring into this subject of Nivedita's reception of Okakura's Pan-Asian ideology, Inaga Shigemi in her essay entitled 'Okakura Kakuzo and India: The Trajectory of Modern National Consciousness and Pan-Asian Ideology across Borders', referring to Tapati Guha Thakurta's, *The Making of a New Indian Modern Art,* has rightly pointed out that for Nivedita, the view of Asia, as outlined by Okakura, provided 'the ideological support for national unity'.[59]

There prevails a belief that Okakura did not know English well, and a greater part of the book was rewritten by Nivedita herself. Such an opinion has been upheld by Nivedita's biographer, Sankari Prasad Basu, in his book entitled, *Nivedita Lokmata.*[60] However, Dinkar Kowshik in his book has strongly refuted this opinion arguing that, both Okakura and his brother had received good schooling, where mostly children of foreigners, who were in Japan at that time, were sent.[61]

Further, we learn that Okakura brought with him the manuscript of the book titled, *Ideals of the East*; regarding its authorship Kowshik has observed: 'For a time, some people talked as though the book was rewritten under her guidance and active participation. But this does not seem to be true. The flavour of Okakura's writing is all his own. The epigrammatic style, the Japanese manner of syntax and imagery is Okakura's.'[62]

Regarding the source of the text *Ideals of the East*, it has been pointed out by scholars like Midori Wakakuwa that, the book is an elaboration of lectures entitled, 'The History of Japanese Art' that Okakura delivered in the Tokyo School of Fine Art. Also, the work was the result of the survey of National Treasures, which was conducted by the Ministry of the Imperial Household, in which Okakura took an important part.[63] Kyoko Niwa, in her doctoral thesis, has also emphatically pointed out that the first draft of the text *Ideals of the East*, had been completed before Okakura's arrival in Kolkata; so it is not possible that the basic ideas of the book was formulated under the influence of Nivedita.[64] Thus, such allegations that the book was rewritten under the guidance of Sister Nivedita, cannot be accepted.

Okakura's second book *The Awakening of the East* was drafted during his stay in India from 1901 to 1902. However, the publication of the text took place posthumously in 1938.[65] Analysing this text, scholars like Midori Wakakuwa and Rustom Bharucha, have drawn our attention to certain passages from Okakura's text, which show resemblance with much of Nivedita's writing. Thus, Midori Wakakuwa in his essay entitled 'Japanese Cultural Identity and Nineteenth Century Asian Nationalism: Okakura Tenshin and Swami Vivekananda', has rightly pointed out the title of the text *Awakening of Asia*, echoes the title of Vivekananda's review *Awakening of India*. Also, for scholars like Bharucha and Wakakuwa, the first sentence of the text: 'Brothers and Sisters of Asia', remind all of us the famous opening address, which Swamiji delivered in Chicago in 1893: 'Sisters and Brothers of America'. Critics like Bharucha have rightly pointed to the frequent invocations to Goddess Kali in Okakura's text, as in the line, 'Om to Steel of honour! Om to the Strong! Om to the Invincible!.[66] Thus, we agree with Bharucha that these invocations to Kali goddess show the influence of Sister Nivedita upon him, the former had just published a book in 1900 entitled, *Kali the Mother*. Okakura and Nivedita shared each other's ideas during their stay in India. Further, they were closely associated and this is evident from Nivedita's letters, in which she fondly nicknamed Okakura, 'Nigu', 'N', etc.[67] However, from Nivedita's letters, and also from her biographies, we learn that later Nivedita also became disillusioned with Okakura. Pravrajika Atmaprana, the biographer of Sister Nivedita has referred to Nivedita's letter to Miss MacLeod, dated, 25 May 1902. The letter clearly shows her disagreement with Okakura: 'My one desire is that he should return home. . . . He was a very incongruous element here, however, and when he announced that he was unfortunately compelled to go, there was a good deal of relief on both sides I fancy.'[68]

One thing can be said about Okakura is that, he remained consistent in his loyalty to his state. If in the *Ideals of the East*, Okakura's belief in the supremacy of Japan, lies implicit within the rhetorical passages of the text representing Asian unity, the idea of Japanese supremacy and even, his advocacy of Japanese imperialism, has been voiced openly in the *Awakening of Japan*, which was published in 1905. The publication of the book overlaps with the beginning of Russo-Japanese War. In this text, Okakura has justified the Japanese government's decision to annex Korea: 'Any hostile power in occupation of the peninsula might easily throw an army into Japan, for Korea like a dagger ever pointed towards the heart of Japan.'[69]

From Marlene J. Mayo, book entitled *The Emergence of Imperial Japan*, we learn that as early as 1871, a section of Japanese ministry was in favour of annexing Korea, from the military stand point of using it as a buffer region.[70] Sister Nivedita, in her article entitled, 'Japan and Korea', which was first published in the *Modern Review*, even before the final annexation of Korea by Japan in 1910, had kept an eye on the accounts of Japan's imperialistic aspiration on Korea. She vehemently protested against Japan's exploitation of Korea's land and her people. A reproduction of the original text is included in the fifth volume of Sister Nivedita's complete works. Nivedita, who earlier found accordance with Okakura's belief in the supremacy of Japanese culture, did not shown any hesitation to denounce Japan's invasion on Korea, in this text:

> What we see here is no friendly suzerainty, no chivalrous protection of the rights of a neighbour against foreign aggression, but on the contrary an invasion and spoliation so cruel, so cold, so pitiless, that it is more like brigandage than anything that we remember even in the blood-curdling annals of imperialization.[71]

The Indian response to this imperialistic aspiration of Japan was critical, as in the case of Nivedita's observation, we have located in this chapter. The following chapter will try to take into account a detailed study of this reaction towards Japan's imperialistic advances that took place in the early twentieth century.

Once again coming back to our previous issue, i.e. Okakura and his impact upon the Bengali intelligentsia of the last century, some other aspects need mention. Okakura's *Awakening of the East* was a posthumous publication, however, his two other books, *The Awakening of Japan* (published in 1905) and *The Book of Tea* (published in 1906), received a good deal of appreciation from the readers of Bengal. This is evident from the reference of the texts, in many essays on Japan, of that period. Priyambada Devi, an educated Bengali woman and poet, maintained her epistolary relationship with Okakura, the latter at that time was residing in Boston. Priyambada Devi's letter dated, 6 October 1912, in splendid poetical expression gives voice to her admiration for Okakura's book *The Book of Tea:* 'Dry shrunken tea leaves, who ever dreamt, held in them yet such green wealth of spring-tide beauty and poetry. . . . Beautifully hast thou, son of Japan, painted eternal life's smiles and tears.'[72]

Priyambada Devi took the task of translating Okakura's book *The Book of Tea*, and it was published in the Bangla magazine *Manashi* (Falgun, 1321 BS). Musing on the cult of Teasim, Okakura, in his *The Book of Tea*, found a suitable occasion to express his views on the supremacy of Asian culture and also about western prejudice. This, according to him, does not allow the West to appreciate the East properly. For Okakura, the cult of tea ceremony is an Eastern attribute, representing the quality of mind to adore 'the beautiful among the sordid facts of everyday existence'.[73]

'When will the West understand, or try to understand the East?'—Okakura raised the question. The text itself may be taken as a befitting literary response to E.M. Foster's *Passage to India*, or similar colonial texts, which upheld the stereotype that the relation between Orient and Occident, is irreconcilable. In the translated text of *The Book of Tea*, by Priyambada Devi, entitled 'Cha Grontho' (included in the *Sekaler Bangla Samoyikpotre Japan*), we notice, how Okakura's ideas about this colonial politics, its supremacy, and racial prejudice, have been aptly conveyed to the Bengali reader:

Kbe proticho bujhibe-kimba bujhibar chesta koribe? Asiabashi amadigoke sombondhe je odvut sotyo o kolponar jal rochito hoy, tahadekhiya amra hotobudhi hoiya jai. Hoy amra podmosugondho somvoge othoba amra chuchundori ebong toilopuyika vojone jibondharon koriya thaki, emon jonosruti sunite pai.[74]

When will the West understand, or try to understand the East? We Asiatics are often appalled by the curious web of facts and fancies which has been woven concerning us. We are pictured as living on the perfume of the lotus, if not on mice and cockroaches.[75]

With reference to Aurobindo's writing, we have already referred to Okakura's *Awakening of Japan,* a text that undoubtedly enjoyed a greater readership, during that time. In the *Awakening of Japan,* Okakura has once again emphasized on Japan's inheritance of a common Asian culture, a theme, which has been dealt in details in many of his books: 'With immense gratitude to the West for what she has taught us, we must still regard Asia as the true source of our inspiration.'[76]

In the first Chapter, dealing with the theme of 'representation', we noticed quite a few times, how the awareness of the strength of Japanese society on the part of the cultural traveller has always been a sad remembrance of the absence of those qualities, in Indian society. With reference to this Okakura's theory of Japanese inheritance of Asian culture, as its real inspiration, rather than borrowing from the West, Jadunath Sarkar in his essay 'Japaner Rajniti' (*Bharati*, Jaistho, 1313 BS) makes an observation, worth noting:

> The fact that Japan's strength lies in the religion and rituals, which she inherited from China and India, and not from the customs of Europe and America, has been again again emphasized by Okakura, in his book *Awakening of Japan.* On the other hand, we Indians are just the opposite of it. Instead of learning, what is worthy to be learnt from others, we remain busy in imitating western lifestyle and food habits. We are borrowing such unsubstantial things from the West, which will be harmful for the people of this country.[77]

Another article on Japan, in which we come across such reference of Okakura, and also, recycling of Okakura's ideals is a Bangla article entitled, 'Japan O Bharotborsho', published in the magazine *Prabasi* (Chaitro, 1310 BS). Fully agreeing with Okakura's idea of 'Yellow Peril, a catchy phrase, Okakura adopted to represent the hysterical reaction of the West towards Japan's advancement, particularly; her military success against Russia, the anonymous author of the article, has referred to an interesting letter that was published in the *London Spectator,* expressing the view that Indian students residing at that time in Japan, were engaged in conspiracy against the empire. For the writer, such conspiracy theory should be taken as a hyper reaction of the West, towards Japan's advancement and its impact upon the colonized races of Asia. The following passage quoted from *The Spectator*, needs mention in this regard:

> 'Sneakingly disloyal Indian students I have myself met both in Japan and elsewhere. It is well that somebody who is competent, as Mr. Norman is, should look into and enquire what they are really doing: silly though their scheming may be, as he assures us. But any sympathy they meet with in Japan will be greatly and justly increased if their country is harshly judged by English' . . . Mr. Seymour's letter to the *London Spectator* quoted in the *Indian Mirror*, 10 February 1904.[78]

Leaving aside these instances of reception to Okakura's writings, another important aspect about his association with the Bengali intelligentsia, needs mention. It is widely known that during the period, Okakura stayed in Bengal, he developed acquaintance with the pioneering leaders of Anushilan Samity, a revolutionary organization in Bengal. In the informal adda (conversation) sessions, he had been urging youths to initiate resistance against the British Raj. Such an impression, we get from quite a few memoirs of the period, recollecting the turbulent period. To begin with, it would be worth recalling Surendranath Tagore's reminiscence of Okakura's presence in Bengal, which was published in the *Visva-Bharati Quarterly*. The article is also included in Dinkar Kowshik's biographical work entitled *Okakura*. The very first question that was asked to Surendranath was, 'What are you thinking of doing for your country'?[79]

The abrupt question, took Surendranth by surprise; however, he managed to provide a repartee, to which, Okakura remarked 'it saddened him to note the tone of despondency in our youth. . .[80] A similar kind of an impression of a catalectic role, played by Okakura, to arouse among youths in Bengal a strong anti–colonial sentiment, has been recorded in many other writings of that period. Among these, a passage from Charuchandra Dutta's memoir entitled *Purano Kotha,* can be mentioned. The memoir speaks of a conspiracy to assassinate Lord Curzon, in which Okakura was involved:

> It was decided that when Lord Curzon would be leading the procession, then an attempt would be taken to assassinate him. Our group included

some eminent personalities—a writer of high repute, an eminent scientist, a famous ship merchant (Hem Mallick) and a world-famous Japanese artist and thinker, Okakura Kakuzo.[81]

The authenticity of this particular document may be questioned. Firstly, as mentioned in Horioka's essay, Okakura left India for Japan on 6 October 1902,[82] almost three years prior to the final implementation of Curzon's decision to partition Bengal.[83] Also, as mentioned in Surendranath's remembrance of Okakura, the second visit of Okakura, took place years later. Thus, Okakura's involvement in a conspiracy to murder Curzon, as mentioned in Dutta's memoir, seems to be a concocted one. However, Okakura's involvement with Anushilan Samity, finds reference in other documents, which cannot be ruled out altogether. A far more reliable document, can be a passage from the *Freedom Struggle and Anushilan Samity*, edited by Buddhadev Bhattacharya, that records a recollection of P. Mitra,[84] how Okakura's words had a deep influence upon him, and determined his political activity in the later period:

> A reception was arranged for Okakura at Jorashanko Thakurbari (the family residence of poet Tagore) . . . reception was attended by top men of the Bengali society of those days, and P. Mitra happened to be present there as an invitee. Okakura while paying tribute to the culture and heritage of the Indian people in words of admiration made a passing reference to India, with a glorious past, being subjected to foreign domination, and expressed surprise that leaders of the country were not seriously taking up the task of shaking foreign rule. Such remarks, coming from a reputed Japanese artist cut into the heart of P. Mitra who, after the reception was over, had a heart to heart talk with Okakura for about an hour. This small incident seems to have further increased P. Mitra's revolutionary zeal.[85]

There are in fact two opposite views; regarding the political activity of Okakura during his stay in India. In an interview given to Nirodbaran, the residential doctor of Pondichery, Aurobindo Ghosh mentioned Okakura's name as the founder of the revolutionary party in Bengal. This oral statement was given by Aurobindo in 1940.[86] It was later published in the *Mother India*, March 1961, (p. 9). The following passage from Aurobindo's statement needs citing: 'Sri Aurobindo . . . I was neither the founder nor the leader.

It was P. Mitter and Miss Ghosal (Sarala Devi) who started it on the inspiration of Baron Okakura.'[87]

However, as Peter Heehs in his book *The Bomb in Bengal* has pointed out, there is difficulty in accepting this statement. According to Heehs, 'Aurobindo's knowledge of Okakura was secondhand'; further, Aurobindo made the remark in order to contradict statements that Aurobindo himself had been the chief mentor of revolutionaries of that period.[88] Even then, the question that remains asking, is why of all people, Okakura's name has been mentioned in quite a few memoirs of that phase?

Others like T.R. Sareen, in his essay entitled 'India and Japan in Historical Perspectives' has observed that, Okakura during his stay in Bengal 'was giving lectures to young Bengali students asking them to adopt revolutionary methods to achieve their goal of freedom'.[89]

T.R. Sareen in his essay has referred to Dinkar Kowshik's biography of Okakura, where we also find references of Okakura's political involvement in Bengal, in meeting youths and discussing with them 'India's bondage and the way they should strive for freedom'.[90] We must not forget that Okakura visited Bengal at a time, when the anti-colonial movements had already started in Bengal. Moreover, the advent of an educated intelligentsia had lost hopes in the British Raj. To substantiate this argument, it would be worth paying a look at Sumit Sarkar's narration of the milieu of Bengal, on the brink of the rise of the Swadeshi movement in Bengal. According to Sarkar, 'Calcutta had become a real metropolis for the educated bhadrolok', the growth of Calcutta at the beginning of twentieth century as a seat of learning, the emergence of a Bengali elite society of service holders during this time, also, the flourishing of Bangla language, the growing number of newspapers and periodicals during this phase, according to Sumit Sarkar, facilitated the educated Bengali class to gain a new confidence.[91] It is this Bengal, just at the brink of the rise of a violent anti-colonial movement, which Okakura visited. Thus, his revolutionary ideas like his conceptualization of Asia, having a common cultural heritage as the source of Asian unity, led to an overwhelming effect upon Bengali youths, cannot be ruled out. Years later, on 15 May 1929, Tagore delivered a speech in Tokyo. Tagore in his speech has recalled how Okakura had gained a wide acceptance among youths of Bengal, at that time: 'He was our guest for a long time and he had immense inspiration for young generation of Bengal in those days which immediately preceded a period of a sudden ebullition of national self- assertion in India.'[92]

It must be noted that, though Tagore mentions Okakura's enormous impact upon Bengali youth, the passage quoted from Tagore's speech entitled, *On Oriental Culture and Japan's Mission*, does not give us any clue about specific political activities, as organizing secret societies in Bengal, or to be a part of it. Okakura's association with some of the founder members of Anushilan Samiti, did not escape the careful vigilance of the British government. With Okakura came Shitoku Hori, a Buddhist scholar, who later became the first international student of Santiniketan. From Hori's diary, translated by Kazuo Azuma, we come to know that on 12 December, he was interrogated by the police regarding Okakura's activities.[93] The fact has also been mentioned in Yasuko Horioka's essay entitled, 'Okakura and Swami Vivekananda', published in the magazine *Prabuddha Bharata*, March 1977. In this essay, Horioka has referred to Nivedita's biographers, who too have upheld the view that Okakura, during his stay, got involved in active politics. However, Horioka in this essay, found difficulty in showing accordance with this view. He has commented that 'Okakura's involvement in the political activity in India' has remained unproven.[94] It seems, like his political ideology, which appears to be enigmatic and inconsistent, as it incorporates often contrary elements like an unquestionable faith in the imperial power of Japan, and also propagating Asian unity, Okakura's direct involvement in Indian politics, seems to be wrapped in mystery. If we put aside these facts and details, what remains is the impression of a Japanese intellectual, who exercised a great deal of influence among the youths of Bengal at that time. Okakura's ideology of Asian unity has been challenged by several critics on the ground that in it, the hierarchical position of Japan has been accepted unquestionably. It would not be irrelevant to find a similarity between Okakura's concept of 'Asian unity' and Goethe's concept of 'world literature'. Goethe, who in an issue of the journal *Uber Kunst and Altertum*, introduced the term 'world literature' in 1827, expressed his firm belief that 'a universal world literature' was in the process of being constituted, in which, Goethe remarked, 'an honourable role' was reserved for the Germans.[95] Thus, for both Okakura and Goethe, their own nation occupies an important place, in their idea of the emergence of a trans-national culture. Further, how far Okakura was committed to the ideal of the 'revival of Asia' is doubtful. We can well agree with Bharucha that one major reason, for which his *The Awakening of the East* was not been published during his lifetime, is that, it was an abandoned text, and Okakura himself 'had lost his interest in *The Awakening of the East*, and was already thinking of Boston, while he was in Calcutta'.[96] In spite of such inconsistencies, and contradictions inherent in Okakura's political thought, the fact that he was greatly admired by a cross-section of Bengali intellectuals of that time, can never be denied. The overwhelming reception that Okakura received in Bengal during his stay, writings from this part of the country as the Introduction of the book *Ideals of the East* that Nivedita authored, and also some other texts, which we have cited, may well be taken as a testimony of the influence of Okakura's Pan-Asian ideals upon the Bengali literate section.

In the above-mentioned texts, one can find an acceptance of Okakura's Pan-Asian ideology of unifying Asia, under the leadership of Japan. However, we can also locate another large group of writings, which seem to challenge this hegemonic domination of Japan over the idea of Pan-Asianism. To sum up this argument, it would not be irrelevant to recall once again an interview given by Tagore to *The Manchestor Guardian* (20 July 1916), where we come across Tagore's vision of Asian unity. We can try to trace how it differs from that advocated by Japanese imperialists, of that time. Commenting on Japan's mission to unite Asia, Tagore has categorically pointed out that Japan alone cannot stand for the fulfillment of this dream, and only by forging association with 'a free China, Siam, and perhaps, in the ultimate course of things a free India', this grand vision of unifying Asia can be materialized.[97]

The vision of unity of Asia, which we find in the above-mentioned interview of Tagore, puts emphasis on giving equal status and positions to different nations of Asia, some of them yet to taste freedom from colonial rule. Needless to say, Tagore's idea of Asian unity was just the opposite of the Japanese ideology of unifying Asia, which desired to substitute a European master by another Asian master. In the following chapter, dealing with Bengal's response to Japan's aggression on neighbouring nations, we will try to delve deep into certain texts, which represent opposition to this idea of Japanese version of Asianism.

To conclude this section, I would like to dwell upon another aspect, i.e. the popularization of *Jujutsu* a Japanese martial art, during this period. This must also be credited to the rise of the strong nationalist voice in Bengal. The rise of a nationalist spirit in Bengal, led to the practice and popularization of physical culture. It is a well-known fact that both the Anushilan Samiti of Calcutta and Dhaka, took initiative in the establishment of *Akhras* (clubs of drills and exercises), where young participants were encouraged to take part in various physical exercises, as an integral part of a greater discourse of the making of the nation. This time, apart from indigenous forms of physical acrobats, *jujutsu* gained popularity in Bengal. From an archival record, kept in the Home Political Branch of the West Bengal State Archives, entitled *History of Agitation against Bengal Partition*, Calcutta, the 25 January 1906, we learn that it was Sarala Devi, who took the pioneering role in arranging *jujutsu* training for Bengali boys. The following excerpt from the above-mentioned document may be cited in this regard:

> In 1903, the Lakhir Bhandar of Cornwallis Street was started by Miss Sarala Devi Ghosal. She edits a journal called *Bharati*, and in 1904, inspired apparently by the success of the oriental in the Russo-Japanese War, she opened an academy at Ballygunj for the instruction of Bengali boys in fencing and *ji-jutsu*, employing as a master an adventurer who called himself Professor Murtaza.[98]

The information, we get about the transplantation of Japanese martial art and the fostering of it, under the influence of a nationalist fervor is a unique one, yet doubt prevails, whether the *jujutsu* taught by an Indian instructor, was a Japanese art, or it was an

Indian version of *jujutsu*. For this, it is needed to be dealt in a separate sub-chapter. This portion, dealing with the topic of reception of *jujutsu* in Bengal, will be incorporated in the later chapter.

As noted earlier, in the next section, we propose to take into account the history of revolutionary movements in Bengal, during the first three decades of the early twentieth century, and their endeavor to seek support from Japan.

THE POLITICS OF JAPAN, IN THE CONTEXT OF THE REVOLUTIONARY MOVEMENTS IN BENGAL AND BEYOND (1900-20)

To begin with, I would like to refer to a document titled *Memorandum on the History of Terrorism in India (1905-33)*, included in the Home Political proceedings of the Archives, West Bengal. The following section, dealing with the history of the establishment of secret revolutionary societies, is derived from the Section II (1905-9) of the said document[99]:

> The revolutionary movement in Bengal grew up on the top of what was known as anti-partition agitation. The idea of training young Bengalis to the use of physical force for political purposes had been planted in Bengal before the partition took place. The success of the Japanese in the war with Russia had demonstrated that an Asiatic nation could by organization and training defeat one of the greatest military nations of Europe, and associations for the promotion of physical culture had sprung up to remove the reproach that Bengalis were a non-martial and effeminate people.

Further, from the details included in Uma Mukherjee's book entitled, *Two Great Revolutionaries,* and also from Jibantara Halder's book, *Anushilan Samitir Itihash*, we learn that prior to the beginning of the anti-partition movement, the Calcutta Anusilan Samiti was founded as a club of physical exercises on 24 March 1902. It was then located at Madan Mitra Lane. Later, in 1905, the Samiti's office was shifted to 49, Cornwalliss Street.[100] Similarly, as noted by Uma Mukherjee, in the curriculum of the Dacca Anusilan Samiti, which was founded on 3 November 1905[101], physical exercises, moral regeneration and philanthropic work, formed an important part. As mentioned in Uma Mukherjee's book entitled,

Two Great Indian Revolutionaries, following the suppression of the Manicktola conspiracy, and also the arrest and deportation of prominent leaders, the first phase of revolutionary movement came to an end for the time being. However, the fervour of protest did not die down. A second phase of more organized revolutionary activities began under the leadership of dauntless men like Rash Behari Bose and Jyotindranath Mukherjee. Uma Mukherjee has observed that men like Rash Behari and Jyotindranath formed a more comprehensive scheme of political action or armed rising against the British Indian Empire. They tried to secure the support of the Indian army, and also took initiative in enlisting the military-cum-financial assistance of some first-class Powers, particularly those inimical to England at that moment.[102] On September 1909, Anusilan Samiti was banned. It was announced as an unlawful organization. Following this event, Chandannagar became the focal point of revolutionary activities.[103]

Also, the first decades of the twentieth century, witnessed the establishment of Indian revolutionary organizations in various parts of America, Europe and Asia. With reference to the establishments of revolutionary groups in different parts of the globe, a significant historical event that deserves mention is, Hardyal's effort in establishing an organization in San Francisco in 1913, which became popular as *Ghadar*, deriving its name from the weekly magazine of the organ, which was *Ghadar* (Mutiny). The Ghadar revolutionaries became successful in establishing a link with revolutionaries of Bengal. Taking the advantage of the war time situation, they tried to ensure German help for the cause of Indian freedom struggle. Thus, in November 1914, Vishnu Ganesha Pingle, an active leader of the Ghadar Party, secretly came to India from America; where, he had been introduced to the Ghadaritre politics. Rash Behari Bose in his memoir entitled *Atmokotha,* has recalled how Pingley met him at the Dasaswamedh Ghat of Varanasi, and ensured him that he was prepared to risk his own life for the sake of his country's freedom.[104] However, the attempt to rouse Indian soldiers stationed in the Lahore barrack, and later, in Meerut, did not materialize. Following the arrest of Pingley, and the failure of this attempt to create an armed rebellion, Bose came back to Chandannagar.

Finally, he complied with the suggestion of his comrades to leave his country. Rash Behari Bose in his memoir has openly stated that he decided to go abroad for securing foreign help to bring arms and ammunitions from abroad, also, to collect money for the cause of freedom struggle.[105] Historians, Arun Coomer Bose in his book *Indian Revolutionaries Abroad, 1905-1922: In the Background of International Developments,* has commented that with the beginning of the First World War, Asian countries bordering on India, like Thailand and China, gained importance in anti-British operations.

With reference to this development of anti-British activities in Asian countries, on the eve of war, it must be remembered that at that time, Japan was a political ally of Great Britain, a fact we have already mentioned in the introduction of this chapter. The Anglo-Japanese Agreement, which was first concluded in 1902, was further revived twice, once in 1905 and next in 1911. According to the Preamble of the third Anglo-Japanese Alliance, it was agreed that both parties, Japan and Great Britain, would be responsible for the maintenance and consolidation of the general peace in the region of Eastern Asia and India.[106] The diplomatic alliance between Great Britain and Japan was an impediment for the Indian revolutionaries to obtain help from Japan. Yet, a study of documents of that period reveals the fact that, even though Japan was a political ally of Great Britain, a steady flow of Indian students to Japan, resulted in the advent of Anti-British revolutionary activities in Japan. We can well agree with T.R. Sareen that 'in spite of the constrains of the Alliance, Japan became an important haven during the First World War for Indian revolutionaries trying to overthrow the British in India by an armed revolt with the help from Germany'.[107]

Also, in Japan during this phase, the idea of Asian unity gained strength, an aspect we have already referred to in the introduction of this chapter. In spite of the Alliance, many political groups were in favour to render help to the Indian nationalists. T.R. Sareen in his essay titled, 'India and Japan in Historical Perspective' has rightly referred to *The Japan Chronicle* which published an article supporting the demand of Congress for *Swaraj*.[108] This change in the political scenario in Japan, during the first decades of the twentieth century, turned out to be favourable for Indian revolutionaries operating in Japan, and her neighbouring countries. With reference to this, a document of the National Archives (Foreign Department) needs citing. This file entitled 'Publication of an article in the newspaper *Keijo Shimpo*, regarding the policy of the Governor-General in Corea' includes a letter of the British Consul General of Seoul, dated, 1 December 1910. The British Consul General in his letter referred to an article that was published in a leading newspaper in Seoul, and has commented that the article was a testimony of the fact that there existed among Japanese, an idea that, Japan should fight the battle of the Asiatic nations. The article referred to, was written by Mr. Y. Takekoshi. It was published in the newspaper *Keijo Shimpo* (27 November 1910). In that article, the author expressed his view that Japan should withdraw her hand from Asiatic mainland, instead, should seize the Dutch East Indies. Thus, it is clear that during the first two decades of the early twentieth century, there existed, contrary opinions among Japanese nationals, regarding the country's diplomatic relations with other Asian nations.

We can also remember Rash Behari Bose's biographer Takeshi Nakajima, who in his biography of Bose, has dealt in detail, the activities of a radical nationalist group in Japan, headed by Michiru Toyama. Toyama provided shelter to Bose, when the deportation order was issued by the Japanese government in November 1915.[109]

Thus, a study of assorted documents of the period such as memoirs, letters, historical account and archival material can reveal two interesting aspects. These are first, the anxiety and effort on the part of revolutionary organs, working both in Bengal and outside, to derive assistance from Japan. Also, a view about the change of international situations just after the end of First World War, which led to the change of Japan's foreign policies, which was benefitting the Indian revolutionaries.

To begin with, I would like to refer to a passage from Dr. Bhupendranath Dutta's book entitled *Oprokashito Rajnoitik Itihash*, recounting the activities of revolutionaries in the Pacific region, on the eve of First World War:

During this time, Indian revolutionaries attempted to sneak into the countries of the Pacific region with the aim of smuggling arms into British India. Thus, revolutionary bodies were formed in China, Japan, and Philippines and in other regions of this area. They received moral support from eminent Japanese personalities like Count Okuma. Their association with Japanese leaders instilled the hope that in time of rebellion against the Raj, the Japanese army would not be deployed to suppress the movement. The revolutionaries also succeeded in getting assistance from Sun Yat-sen, the Chinese revolutionary leader.[110]

As regards Dutta's claim of Indian revolutionaries in the Pacific region, having obtained some definite help from Sun Yet-sen, it must be noted that in Arun Coomer Bose's book entitled, *Indian Revolutionaries Abroad*, it has been mentioned that Vishnu Ganesh Pingley while coming from U.S.A., also met Dr. Sun for his advice and cooperation.[111]

Dutta in his book has recounted the operation of Indian revolutionaries in the Pacific region on the eve of the First World War. However, from other sources, we come to learn that Indian revolutionaries started working in Japan, even before that period. According to the information we get from Arun Coomer Bose's book *Indian Revolutionaries Abroad*, the first Indian to settle in Japan for organizing revolutionary activities was Surendramohan Bose. As mentioned in Bose's book, he reached Japan in 1906; nothing much is known about him, only he was disappointed and left Japan in 1907.[112] T.R. Sareen in his essay entitled, 'India and Japan in Historical Perspectives', has noted that after the First World War, there began a steady stream of Indian students to Japan, many of them got involved in revolutionary politics. Both from the accounts of T.R. Sareen's essay, and from Arun Coomer Bose's book, we learn that it was only after Mohammed Barkatullah's arrival in Japan in 1909, that anti-British agitation by Indians residing in Japan, started taking place. Barkatullah came to Japan from U.S.A. in 1909; he started teaching Urdu at Tokyo University. During his stay in Japan, he got involved in the pan-Islamic politics and was one of the key publishers of the revolutionary journal *Islamic Fraternity*. However, the Japanese government yielded to the pressure of the British Government in accordance with the terms and conditions of the Anglo-Japanese Alliance. This resulted in the suppression of the publication of the *Islamic Fraternity*. Barkatullah finally left for U.S.A. in 1914. We can well agree with Arun Coomer Bose's observation in his book that the 'contribution of Barkatullah and his associates, however lay primarily in creating a favourable climate of opinion for India and in establishing valuable contacts with Japan'.[113] Bose in his essay entitled, *Indian Revolutionaries in Japan*, has pointed out that Barkatullah managed to get powerful patrons in Japan like Count Taisuki Itagaki, Dr. Toru Terao, Tsuyoshi Inaku and Michiru Toyoma. Michiru Toyoma was the right-wing ideologue of Japan at that time, whose involvement in saving Rash Behari Bose has already been narrated.

The Komagata Maru incidents in 1914, and the Singapore uprising, that took place in the following year, are two historical events of this period, in which the Ghadar revolutionaries had an important role to play. Both of these events created a ripple in British India. To an extent, they also contributed to the development of public opinion in Japan, towards the nationalist movement in British India.

The Komagata Maru was a Japanese vessel, which was chartered by Gurdit Singh, a wealthy businessman of Hong Kong. The boat carrying mostly Sikh immigrants, intending to get jobs after landing at Vancouver, was forced to leave Vancouver on 24 July 1914, exposing the racist Canadian immigration policies. For two months, the passengers of the Komagata Maru were denied fresh water and food, in order to force them to return back to India. Many books have been written on this tragic incident. On the centenary of the Komagata Maru incident, a host of online documents have also been published on the internet. Sho Kuwajima in his book *Indian Mutiny In Singapore*, dealing with the backdrop of the mutiny, has brought out a detailed study of the reaction of the Japanese consul in Vancouver, and that of the Japanese press, regarding the Komagata Maru incident. According to the author of this book, the main concern for the Japanese Consul at Vancouver was to ascertain the safety of the Japanese crew and the ship. Thus, referring to Japanese Foreign Minister's note to the Japanese Consul at Vancouver, Sho Kuwajima has rightly pointed out that the attitude of the

Japanese government was that as it was a private ship, and they had nothing to do in this regard.[114] However, the situation on board was becoming pitiable for the passengers, the author referring to Gurdit Singh's recounting of the condition of passengers, has narrated how following the exhaustion of food and water on board, looting of water from Japanese sailors took place. This led to an uneasy situation between the Japanese crew and the passengers.[115] Sho Kuwajima in recounting the Komagata Maru incident, has taken into account Gurdit Singh's association with Ghadar party, also, has mentioned that during the return voyage, Ghadar Party rendered help to the hapless passengers at various points, and in Yokohama also. However, the author has clearly stated that the majority of the passengers were 'loyal subjects of the British Raj and the purpose of their journey was not political, but to get jobs after landing Vancouver'.[116] The author has also referred to the coverage of the *Japan Chronicle*, English daily, regarding the condition of passengers, once they reached Kobe. According to Sho Kuwajima, the Japan Chronicle expressed its sympathetic attitude towards the role of the British Consul-General at Kobe, and concluded that the Consul Officers had done their best for the passengers.[117] However, *The Japan Chronicle* of 27 August 1914, brought out the hapless condition of the passengers at Kobe, where they were allowed to land:

> Meanwhile the position of the Indian passengers is pitiable. They are all destitute, and have not even the money to buy fruit and fresh vegetables in Kobe. . . . The food on board is of the poorest kind, and consists almost entirely of pulses. They have not even the means to telegraph to India for help.[118]

The author has also referred to another issue of *The Japan Chronicle* (30 August 1914), from where we learn that the passengers behaved exceedingly well at Kobe. Also, Gurdit Singh had a great influence on the passengers.[119] It must be noted that in spite of being deprived of the basic amenities at boat, Gurdit Singh and men tried their best to refrain from falling out with the Japanese crew. It is a well-known fact that when the ship's passengers finally got down at Budge Budge, a fight broke out between the passengers and the police, following which about 17 Sikh passengers died in police firing. Many were arrested and sent to jail for rioting.[120] The Home Political File of West Bengal State Archives, entitled *Riot by passengers of the S.S. 'Komagata Maru' at Budge Budge*, contain a statement of Captain Yamamoto, recorded by Mr. Humphreys and interpreted by Captain Curdew. The statement of Captain Yamamoto also records that Gurdit Singh had told the captain that he had no ill will against the Japanese, but was against the whites. The Home Political File of West Bengal State Archives entitled *Riot by passengers of the S.S. 'Komagata Maru' at Budge Budge*, also speaks of seditious activities of the passengers under the influence of the Ghadar Party: '. . . Two most dangerous from the point of view of the Government are the two who came on board at Kobe. Gurdit Singh was always talking of revolutions; used to say that the present time of war was the time to stir up trouble.'[121]

It is no wonder that in the police file, there remains no reference of the destitution of the passengers, which they faced on board. It does not also speak of the racist policies of Canadian government, which was the source of the trouble. To conclude, the *Komagata Maru* incident demonstrated that the standpoint of Japan at that time was to comply with the western powers. We can agree with Sho Kuwajima's observation that 'the *Komagata Maru* affair, was a diverging point of Indian nationalism and Japanese nationalism, though both seemed to sail in the same ship for some time'.[122]

Sho Kuwajima's study of the events of the *Komagata Maru* incident reveals it to be a prelude to the mutiny of Indian soldiers in Singapore. This incident took place only a few months after the ship had left Kobe. The Japanese Navy, in accordance with the Anglo-Japanese Alliance, was used by the Japanese Government to suppress the mutiny.[123] Dr. Bhupendranath Dutta in his book, entitled *Oprokashito Rajnoitik Itihash*, has given a short account of the course of the mutiny, based on the Berlin Report, during the time he stayed there:

> It was in Singapore that the Sikh soldiers serving the British army, revolted at first. The Berlin Committee received a report of this rebellion. The rebel soldiers became successful to get hold of the city for a week, and also freed the German prisoners. However, the Germans declined to fight against the

British forces. The rebel soldiers lacked efficient leadership and finally were forced to give in.[124]

Regarding the role of the Japanese navy in suppressing mutiny, the report referred to by Dutta, speaks of two opposed opinions: 'The report mentioned that the Japanese army did not raise their weapons against the Indian soldiers. However, there were controversial reports; some said that the Japanese forces also fought against the rebel soldiers.'[125]

Sho Kuwajima in his book entitled *Indian Mutiny in Singapore,* has brought out a detailed study of the response of the Japanese newspapers, and also of the Japanese politicians, regarding the involvement of Japanese navy to suppress the mutiny. Thus, the writer has referred to *The Tokyo Asahi Shimbun* (19 February 1915), which justified the decision of the Japanese government to send Japanese Navy to suppress the mutiny.[126] However, as in the German report referred to by Dutta, Sho Kuwajima's study of Japanese newspapers reports; represent contradictory versions regarding the exact role played by the Japanese navy during the mutiny. The author has referred to another English daily of Japan, *The Japan Time* (23 February), that wrote that 'at first the Japanese army and naval authorities had the intention of landing blue jackets from the Japanese warships in the neighbouring waters to assist in the pacification of the disturbances, but this was given up as it was feared to give rise to international complications'.[127]

Sho Kuwajima has also referred to Sumei Ohkawa, who in his book entitled, *Indo ni Okeru Kokumin undo no Genjyo ooyobi sono Yurai (History and Present Condition of the National Movements in India)*, has criticized the role of Japanese navy to suppress the mutiny. With reference to this critical opinion among a cross-section of Japanese leaders, regarding Japan's blind allegiance to suppress a mutiny of Indian soldiers stationed in Singapore in 1915, Sho Kuwajima's observation may be taken into account:

One main factor was that there had been some contacts between Japanese political and opinion leaders, and Indian nationalists who were conducting their activities in Japan after the Russo- Japanese War. These Japanese came to be influenced by the national awakening in India. Another factor was the friction between Japan and Britain in connection with their China policy, which led some Japanese leaders to the reconsideration of usefulness of the Anglo- Japanese Alliance.[128]

We have already taken account of the critical response of Japanese people, with reference to the deportation order of two Indian revolutionaries in Japan, Rash Behari Bose and H.L. Gupta.

We have also referred to Rash Behari Bose's autobiography, a text, in which he himself stated that, one of his reasons for leaving India was seeking foreign aid for the cause of the freedom struggle. After Rash Behari Bose reached Kobe on 5 June 1915, he did not waste time but got involved in this mission. The Jugantar group of Bengal and other revolutionary groups of Bengal were keen on obtaining assistance from Japan. From the C.I.D. file entitled *Proscription of the Book*, entitled *Biplabi Abani Mukherjee*, preserved in the West Bengal State Archives, also, from Abani Mukherjee's biography written by Professor Gautam Chattopadhyay entitled, *Abani Mukherjee: A Dauntless Revolutionary and Pioneering Communist*, we come to know that shortly after Rash Behari had left for Japan, Jatindranath Mukherjee, popularly known as Bagha Jatin, became anxious to obtain definite information about German aid. As advised by Jatindranath, Abani left for Japan in 1915.[129] From these two sources, we get fascinating glimpses of Abani's Mukherjee's political activities, during his stay in Japan.

Abani Mukherjee during his stay in Japan, met Binoy Kumar Sarkar and Shiva Prasad Gupta, both of them were staying in Japan at that time. With their help, Abani met Lala Lajpat Rai and the Chinese leader Sun Yat-sen, who was staying in Tokyo at that time. From the *Sedition Committee Report, 1918, Calcutta*, quoted in Professor Gautam Chattopadhyay's biography of Abani Mukherjee, we further come to know that it was SunYat-sen, who introduced Abani Mukherjee to Rash Behari Bose, who had arrived in Japan, some time before Abani reached there.[130] Also, Abani Mukherjee met Bhagawan Singh, who too was hiding in Japan at that time. From Bose's biography written by Takeshi Nakajima, entitled *Bose of Nakamuraya: An Indian Revolutionary in Japan*, we learn that the three of them managed to buy a large number of pistols and cartridges from Japan. Abani reached Shanghai from

Tokyo, from where he boarded a ship for India. However, their mission to smuggle weapons from Japan, and her neighbouring countries, also turned out to be a failure.[131] From Rash Behari Bose's English writing, entitled *Our Struggle,* included in *Rash Behari Bose: Collected Works,* we come across his recollection of the political activities and comrades, during the time they stayed in Japan:

> With the aid of Germany, I was able to send home two ships load of arms and ammunition but unfortunately, they were confiscated before reaching India.[132]

Rakhal Chandra Das of Dhaka (previously spelt as Dacca) in the late twenties, published a biography of Abani Mukherjee, entitled *Biplabi Abani Mukherjee.* The book was proscribed by the British government. The C.I.D. Intelligence Branch of the West Bengal State Archives contains an English translation of the said text, entitled *Proscription of the Book, entitled Biplabi Abani Mukherjee.* This translated document is resourceful in enlightening us about the period Abani spent in Japan. It narrates the political activities, in which he got involved and also, his final disillusionment with Japan's role in liberating India. From this document, we learn that Abani after arriving in Tokyo managed to make acquaintance with the Japanese political leaders; he tried his best to persuade them to obtain help for the sake of initiating an armed rebellion against the British rule in India. However, his hopes turned to be futile, as it has been narrated in the translated document:

> . . . all the hopes held out by the political leaders of Japan proved to be false. Japan was then busy, trying to strengthen the foundation of her own Imperialism. Britain, the mightiest Imperial power, was therefore, her chief rival. Japan did not shirk from achieving her own selfish interests in small measures by cheating this white Power. But how can she tolerate India standing as an independent power in the East? Hence, Abani met with failure only, though he tried heart and soul.[133]

An important document that needs citing, with reference to Japan's relation with British India during the period of First World War, is a secret report of Government of India, entitled *Trade After the War: Japanese Activities* (no. 36 of 1919), included in the West

Bengal State Archives (Home Political). The said document expresses the view that taking the advantage of the war time situation, Japan succeeded in increasing her overall trade with British India. Thus, the Anglo-Japanese Alliance, which was revived for the third time in 1911, turned out to be profitable for Japan, which succeeded in capturing the Indian market, as mentioned in the said document. It is thus no wonder that till the end of First World War, all attempts made by Bengali revolutionaries to win support from Japan, ended in failure.

From M.N. Roy's autobiography, entitled *M.N. Roy's Memoir,* we learn that M.N. Roy, after failing to smuggle ammunitions from Indonesia with the help of German Consul General there, left for Japan with the hope of getting Rash Behari Bose's help, who had reached Japan prior to him However, Roy has described his disillusionment with Japan and also with Rash Behari Bose, who according to Roy, had been able to receive a 'safe and comfortable political patronage' in Japan at that time:

> Rash Behari Bose was there with an identical mission; he would certainly help me. But I was rather surprised to find that he now believed that our mission of liberating India would be accomplished only in consequence of bigger mission of Japan to free Asia from White domination. I was still a full-blooded nationalist, and as such believed in the doctrine of racial solidarity. Nevertheless, I could not forget the fact that Japan was Britain's ally. How could we rely upon her helping us in our struggle against British domination?[134]

M.N. Roy's memoir also speaks of his disillusionment with the Chinese nationalist leader Sun-Yat-sen, who like Rash Behari Bose, was in exile in Japan. Moreover, like Bose, he had a great reliance on Japanese politicians:

> Sun Yat-sen believed in the liberating mission of Japan. He argued that it was in Japan's own interest to help other Asiatic peoples to free themselves from the domination of European Powers. . . . But my faith in racial solidarity was shaken rudely by the refusal of the prophet of Asiatic nationalism to help India against Britain.[135]

From M.N. Roy's memoir, we come to know that his mission of seeking assistance from Japan, turned out to be a failure, and he had to leave Japan very soon.[136]

The accounts we come across in Abani Mukherjee's biography, and also in M.N.Roy's Memoirs, well establish the fact that till the end of First World War, Japan was obliged to keep her diplomatic tie with England. In the introduction of this chapter, I have already referred to the deportation order of Rash Behari Bose and H.L. Gupta, and also of the fact that this deportation order, fell under pungent criticism in Japan.[137] With reference to Bose's biography, *Bose of Nakamuraya: An Indian Revolutionary in Japan*, we have already narrated the daring attempt of the members of the Genyosha, a right-wing nationalist party headed by Michiru Toyoma, which saved the life of Rash Behari Bose.

The diplomatic tie between Great Britain and Japan, which prevailed during the war time, altered after the end of war. Bose's biographers, Takeshi Nakajima and, J.G. Ohsawa have referred to the *Tenyo-maru* incident, which according to them played an important part in worsening the diplomatic tie between Japan and Great Britain. A British naval ship opened fire upon the Japanese liner *Tenyo-maru* and raided it. The incident led to a strong protest in Japan and according to Bose's biographer, Takeshi Nakajima, 'the Japanese Foreign Ministry of Japan made a strong official protest to England and took it as an opportunity to withdraw the deportation orders against Bose and Gupta'.[138] Moreover, we have earlier referred to Sho Kuwajima's observation that the friction between Japan and Great Britain, in connection with their attempts to exercise power over Chinese territory, also led to the worsening of Anglo-Japanese Alliance. Again, it must also be remembered that as early as from the Russo-Japanese War (1905), a cross-section of the Japanese nationals held the view that Japan should severe its diplomatic tie with Great Britain. A file of the Foreign Department of the National Archives, can give a glimpse of the change of attitude about Great Britain among the nationalists of Japan. The title of the file is *Publication of an Article in the Japanese Newspaper 'Keijo Shimpo'.* The file contains a letter of the British Consul General of Seoul, dated 1 December 1910, in which the writer has referred to a translation of an article, which was published in leading Japanese newspaper in Seoul. As mentioned in this document, the article was written by Mr. Y. Takeko, and it was published in the news week *Keijo Shimpo* (27 November 1910). From this letter, we further come to know that the writer of the article expressed his view that Japan should withdraw from Asiatic lands, instead, should seize the Dutch Indies. Commenting on this article, the British Consul General of Seoul remarked that the article itself was a testimony to the fact that there existed among Japanese, an idea that Japan should fight the battle of the Asiatic nations.[139]

With reference to this weakening of the diplomatic ties between Japan and the West, it must also be remembered that Japan, like other Asian countries, also experienced racial discrimination from the West. The awareness of it played a significant part in rousing anti-European sentiment among Japanese people, during the early twentieth century. Yumiko Iida in his article entitled *Fleeing the West, Making Asia Home: Transposition of Otherness in Japanese Pan-Asianism, 1905-30*, has rightly related this issue of racial discrimination from the West to this greater discourse of Asian solidarity. Iida has rightly pointed out that in 1919, just after the Paris Conference Japan proposed a clause of racial equality in the League of Nations Covenant; the rejection of this proposal shocked the Japanese public opinion.[140]

We have earlier traced how the Journals published from Bengal, were extremely receptive to any new development in Japan. *The Modern Review* for May 1919, published a declaration taken by the 37 societies of Japan, opposing all forms of discriminatory treatment that existed till then in international intercourse and which, according to them, was opposed to all principles of liberty and equality. The declaration was taken in a meeting, held on 5 February 1919, in Japan.[141]

Essays on racial discrimination against Japanese people living abroad, chiefly, in the United States, has also been published in vernacular magazines as in *Bharati*. The essay is 'Markine Japani Mlecho', was published in the magazine *Bharati* (Magh, 1322 BS). Sri Binoy Kumar Sarkar, the writer of this article, has rightly pointed out that Japan's sudden economic growth was the prime reason for such racial hatred from the West: 'The sudden rise of the yellow people of Japan has created fear among Americans. The rise of

Japan has also inspired the Yellow people of China, and also of other parts of Asia. Thus, America has become determined to pose impediment to Japan's material success.'[142]

Racial hatred against Japanese and other Asian people, residing in the United States, as witnessed by the writer, reached to such an extent, that he has observed that the term 'Asiatic' in Europe and America, of his time, was used in a derogatory sense: 'Nowadays, the word "Asiatic" is used as a synonymous expression for the word "heathen".'[143]

Rash Behari Bose in one of his English writings originally published in *The Standard Bearer* (vol. III. no. 20 (16-1-23), and also included in *Rash Behari Bose: Collected Works*, has vehemently opposed and criticized a verdict of the Supreme Court of United States in the early 1920s, barring the naturalization of Japanese residing in America, during that time. Bose, referring to an interview of Sun Yat-sen, in which the later criticized Japan's alliance with the western powers, during the World War period, has urged Japan to shed her tie with the allied power, and to take initiative in uniting the Asiatics.[144]

It is this change in the international situation, as we have already discussed earlier, which led to the rise of anti-western sentiment in Japan. This situation made favorable for Indian revolutionaries like Rash Behari Bose, who were keen to seek, Japan's assistance for the cause of Indian freedom struggle. After the deportation order was withdrawn in the year 1916, by the Japanese government, it became easier for Rash Behari Bose to carry out his activities in Japan. Rash Behari Bose became a citizen of Japan in July 1921.[145] During the twenties, Rash Behari Bose played an important role in hosting the First Pan Asiatic Conference that was held in Nagasaki, in August 1926. The Bangla newspaper *Bengalee*, published from Kolkata (24 September 1926), brought out a report on the proceedings of the Pan-Asiatic Conference. A copy of the said document has been included in a file of the Foreign and Political Department of the National Archives entitled, *Pan-Asiatic Conference*. From this newspaper report, we learn that the conference was held in Nagasaki, on the first three days of August in 1926. Further, the objective of this conference was to 'discuss the future of Eastern nations and to establish an organization for promoting their welfare'. It was attended by 70 delegates representing India, Turkey, Japan, Mongolia, China, Siam, the Phillipines Islands and the Malay States. The conference resulted in the formation of a Pan-Asiatic Union, having it's headquarters in Tokyo. The file entitled *Pan-Asiatic Conference* also includes a summary of the speech Rash Behari Bose delivered at the conference. As it has been recorded in the said document, Bose in his speech thanked wholeheartedly Mr. Imazato, who was a member of the Diet at that time, for taking the initiative to arrange the conference. He expressed his opinion that as Europeans had organized the League of Nations, Asiatics should organize a Pan-Asiatic League. Bose in his speech, delivered at the conference, also spoke of the rich heritage of Asiatic civilization, and its supremacy over the modern European civilization.[146] However, from the report published in the newspaper *Bengalee* (24 September 1926), also, from the account of the proceedings of the conference, described by Bose's biographer Takeshi Nakajima, we come to know that the proceedings of the conference exposed conflicting standpoints being taken by representatives of nations. The newspaper report held the view that the role played by Japanese representatives during the conference was far removed from its lofty objective of emancipating Asiatic countries from European domination. The report has rightly pointed out that the Japanese delegates as a whole, created a bad impression by trying to avoid discussion of the treaties that had given Japan a political and commercial hold on China. As expressed in this report, these treaties, known as the Twenty-One Point Demand, had been forced upon China against her will. This report which was published in the newspaper *Bengalee*, has rightly doubted the idea of the emergence of an Asia, free from colonial domination, and aptly concluded that for the proper functioning of Pan-Asiatic Union, an organization, whose sole aim is to foster the emancipation of all Asians, it was primarily needed that one Asiatic country should remove oppression on another.[147] Thus, the Pan-Asiatic Congress exposed the double standards maintained by Japan, advocating the ideal of Asian solidarity on one hand, and again continuing to keep her domination on parts of Asia, on the other. From the narration of the proceedings of the Conference, as done by Bose's biographer Nakajima, we also get a similar picture. Nakajima, in his description, has pointed out that during the conference, the Korean representative, in spite of being present was barred from delivering his speech. As Korea was a colony of Japan, her representative was deprived of having equal status, like other Asian delegates during the conference. Takeshi Nakajima has observed that the denial of Korean representation, during the conference, exposed the public view that the Asianism advocated by Imazato, did not guarantee equality to all Asian races, in the real sense.[148] The Foreign and Political file, we have already referred to, includes a letter, written by John Tilley of the British Embassy, Tokyo, to Sir, Austen Cumberlain, dated, 13 August 1926, in which the writer has expressed his view that the conference did not succeed in getting much support from the influential Japanese circles. John Tiller, in support of his observation, has referred to the fact that Mahendra Pratap, the Afghan delegate, who secured admittance in Japan, was first detained at Kobe, later, he was allowed to land at Osaka, on condition that he would not attempt to go to Nagasaki, to attend the conference.[149]

From these documents relating to Pan-Asiatic Conference, it is evident that Japan, though being the host of such a conference, showed extreme calculations in providing support to anti-colonial struggle in British India, or in other parts of Asia. Moreover, Japan contesting with other super powers of the West, was also engaged in exercising power over her neighbouring countries. The file entitled, *Pan-Asiatic Conference*, of the Foreign and Political Department of the National Archives, also include another letter written to Sir John Tilley, Ambassador to Tokyo, dated 4 August 1926. The letter has rightly pointed out that the main bone of contention between the Chinese and Japanese delegates attending the conference was regarding the unequal treaties, which had been forced on China by Japan.[150] It has also been stated that the Chinese delegates proposed the condemning of the Twenty-One Treaties that faced opposition from the later.

According to Takeshi Nakajima, the Pan-Asiatic Conference was a turning point in Rash Behari Bose's exiled life in Japan. Nakajima has observed that after the Conference, 'Bose refrained from criticizing Japan in public as far as possible'. Further, he tried his best to strengthen his relationship with important people of Japan; and to win their support for India's freedom struggle. During this period, Bose regularly contributed articles in Japanese magazines.[151] A close study of his English articles published during the 1920s, in the *Standard Bearer*, reveals the fact that Bose, from a pragmatic point of view took the task of advocating in favour of Japan. He has tried to justify Japanese advancement in neighboring countries. Thus, in an article entitled, 'Japan's Budget Estimate For 1923-4', which was published in the *Standard Bearer*, vol. III, Bose has dished out details of Japan's Budget, in order to point out the fact that Japan, in contrast to England, and other European countries, has provided a lot of subsidies to her colonies. As mentioned in the article, this aid was provided to Korea, Kwantung (China), Saghalien and South Sea Regions. Bose has concluded that since the time of annexation of Korea, Japan had been spending a considerable sum every year, for the development of Korea.[152]

Even if we agree with Bose's argument, the question that remains is, how can colonization of a foreign territory be justified, even if the colonizer undertakes development measures? Needless to say, Bose's arguments in favour of Japanese imperialism seem to be a reincarnation of the 'white men's burden' hypothesis.

Another important aspect of the political writings of Rash Behari Bose, which needs mention, is his positive attitude towards the newly formed Bolshevik Russia. In an article, entitled, 'Russo-Japan Relations', Bose has earnestly wished that both Russia and Japan, would succeed in becoming a strong ally:

> If Japan could secure Russian friendship, she will not experience any difficulty in obtaining raw materials even in times of war. And the third, rather the most important motive is political. Japan is already feeling the menacing pressure from the Anglo-Saxon imperialism in various ways. . . . In order to extricate herself from this dangerous situation, the only thing which she should do is to effect an equally strong combination. In the absence of a free India and a strong China, her natural allies, she has no other alternative but to seek the help of Russia, a semi-Asiatic country, having common interest so far as the Anglo-Saxon imperialism is concerned.[153]

It seems from this article that, Rash Behari Bose during the 1920s cherished the hope that a grand alliance of Russia and Japan would take place. This would facilitate anti-colonial struggle in many Asian countries. However, the course of historical events moved in a different direction, than materializing his dream. From a document of the I.B. of the West Bengal State Archives entitled, *Proposal to Send Revolutionaries to the Far East in Connection with Arms Smuggling* (3/4/1927, Sl. no. 164/1927)[154], it is evident that even in the late 1920s, the Jugantar Dal, maintained relations with Rash Behari Bose. This revolutionary outfit sought monetary help, and also assistance, for the purpose of smuggling arms and ammunitions from Japan. However, Bose during the 1920s was more engaged in winning the support of important Japanese politicians, than taking active role in sending arms to India, which he did before.

To conclude this section, it can be said that, the possibility of obtaining foreign assistance, for carrying out armed resistance against the empire, which brightened on the eve of the First World War, lost its significance during the 1920s. Firstly, Germany lost the war. Moreover, though Japan's diplomatic ties with England worsened, Japan, as we have noticed, was more preoccupied in keeping up her control over vast part of Asia, than facilitating anti-colonial movement in British India, and in other parts of Asia. The news of Japan's aggression on her neighbouring nations did not miss the attention of the reading public of Bengal. It generated a strong reaction against Japanese imperialism. The following sub-chapter will attempt to locate the reaction of the writings from Bengal, with regard to Japan's expansionism during the first three decades of the last century.

ANNEXATION OF KOREA, AND AGGRESSION ON MANCHURIA: DISILLUSIONMENT WITH JAPAN'S POLITICAL ROLE AMONG THE INTELLIGENTSIA OF BENGAL

T.R. Sareen in his article entitled 'India and Japan in Historical Perspectives', has observed that initially Indian leaders had been receptive to the ideology of Pan-Asia sponsored by Japan. However, Japan's aggressive policy in China moved them away from Japan.[155] It is true that it was after the sudden aggression on Manchuria, by the Japanese army in September 1931, which led to a strong reaction against Japanese imperialism among Indian national leaders. However, it must also be noted that, this change of attitude towards Japan did not happen overnight. A close study of articles published on Japan in different magazines from Bengal, of the early twentieth century, such as *Bharati* or *The Modern Review*, can ascertain the fact that this disillusionment with Japan's political role, happened much beforehand than Japan's invasion on Manchuria in 1931. We have already referred to Sister Nivedita's denouncement of the annexation of Korea in 1910, in her article 'Korea and Japan'. The article was published in the *Modern Review* (1907), even before the formal annexation of Korea, by the Japanese government in 1910. The news of Japan's annexation of Korea was published in *The Modern Review* (September 1910, p. 345). The editor has observed that the response of the British newspapers, with regard to this important event, was only restricted to expressing their anxiety regarding ensuring Great Britain's commercial interests with Korea. Further, we learn from this news that following the annexation of Korea, the new Resident General of Japan in Korea made a statement, which announced that all measures would be taken by Japan to ensure Koreans, and the world, to make them feel that Japan's rule over Korea was beneficent. An ambivalent observation made by the editor of *The Modern Review* in this regard, deserves mention: 'This assurance will be to the Koreans what the Queen's Proclamation of 1858 has been to the Indians.'[156]

Thus, it is from the time of Korean annexation (1910), we notice that the educated classes of Bengal were keenly observing every advance made by Japan. As time rolled on, the earlier jubilant acceptance of Japan, as the saviour of the East, was substituted by an air of skepticism.

An interesting article that needs citing is Jyotirindranath Tagore's 'Adhunik Japan'. It was published in successive serials in the Bangla magazine *Bharati*. In the last sequal of this essay, published in *Bharati* (Ashin, 1315 BS/1908), we notice Jyotirindranath questioning Japan's imitation of the political machinery of the European nation state. It must be noticed that the publication of this article took prior to the time of annexation of Korea in 1910. Still, the essay gives an illuminative glance on the history of the emergence of Japan's imperialism, which ran parallel with the process of modernization of Japan. According to the writer, it was the need of self-protection, which led to the rise of militarism in Japan:

> It is regretable that following Japan's rapid armament, Japan's international policy has undergone a change. The patriotic feeling of the Japanese people has now turned the nation into an aggressive and ruthless one. Earlier, Japan was empathetic towards the suffering of other nations, in our times, Japan is engaged in creating her 'Yellow empire'. The advent of Japanese imperialism, may well be termed as 'pan-japanism'.[157]

This imperialistic ambition of Japan, as pointed out by the author, has led to the transformation of Japanese nation state, according to western standard:

> Japan became keen on winning equal status and equal treatment from the West. This led to the transformation of Japanese state policies and governance, according to European standard. The Japanese emperor Mikado himself took initiatives to change the functioning of the Japanese government, following western standard.[158]

It is this borrowing by the Japanese, ideals of a European nation state, against which, Rabindranath Tagore has raised his arguments in his seminal text *Nationalism*:

> What is dangerous for Japan is not the imitation of the outer features of the West, but the acceptance of the motive force of western nationalism as her own.[159]

Thus, Jyotirindranath Tagore's opinion regarding the emergence of Japanese imperialism seems coherent with Tagore's denouncement of Japanese nationalism in his text *Nationalism.* The other significant aspect of this essay, which demands attention, is Jyotirindranath's coinage of the term 'Pan-Japanism'. In this context, it would be worthy to pay attention to Seven Saaler's observation regarding the terms 'Pan-asianism' and 'Asianism', and his preference for differentiating these two terms, with another term, 'Greater Asianism', in his article 'Pan Asianism in Meiji and Taisho Japan-A

Preliminary Framework'. Seven Saaler has studied the ideology of Pan-Asianism in the context of the history of Japan of the Meiji, and the Taisho era (1912-26). He has concluded that the term Pan-Asianism and Asianism, may be used synonymously; however, it is different from the term, Greater Asianism, a term, which gained popularity in the 1920s, and 1930s, as an ideological state apparatus of Japan's imperialistic and expansionist policy.[160] Jyotirindranath's coinage of the term Pan-Japanism, seems to bear similarity with Greater-Asianism, the ideology of Asianism, advocated by Japanese politicians, to justify Japan's imperialistic ambition, on the ground of consolidation of nations, based on racial affinity.

We have earlier referred to Sarala Devi's memoir *Jibaner Jhora Pata*, where Sarala Devi has recounted how the news of Japanese victory filled them with enthusiasm. Sarala Devi, in the same memoir, has recounted her later disillusionment in finding Japan's repression on her neighboring countries:

> Our attitude towards Japan has changed formidably, in comparison to that of earlier period. During that time, Japan became successful to defeat a strong European nation, namely, Russia. This military success against a European nation inspired other subjugated nations of Asia. Thus, Japanese ideology of unifying Asia, under the catchy phrase 'Asia is one' stimulated the minds of many. Now, we can see the deception of that ideology, which seemed to be a desire of unifying Asia, and became successful to hide the imperialist design of Japan to colonise the whole of Asia.[161]

Thus, Sarala Devi in her writing has rightly pointed her finger towards the double standard of Japanese Asianism, an ideology that propagated Asian solidarity on one hand, and on the other hand, justified Japan's expansionist policies. Following the Korean annexation in 1910, Japan turned out to be an important power in Asia. Japan's imperialistic ambition soared high, and during the period of the First World War, taking the advantage of Japan's alliance with England, Japan succeeded in exerting power and control over Manchuria and China. In early 1915, the Japanese government imposed upon China a series of demands, known as the Twenty-one Demands. These demands included certain financial privileges, and also control over trade and commerce, in the Shangtung province, and also in South Manchuria.[162] No doubt, these advances of Japan on Manchuria and China, did not escape the notice of Bengali readers. As mentioned earlier, in many articles published during the 1920s and 1930s, we come across a sceptic attitude towards Japan's role, as a leading nation of the East. In this context, among many, I would like to refer a particular article, which was published in the Bangla magazine *Prabasi* (1343 BS, Poush). The article is entitled 'Japanider Bharatborshe Boudhdhormo Prochar Chestha'. The writer, in this article, has referred to the news of a construction of a Buddhist temple in Delhi, which received funding by the Japanese government, of that time. Also, similar instances of construction of Buddhist monasteries in East Bengal, which were constructed by the Japanese government, have also been mentioned in this essay. For the author, this sudden enthusiasm in promoting Buddhism in India turns out to be a mysterious one. In regard to this, his caustic observation, with reference to this issue, needs mention:

> The whole thing seems to be shrouded in mystery. Western missionaries came to India and founded many monastries. Now, if Japanese Buddhists start setting up Buddhist associations in India, it cannot be objected. However, we must not forget that the proces of colonizing many countries, took a strange course. At first, they came with *Bible* in their hands, then, bottles (alcoholic beverage) were distributed among the natives. Finally, with the employment of force, colonization became complete. Will the Japanese step into the shoes of their white masters?[163]

It is with reference to this reaction against Japanese imperialiasm in the writings from Bengal, during the early twentieth century, that it would be worth noting once again, Tagore's criticism of Japanese nationalism in his seminal text *Nationalism.* Also, the lectures he delivered during his visit to Japan, deserve a close reading. During his successive visits to Japan, Rabindranath might have been shown a display of war trophies won from China. With regard to this, we note his contemptuous observation, as recorded in Uma Dasgupta's edited text entitled *Rabindranath Tagore: My Life in My Words:* 'When I came to Japan, I had a chance of observing something that deeply hurt my mind. I saw trophies won from the Chinese people being exhibited there. It was just after China had been humiliated by the Japanese people.'[164]

For Tagore, it is because of the intense nationalism that Japanese found no wrong in displaying such war trophies won from China.[165]

Tagore's *Nationalism* and his famous novel *Gora* were written almost in an overlapping period. The novel explores his idea of *Bharatbarsa*; and it has been so poignantly explored in the delineation of the character of Gora, the protagonist of the novel. If Tagore was a severe critic of western concept of nation, which relies on the use of power, he equally rejected the ultra-Hindu concept of Indian nation, as the space for one religious' community. Needless to say, this has been Gora's final realization, when he came to know about his parental origin, that he was not born of a Hindu family, but of Irish parents, who lost their lives during the 'Revolt of 1857': 'Today give me the *mantram* of that Deity who belongs to all, Hindu, Mussulman, Christian and Brahmo alike—the doors to whose temple are never closed to any person of any caste whatever—He who is not merely the God of the Hindus, but is the God of India herself!'[166]

This profound utterance of Gora represents Tagore's ambivalent attitude towards East and West. In the concluding part of the first Chapter, we have already discussed at a length that for Tagore, Japan is essentially a child of the East; and he heavily stresses on Japan's legacy of the culture and civilization of the East. Also, Tagore opposes the political machinery of the western world. Yet, his view must not be seen as identical with the representation of Orient, we come across in so many European writings. Rather, Tagore in all his lectures, as in *The Message From India to Japan*, a lecture, which he delivered in Japan, has warned Japan from being a thoughtless imitator of the political machinery of the West: 'Japan has imported her food from the West, but not her vital nature. Japan cannot all together lose and merge herself in the scientific paraphernalia she has acquired from the West and be turned into a mere borrowed machine.'[167]

In a more categorical manner, Tagore in his *Nationalism* has pointed that it is not the imitation of the outer features of the

West, that he opposes, but the 'acceptance of the motive force of western nationalism as her own'.[168] Truly, Tagore views the modern nation of the West, as a monstrous machine, and all his arguments are directed against this incorporation of the modern state machinery in an Asian country, like Japan: 'The political civilization which has sprung up from the soil of Europe and in overrunning the world, like some prolific weed, is based upon exclusiveness. . . . It is carnivorous and cannibalistic in its tendencies.'[169]

In *Nationalism*, Tagore has rightly pointed out that there is nothing objectionable in Japan's acquiring of modern weapons for self-defense. However, the poet emphasizes that, 'this should never be allowed to go beyond her instinct of self-preservation'.[170]

As opposed to the ideology of the political civilization of the West, Tagore professes a kind of Asianism, which is also antithetical to the Asianism advocated by Japanese politicians during that time. The ideology of Asianism, advocated by Japanese politicians was as an ideological state apparatus, intended to exert their control over large territories of Asia. Tagore's ideals of Asian civilization, which he believes to be the lineage of Japan, is not dependant on the use of power, but on *maitri* (harmony), a term he coins in his essay *Nationalism*, and also in other lectures and essays: 'The ideal of *maitri* is at the bottom of your culture-*maitri* with men and *maîtri* with nature.'[171]

In all his lectures, which Tagore delivered in Japan during his successive visits, he tried to convey his message of pacifism to the Japanese people. Tagore warned Japan, to refrain from the path of imperialism, which according to Tagore was borrowed from the West: ' Be gentle, be patient; for that will save you; that will make you live; that will give you life everlasting . . . not machine guns, not poison gas, not bomb throwing aeroplanes; in the end man will only survive where he is human, and not where he is demonically making profits.'[172]

The critical response of Japanese intellectuals towards Tagore's pacifism has been dealt in details, in Stephen Hay's *Asian Ideas of East and West*, also, in Kyoko Niwa's article entitled *Rabindranath Tagore and Japan*. It is no wonder that Tagore's call for pacifism fell flat, and he was viewed by Japanese intellectuals, to be a spokesman of a defeated nation. Hay, referring to Kanokogi Kazunobu's observation that Tagore was 'the beautiful flower of a ruined country'[173], has pointed that it was not Kanokogi alone, who considered Tagore to be a representative of a defeated nation, but this idea was predominant among most of the leading intellectuals of Japan, at that time. Hay has concluded that, 'proud of Japan's independent status and her rise to equality with the world's great powers, these intellectuals looked down on India as a pitiful country that had lost out in the struggle for survival'.[174]

Kyoko Niwa in her article entitled 'Rabindranath Tagore and Japan: On His Visit with His Message and its Results', commenting on the enthusiasm of the Japanese people on the occasion of Tagore's first visit in 1916, and the weaning of it afterwards, has rightly pointed out that, the 'Tagore boom' in 1915 was caused by the reception of Nobel Prize, and a rumour of his visit to Japan'.[175] According to Niwa, the popularity of Tagore was hardly caused by a true understanding of Tagore and appreciation of his aesthetics.[176] Kyoko Niwa, in the same article, referring to C.F. Andrews' recounting of Tagore's visit to Japan in 1916, has rightly pointed out that no sooner had Tagore voiced against Japanese nationalism, than the enthusiasm about Tagore, that was created by the news of his reception of Nobel Prize, started to withdraw:

> But when he spoke out strongly against the militant imperialism which he saw on every side in Japan and set forward in contrast his own ideal picture of the true meeting of East and West, and its vista of world brotherhood, the hint went abroad that such 'pacifist' teaching was a danger in war-time, and the Indian poet represented a defeated nation. Therefore, almost as rapidly as the enthusiasm had arisen, it subsided.[177]

In July 1937, the Japanese army made sudden military advances in portions of Northern China, and this led to her war with China. The news of Japanese aggression in China created a strong reaction among many Indian leaders. The Congress condemned Japan and called for a boycott of Japanese goods. The Congress also sent a medical mission to China, in solidarity with her people. This reaction against Japanese aggression was not confined to the Indian nationalists alone. Tagore also, condemned this aggression on China by Japan, as a 'virulent infection of imperialistic rapacity imported from West'; his reaction was printed in the *Visva-Bharati News*, 7, no. 1 (July 1938).

Uma Mukherjee, another of Rash Behari Bose's biographer, has observed that for Rash Behari Bose, the anti-Japanese standpoint taken by the Congress, as well as a formidable portion of Indian intelligentsia, turned out to be irrational and inimical to the national interest. Thus, to mend Indo-Japanese friendship, Rash Behari Bose took an initiative to invite Tagore to Japan. Uma Mukherjee has referred to the cable, which was sent to Tagore, conveying the invitation. Tagore sent a decent reply to Bose on 10 October 1937. Tagore's letter shows his admiration for Japan on one hand, and his horror and contempt at the Japanese invasion in China, on the other. Tagore finally declined Rash Behari's invitation. A portion of the letter, quoted by Uma Mukherjee, needs citing in this context:

> I know in making this appeal you counted on my great regard for the Japanese, for I, along with the rest of Asia, did once admire and look up to Japan and did once fondly hope that in Japan Asia had at last discovered its challenge to the West, that Japan's new strength would be consecrated in safeguarding the culture of the East against alien interests. But Japan has not taken long to betray that rising hope and repudiate all that seemed significant in her wonderful, and, to us symbolic awakening, and has now become itself a worse menace to the defenseless people of the East.[178]

It is Japan's sudden aggression on China in 1937, which led to a well-known epistolary debate between Tagore and Yonejiro Noguchi. From Kyoko Niwa's essay entitled 'Rabindranath Tagore and Noguch Yonejiro', an article in which the author has dealt in detail Noguchi's cosmopolitan background, and also his previous associations, and what led to Noguchi's criticism of Tagore, following the latter's condemnation of Japanese aggression on China. According to Niwa, Noguchi, who was brought up in the West, and started his literary career firstly in English language, suffered from an identity crisis in Japan. It was out of his earnestness to emphasize his belonging to Japan, he openly advocated in favour of Japanese military advances in China, and took up his pen to criticize Tagore. There is no reason to deny the argument raised by Niwa, if we once again read Noguchi's impulsive comments, in which he tried to put forward his support of Japan's war against China, and its consequent human carnage:

> But if you take the present war in China for the criminal outcome of Japan's surrender to the West, you are wrong because, not being a slaughtering madness, it is I believe, the inevitable means, terrible it is though, for establishing a new great world in the Asiatic continent, where the 'Principle of live and let live' has to be realized. Believe me, it is the war of 'Asia for Asia'.[179]

The passage quoted above, can clearly point out how the hegemony of Japanese Asianism, eclipsed Noguchi's ideas. He considered this brutal war against Chinese people, to be the inevitable means of creating Asia for Asiatic people. Needless to say, this opinion of Noguchi must have been a shock for Tagore. From biographical details regarding Tagore-Noguch relationship, that we come across in Niwa's essay, we learn that in 1935, Noguchi paid a visit to Tagore Santiniketan.[180] Tagore's reply letter to Noguchi, dated, 1 September 1938, voices Tagore's condemnation of this brutal war, which Japan imposed on Chinese people and also a refutation of Noguchi's arguments:

> Humanity, in spite of its many failures, has believed in a fundamental moral structure of society. When you, speak, therefore, of 'the inevitable means, terrible it is though, for establishing a new great world in the Asiatic continent'—signifying, I suppose, the bombing of Chinese women and children and the desecration of ancient temples and universities as a means of saving China for Asia-you are ascribing to humanity a way of life which is not even inevitable among animals and would certainly not apply to the East, in spite of her occasional aberrations. You are building your concept of Asia which would be raised on a tower of skulls.[181]

We have earlier referred to Rash Behari Bose's attempt to enlist Tagore's support for Japan. In 1938, Rash Behari tried once again to persuade him to visit Japan. From the editorial notes provided by Krishna Dutta and Andrew Robinson in the *Selected Letters of Rabindranath Tagore*, he come to know that at that time, Japanese bombing on China was taking place, Guangzhou (Canton) had been captured by Japanese army; all these led Tagore to decline Bose's offer once again:

> ... But as I am doubtful whether the military authorities of Japan, which seem bent upon devastating China in order to gain their object, will allow me the freedom to take my own course, I shall never forgive myself if am tempted for any reason whatever to pay a friendly visit to Japan just at this unfortunate moment and thus cause a grave misunderstanding.[182]

Benode Behari Mukherjee reached Japan at a time, when Japan's entry into the war had become imminent.[183] Benode Behari in his *Chitrakar*, has written that Japan was preparing for the war that was about to break out. In the streets of Tokyo, national flags of Japan and Germany, were unfurled to commemorate the political alliance of Germany and Japan. Also, there was regular machinegun practice in the outskirts of the city, the sound of which resounded everywhere.[184] During his stay in Japan, through Rash Behari Bose's initiative, Benode Behari was introduced to an organization, which endeavoured to establish cultural ties between Japan and other parts of the Orient. The organization provided him a young guide whose name was Hango, with whom the painter was on friendly terms. He took Benode Behari into his confidence, and expressed his disillusionment with Japanese painters like Taikan Yokohama, who had become spokesmen of the military regime:

> I never found him voicng against Japanese inheritance of the Chinese tradition of art. Rather, he said that they (Japanese) have learnt many useful things from China. Hango was of the opinion that an artist should not have any direct involvement in politics. He further pointed out that Taikan, who earlier voiced in favour of freedom for artists, has become a turncoat. He has received patronage from the Japanese government. He has been sent to Germany, and to Italy, as a cultural representative of Japan. Thus, Taikan's views have changed completely. He has become the spokesperson of the Japanese government.[185]

Hango's criticism of Taikan, for becoming a spokesman of the military regime in Japan, during the war time, reminds us of Tagore's reproach of Noguchi, and of other intellectuals, who could have played an important role to resist the hegemony of the Japanese warmongers:

What is not amusing is that artists and thinkers should echo such remarkable sentiments that translate military swagger into spiritual bravado. In the West, even in the days of war madness, there is never dearth of great spirits who can raise their voice above the din of battle, and defy their own warmongers in the name of humanity.[186]

It can be concluded that Tagore-Noguchi's epistolary debate in 1938, almost marks the end of a chapter, of a long interaction between the Japanese intellectuals and their Bengali counterpart. It is this Japan's war against China and her people, which eventually led to the dilution of the ideology of Asian solidarity, which was propounded by Pan-Asian ideologues like Tenshin Okakura. We have also mentioned that the Congress took a standpoint to oppose Japanese aggression on China. In 1938, in the Haripura session, the Congress took a decision to boycott Japanese goods. With reference to this issue of Japanese invasion of the Chinese mainland, an interesting article referred to by Subhas Bose's biographer Sugata Bose, needs mention. The October 1937 issue of the *Modern Review*, brought out a long essay by Bose, entitled 'Japan's Role in the Far East', in which the author, despite being an admirer of Japan, has offered a criticism of the advent of militarism in Japan. 'Could not Japan's aim be achieved', asked Subhas Bose, 'without imperialism, without dismembering the Chinese Republic, without humiliating another, proud, cultured and ancient race'?[187]

Thus, historians like Bipan Chandra, have observed that in the course of anti-imperialist struggle, the Indian people developed a policy of solidarity towards anti-imperialist movement in other parts of the world. Bipan Chandra has cited the resolution adopted at the Haripura session in 1938, condemning the Japanese invasion of China.[188] However, it would be another oversimplification to derive that all segments of Indian political organizations, consented to this policy. With Japan's entry into the Pacific War, the possibility of seeking Japanese help for the sake of India's Independence, once again revived. On 8 December 1941, the Greater East Asia War broke out. With Japan's entry into the Second World War, Japanese politicians once again sought to ensure the cooperation of Indian nationalists, for their war against the Allied forces.

Thus, on 16 February 1942, Prime Minister Tojo issued a declaration in both the houses of Parliament, referring to the cause of Indian freedom struggle:

> This is the best opportunity for India to rid itself of the despotic policy of oppression by the British and participate in building the Greater Asia Co-prosperity Sphere. The Japanese Empire hopes to restore India to its original status, whereby the nation belongs to Indians, and will provide all help to the patriotic efforts of the Indian people.[189]

How far the Congress yielded to these promises offered by Japan, may well be doubted. For instance, Maulana Abdul Kalam Azad in his book *India Wins Freedom*, has refuted the view of a cross-section of nationalists, who were in favour of Japan: 'I sharply criticized those who believed or said that Japan would give India freedom. National self- respect demanded that we should not think in terms of a change of masters.'[190]

However, for Rash Behari Bose, this new situation seemed to be a fulfillment of his dream. From the biographical details provided by J.G. Ohsawa in his book, *The Two Great Indians in Japan*, we come to know that Rash Behari, on 13 March 1942, carried out radio broadcasting from Tokyo.[191] Rash Behar Bose's *Collected Works*, edited by Asitava Das, include transcribed versions of his radio broadcast from Japan, his speech, which he delivered in Japan on 26 January 1943 and also his letters and messages to the leaders of Congress, like Sardar Vallabhbhai Patel, Jawaharlal Nehru and others, seeking the cooperation of the Indian nationalists and asking them to take side with Japan, in her war with Great Britain: 'I entreat the Indian Congress Leaders in the name of Indians in East Asia, to rise to this occasion and sever the shackles of British imperialism and all that it stands for and assert India's right to self-determination and complete Independence.'[192]

The history of the making of the I.N.A, and the role of Rash Behari Bose and Subhas Bose, in leading Indian freedom struggle during the Second World War, involve a detailed study of a plethora of documents, which remain beyond the scope of this chapter, intended to be restricted to a time span of 45 years, from 1893 to 1938. Yet, I will try to refer to a few documents, which deserve mention with reference to this history of Indian freedom struggle that received some definite assistance from Japan, during the period of the Second World War. Nikki Kimura in his remembrance of Rash Behari Bose, entitled 'My Memory about the Late Rash Behari Bose', included in the book *Rash Behari Bose: His Struggle for India's Independence,* has given an account of Rash Behari's involvement with I.N.A., and how he was chosen as the leader of this mission. In short, following the outbreak of the war, when Japanese army advanced to Singapore and Malay, Mr. Tojo Hideaki, the then Prime Minister of Japan, sought for the assistance and cooperation of Indians residing outside India, but in Asian countries. It was then, Nikki Kimura was chosen as the adviser to the Japanese Army General Staff Office, by the then Prime Minister of Japan. Kimura suggested the name of Rash Behari Bose as the leader of the volunteer corps.[193] It is well known that the process of organizing the I.N.A faced many impediments at first.[194] However, after Subhas Chandra Bose reached Japan, the activities of I.N.A. received some stimulus. Subhas Bose reached Japan on 2 July 1943, a meeting of the Indian Independence League was arranged in Singapore on 4 July. Rash Behari in that meeting introduced Subhas Chandra Bose to the audience, and proposed his name, as the representative of Indian Independence League.[195] K.K. Ghosh in his book entitled, *The Indian National Army*, has given a detailed account of the history of I.N.A. and its war against the Allied forces, in Arakan and Imphal sector. From this book, we further come to know that between February and May 1944, the I.N.A. succeeded in 'crossing into Indian soil in the Arakan sector and in the Bishenpur in the Imphal sector'.[196] However, the course of the war, turned out to be far from the hopes and expectation of both Rash Behari and Subhas Bose. Japan's unconditional surrender to Allied force on 15 August 1945 brought an end to the Greater East Asia War.

Bengal's association with the politics of Japan will remain incomplete, without referring to the name of Radhabinod Pal, and his dissenting judgment at the Tokyo Tribunal. Radhabinod Pal, who was appointed to serve the International Military Tribunal for Far East, submitted a dissenting note, for which he holds a position of high esteem among Japanese, still today. While admitting the charge brought against the Japanese armed forces, of atrocities carried out against civilians and prisoners of war, during the war time, Radhabinod Pal, in his judgment questioned the legitimacy of the tribunal and its verdict. Justice Pal opposed the prosecution for crime against peace, and crime against humanity, as defined in the Tribunal Charter, 'because these crimes had no previous grounds in the international laws'.[197] Also, Pal considered the atomic bombing of the cities, Hiroshima and Nagasiki, to be the worst atrocities of the war.[198] Commenting on the reason, why Pal is still honoured in Japan, T.R. Sareen has observed that 'the Pal Judgement raised Japanese morale, which was very low due to their defeat'.[199] Also, Norimitsu Onishi in his article entitled 'Decades After War Trials, Japan Still Honours a Dissenting Judge', has referred to a 'Nippon Hoso Kyokai' broadcast dealing with Pal's life, the publication of scholarly books on Judge Pal, and also the erection of a monument to the judge, at Yasukuni Shrine in Japan. According to Onishi, Judge Pal seemed to have mixed feelings towards Japan. The writer has rightly pointed out that this was also shared by many Indian anti-colonialists of Pal's generation. Japan's success as an Asian nation was an inspiration for Indians. However, her colonial ambition was looked upon critically. Onishi has cited historian Sugata Bose's opinion regarding his great-uncle, Subhas Chandra Bose, who, according to Sugata Bose, 'criticized Japan's invasion of China but allied himself with Japan against the British'. Interestingly, the news of Radhabinod Pal's dissenting role at the Tokyo Tribunal, was published in the miscellaneous section of *Prabasi* and is entitled, 'Japani Samorik Netribrinder Bichar' (1355 BS, Agrahan). The report can once again testify how Bengal's sympathy went with Japan, the defeated and not the victor:

Most of those German generals, who were convicted at the Nuremberg trial, met with the gallows. They were even deprived of the honour of dying, facing the firing squad. These facts have almost passed into oblivion. The recent Tokyo Tribunal reminds us of the fact that the victors of the war, never refrain from taking revenge against the defeated. Justice Radhabinod Pal, a Bengali judge, was one among the 11 juries of this tribunal. The majority of the jury held the view that the accused Japanese generals were guilty of committing atrocity against civilians and prisoners of war. Owing to these charges against the accused, six prisoners were sentenced to death, and 11 others were given life-time imprisonment. It is not difficult to understand that the Japanese have not committed so great a crime against humanity during the war time that they can be charged with such offence. The dissenting note of Radhabinod Pal showed us that the Tribunal turned out to be nothing other than victor's justice.[200]

The ideology of Pan-Asianism, which is rooted in the notion of a spiritual and cultural affinity among Asian countries, evolved as an isolated intellectual discourse, observes Seven Saaler, in his article entitled, 'Pan-Asianism in in Meiji and Taisho Japan—A Preliminary Framework'. However, according to the writer, during the 1930s in Japan, it played a significant part in forming Japan's foreign policy. Saaler has defined this type of Pan-Asianism as 'the hegemonic pan-movement, justifying and legitimizing Japan's ambitious project of colonizing parts of Asian continent'.

To conclude, it can be said that Bengal's response to this ideology of Pan-Asianism, was one of accord and discord. Japan became an inspiration for many, in her rapid material advancement. However, the news of Japanese atrocity on the people of Japan's neighbouring nations, Korea and China, created a sentiment of discontent and of suspicion. In spite of its pervasive impact in being the hegemonic tool of Japan's empire building process, we must also admit that the ideology of Pan-Asianism, for the first time, upheld the idea of collaboration of Asian countries. And, this had a deep impact upon the subjugated races of Asia. During the post-Independence period in India, Pan-Asianism, had a lingering effect in developing India's foreign policy, observed T.A. Keenleyside. The writer in his essay entitled, 'Nationalist Indian Attitudes Towards Asia', has referred to the Jaipur session of Indian National Congress in 1948, which declared that close cooperation would be developed among Asian nations. According to T.A. Keenleyside, Nehru himself was responsible for keeping the Pan-Asian idea alive during the 1950s. The bilateral peace treaty, which was signed between Japan and India in June 1952, may be viewed as an important step with regard to Asian solidarity.

The task of ensuring cooperation and solidarity among Asian

countries, during the cold-war period, witnessed many impediments. For instance, Japan and India, during the later part of the last century drifted away, due to their allegiance to opposed global camps. A sea change in international politics and in economy also started with the dissolution of the Soviet Union in the 1990s, and also under the impact of economic liberalization, that dawned during the same time. In keeping with this spirit of change in the global scenario, the Asia Cooperation Dialogue (ACD)[201] has been created on 18 June 2002. We can hope that Asian countries will be able to foster solidarity and cooperation among themselves, in near future, to ensure peace, prosperity and progress in this continent.

NOTES

1. Marlene J. *Mayo*, 'Introduction', *The Emergence of Imperial Japan,* ed. Marlene J. Mayo (Massachusetts: D.C. Health & Co., 1970), p. vii.
2. Brij Tankha and Madhavi Thampi, *Narratives of Asia from India, Japan and China* (Kolkata: Sampark, 2005), p. 39.
3. Tankha, *Narratives of Asia,* p. 43.
4. Ibid., p. 44.
5. Ibid., p. 46.
6. Matsumoto Kenichi, 'Okakura Tenshin and the Ideal of Pan-Asianism', *Shadows of the Past: Of Okakura Tenshin and Pan-Asianism,* ed. Brij Tankha, (Kolkata: Sampark, 2007), p. 26.
7. Ibid.
8. Yumiko Iida, 'Fleeing the West, Making Asia Home: Transpositions of Otherness in Japanese Pan-Asianism, 1905-30', *Alternatives: Global, Local, Political,* 32. 3 July to September (1997), http://*www.jstor.org,* (accessed on 23 May 2014), p. 417.
9. Ibid., p. 418.
10. Takeshi Nakajima, *Bose of Nakamuraya: An Indian Revolutionary in Japan* (New Delhi: Promilla & Co., 2009), p. 76.
11. Ibid., p. 101.
12. Marlene J. Mayo, *The Emergance of Imperial Japan,* op. cit., p. 55.
13. Govt. of West Bengal, I.B. Records of the State Archives, proscription of a Bengali book entitled *Sun Yat-sen* by Sri Narendranth Roy, F.N. 350/1925, pp. 95-6.

14. Eri Hotta, *Pan-Asianism and Japan's War (1931-45)*, (New York: Palgrave Macmillan, 2007), pp. 7-8.
15. Iida, 'Fleeing the West, Making Asia Home: Transpositions of Otherness in Japanese Pan-Asianism, 1905-30', p. 418.
16. Kenneth Scott Latourette, *The History of Japan*, p. 145.
17. Kamaladevi Chattopadhdhya, *Japan: Its Weakness and Strength* (Bombay: Padma Publishers, 1944), p. 1.
18. 'Japane Bharatiyo Chatro', *Bharati*, Poush (1309 BS, 1902), p. 893 (Anonymous text).
19. 'Swami Vivekananda: The Abroad & the Problems at Home' (*The Hindu*, Madras, February 1897), *Complete Works*, 4th edn., vol. 5 (Kolkata: Advaita Ashrama, 1936), p. 139.
20. Ibid., p. 140.
21. Vivekananda, 'Conversations and Dialogues', *Complete Works,* 4th edn. vol. 5 (Kolkata: Advaita Ashrama, 1936), p. 288.
22. Ibid.
23. Amitava Acharya, 'Asia is Not One', *The Journal of Asian Studies*, 69, 4 November 2010, http://*www.jstor.org*. (Accessed on 23 June 2014), p. 1004.
24. Ibid.
25. W.W. Pearson, 'On an Indian Image Found in Japan', *The Modern Review*, September (1917), p. 261.
26. Yasuko Horioka, 'Okakura and Swami Vivekananda', *Prabuddha Bharata*, January (1975), p. 31.
27. Ibid., p. 30.
28. Ibid., p. 31.
29. Aurobindo Ghosh, 'India and Mongolian', *Bande Mataram*, 1 April, (1908), rpt. in *Bande Mataram: Political Writings and Speeches (1890-1908*, vol. 6 & 7, *The Complete Works of Sri Aurobindo* (Pondichery: Aurobindo Ashram Press, 2002) http://*www.aurobindo.ru*, (accessed on 15 June 2015), p. 989.
30. Ibid., p. 990.
31. Ibid., p. 989.
32. Okakura Kakuzo, *Awakening of Japan* (New York: The Century Co., 1905), https://www.gutenberg.org/ (Accessed on 31 December 2012).
33. Tankha, *Narratives of Asia*, p. 23.
34. Aurobindo Ghosh, 'Asiatic Democracy', *Bande Mataram*, 1 April 1908, p. 6.
35. Aurobindo Ghosh, 'India and Mongolian', *Bande Mataram*, p. 988.
36. Records of the State Archives, Govt. of West Bengal, Home Political, *Report on the Indian Newspapers and Periodical*, January-March 1906.

37. Aurobindo, 'India and the Mongolian', *Bande Mataram*, p. 989.
38. Ibid., p. 990.
39. Sumit Sarkar, *Modern India* (New Delhi: Macmillan India, 1983), p. 109.
40. Kenneth Scott Latourette, *The History of Japan*, p. 147.
41. Bandyopadhyay, *Japan*, p. 51.
42. Jadunath Sarkar, 'Mikado', *Bharati*, Ashin (1319 BS, 1912), p. 666.
43. Takeda, *Bango Mahilar Japan Jatra*, p. 35.
44. Bandyopadhyay, *Japan*, p. 35.
45. Hay, *Asian Ideas of East and West*, p. 70.
46. Rathindranath Tagore, *On the Edges of Time* (Kolkata: Visva Bharati, 2010), p. 58.
47. Sarala Devi, *Jiboner Jhora Pata*, p. 137.
48. Hemchandra Kanungoe, *Banglai Biplab Prachesta* (Kolkata: Radical Impression, 2016), p. 50.
49. Nagendrachandra Some, 'Japani Akhanmala' [*Narratives of Japan*; in Bengali], in *Prabasi* (Ashin 1311 BS/1904), pp. 304-20.
50. Hotta, *Pan-Asianism and Japan's War (1931-1945)*, pp. 7-8.
51. Okakura, *The Ideals of the East*, p. 9.
52. Ibid., p. 11.
53. Ibid.
54. Ibid., p. 12.
55. Bharucha, *Another Asia*, p. 18.
56. Kowshik, *Okakura*, pp. 56-8.
57. Okakura, *Ideals*, p. 3.
58. Midori Wakakuwa, 'Japanese Cultural Identity and Nineteenth Century Asian Nationalism: Okakura Tenshin and Swami Vivekananda', *Shadows of the Past: Of Okakura Tenshin and Pan-Asianism*, ed. Brij Tankha (Kolkata: Sampark, 2007), p. 37.
59. Inaga Shigemi, 'Okakura Kakuzo and India: The Trajectory of Modern National Consciousness and Pan-Asian Ideology Across Borders', tr. Kevin Singleton, *Review of Japanese Culture and Society*, December (2012): http:// www.jstor.org (accessed on 23 May 2014), p. 41.
60. Sankari Prasad Basu, *Nivedita Lokmata*, vol. 2 (Kolkata: Ananda, 2007), p. 114.
61. Kowshik, *Okakura*, p. 17.
62. Ibid., 67.
63. Midori Wakakuwa, 'Japanese Cultural Identity and Nineteenth Century Asian Nationalism: Okakura Tenshin and Swami Vivekananda', *Shadows of the Past: Of Okakura Tenshin and Pan-Asianism*, p. 37.

64. Kyoko Niwa, 'Rabindranath Tagore and Japan', Thesis, Jadavpur University, 1987.
65. Rustom Bharucha: *Another Asia*, p. 29.
66. Ibid., p. 166.
67. We can well agree with Dinkar Kowshik that 'Nivedita was apprehensive that Okakura might get into trouble with the Intelligence Department'. Hence, Nivedita in her letters, restrained herself from mentioning Okakura's name (*Okakura* , pp. 67-8).
68. Pravajika Atmaprana, *Sister Nivedita* (Kolkata: Sister Nivedita Girls' School, 2007), p. 137.
69. Okakura, *Awakening of Japan*, p. 208.
70. Mayo, in his introduction, has referred to Soejima Taneomi, the Foreign Minister of Japan (1871-3), who during his tenure favoured expedition to Korea and Taiwan.
71. Nivedita, 'Japan and Korea', *The Modern Review* (July-December, 1907), rpt. in *The Complete Works of Sister Nivedita*, vol. 5 (Kolkata: Advaita Ashram, 1999), p. 243.
72. Kowshik, *Okakura*, p. 110.
73. Okakura, *The Book of Tea*, p. 1.
74. Priyambada Devi, 'Cha Grontho', *Manashi*, 1321 BS (1914), rpt. in *Sekaler Bangla Samoyikpotre Japan*, ed. Subrata Kumar Das (Dhaka: Nabajuga Prokashoni, 2012), p. 147.
75. Okakura, *The Book of Tea*, p. 3.
76. Ibid., p. 5.
77. Sarkar, 'Japaner Rajniti', p. 177.
78. 'Japan O Bharotborsho', *Prabasi* Chaitro (1310 BS, 1903), p. 514.
79. Kowhik, *Okakura*, p. 92.
80. Ibid., p. 93.
81. Charuchandra Dutta, 'Uposonghar', *Purano Kotha* (Kolkata: SIB, 1420 BS 2013), p. 256.
82. Yasuko Horioka, 'Okakura and Swami Vivekananda', *Prabuddha Bharata* March 1977, p. 2.
83. Sekhar Bandhyopadhyay in his book *From Plassey to Partition* has remarked that 'the agitation against partition had started in 1903, but became stronger and organized after the scheme was finally announced and implemented 1905, p. 255.
84. Promothanath Mitra was a founder member of the Calcutta Anushilan Samiti. For details, see *Anushilan Samitir Itihash*, Jibantara Halder, p. 81.
85. Buddhadev Bhattacharya & Niharranjan Roy, *Freedom Struggle and Anushilan Samiti* (Kolkata: Anushilan Samity, 1979), pp. 21-2.

86. Peter Heehs , Appendix 1, 'The Bomb in Bengal', p. 261.
87. qtd. in 'Grantho Parichoy', *Japan,* Jatri, p. 136.
88. Peter Heehs, *The Bomb in Bengal* (Oxford: Oxford University Press, 2004), p. 260.
89. T.R. Sareen, 'India and Japan in Historical Perspctives', *India and Japan in Search of Global Roles,* ed., Rajaram Panda, Yoo Fukazawa (New Delhi: Promilla & Co., 2007), p. 34.
90. Kowshik, *Okakura,* p. 68.
91. Sumit Sarkar, *Modern India* (New Delhi: Macmillan India, 1983), p. 108.
92. qtd. in 'Introduction , *Japan Jatri,* p. 136.
93. Kazuo Azuma, tr. *Shitoko Harir Dinoponji,* p. 63.
94. Horioka, Yasuko, 'Okakura and Swami Vivekananda', *Prabuddha Bharata* (March 1975), p. 121.
95. John Pizer, 'Goethe's 'World Literature' Paradigm and Contemporary Cultural Globalization', *Comparative Literature,* vol. 52, no. 2, Summer (2000), http://*www.jstor.org/stable/1771407* (accessed on 26 October 2014), p. 215.
96. Bharucha, *Another Asia,* p. 36.
97. qtd. in Hay, *Asian Ideas of East and West,* p. 67.
98. Records of the State Archives, Govt. of West Bengal, Home Political, *History of Agitation against Bengal Partition,* Calcutta, 25 January 1906, F.N. 25/ 1906, p. 9.
99. Records of the State Archives, Govt. of West Bengal, Home Political, *Memorandum on the History of Terrorism in India, (1905-1933).*
100. West Bengal State Archives, Home Political, *Riot by Passengers of the S.S. 'Komagata Maru' at Budge Budge,* p. 31.
101. Uma Mukherjee, *Two Great Revolutionaries* (Kolkata: Firma K.L. Mukhopadhyay, 1966), p. 23.
102. Ibid., p. 2.
103 Ibid., p. 37.
104. Asitava Das, ed., '*Rash Behari Basur Jibankatha O Rachanasangraha,* Kolkata: Patrolekha, 2014, p. 63.
105. Ibid., p. 66.
106. Sho Kuwajima, 'Appendix 2', *Indian Mutiny in Singapore* (Kolkata: Ratna Prakashan, 1991), pp. 147-8.
107. Sareen, 'India and Japan in Historical Perspectives', *India and Japan in Search of Global Roles,* ed. Rajaram Panda and Yoo Fukarawa, (New Delhi: Promilla & Co. 2007), p. 34.
108. Ibid., p. 33.
109. Takeshi Nakajima, *Bose of Nakamuraya: An Indian Revolutionary in Japan* (New Delhi: Promilla & Co., 2009), pp. 71-8.

110. Bhupendranath Dutta, *Oprokashito Rajnoitik Itihash* (Kolkata: Nabobharat Publishers, 1959), p. 22.
111. Arun Coomer Bose, *Indian Revolutionaries Abroad, 1905-1922: In the Background of International Developments* (Patna: Bharati Bhawan, 1971), p. 132.
112. Ibid., p. 67.
113. Ibid., p. 69.
114. Sho Kuwajima, *Indian Mutiny in Singapore* (Kolkata: Ratna Prakashan, 1999), p. 115.
115. Babu Gurdit Singh, *Voyage of Komagata Maru, or India's Slavery Abroad,* pp. 72-4.
116. Kuwajima, *Indian Mutiny in Singapore,* p. 13.
117. Ibid., p. 22.
118. qtd. in Kuwajima, p. 21.
119. Ibid., p. 22.
120. Home Political, *Riot by Passengers of the S.S. Komagata Maru' at Budge Budge.*
121. Records of the State Archives, Govt. of West Bengal, Home Political *Riot by Passengers of the S.S. Komagata Maru at Budge Budge*, F.N. 322/ 1914.
122. Kuwajima, *Indian Mutiny in Singapore,* p. 23.
123. Ibid., p. 47.
124. Dutta, *Oprokashito Rajnoitik Itihash,* p. 23.
125. Ibid., p. 24.
126. Kuwajima, *Indian Mutiny in Singapore,* p. 44.
127. Ibid., pp. 45-6.
128. Ibid., p. 77.
129. West Bengal State Archives, C.I.D. Intelligence Branch, *Proscription of the Book,* entitled, *Biplabi Abani Mukherjee,* File no. 11-1930, p. 15.
130. Gautam Chattopadhyay, *Abani Mukherjee: A Dauntless Revolutionary and Pioneering Communist* (Kolkata: People's Publishing House, 1976), p. 121.
131. Takeshi Nakajima, *Bose of Nakamuraya: An Indian Revolutionary in Japan,* p. 58.
132. 'Autobiography', trans. Asitava Das, rpt. in *Rash Behari Bose: Collected Works,* ed. Asitava Das (Kolkata: Kisholoy Prakashon, 2006), p. 179.
133. Govt. of West Bengal, I.B. Records of the State Archives, *Proscription of the Book,* entitled *Biplabi Abani Mukherjee,* F.N. 11/ 1930,16.
134. M.N. Roy, *M.N. Roy's Memoir* (Bombay: Allied Publishers, 1964), p. 5.
135. Ibid., p. 6.
136. Ibid., p. 7.

137. J.G. Ohsawa in his book entitled, *Two Great Indian in Japan: Rash Behari Bose & Subhas Chandra Bose*, has observed that on the next day, following the day of the publication of the deportation order, 'almost the entire Japanese press opened fire on Foreign Affairs'.
138. Nakajima, *Bose of Nakamuraya: An Indian Revolutionary in Japan*, p. 110.
139. Govt. of India, Records of the National Archives, Foreign and Political Department. Publication of an article in the Japanese newspaper, '*Keijo Shimpo*', F.N. 41-42/1911.
140. Iida, *Fleeing the West, Making Asia Home: Transposition of Otherness in Japanese Pan-Asianism, 1905-1930*, Alternative: *Global, Local Political*, 32, 3 July to September 1997, http://www.jstor.org (Accessed 23 May 2014), p. 420.
141. 'Declaration taken by the thirty-seven societies of Japan', *The Modern Review*, May (1919), pp. 558-9.
142. Binoy Kumar Sarkar, 'Markine Japani Mlecho', *Bharati*, Magh (1322 BS, 1915), p. 953.
143. Ibid., p. 954.
144. Bose, 'Notes from Japan', *The Standard Bearer* III, 20. 16-1-23, rpt. in *Rash Behari Bose: Collected works*, ed. Asitava Das (Kolkata: Kisholoy Prakashon, 2006), p. 214.
145. Nakajima, *Bose of Nakamuraya: An Indian Revolutionary in Japan*, p. 133.
146. National Archive, Foreign and Political Department, *Pan-Asiatic Conference*, p. 24.
147. Ibid., p. 5.
148. Nakajima, *Bose of Nakamuraya*, p. 171.
149. National Archive, Foreign and Political Department, *Pan-Asiatic Conference*, p. 7.
150. Ibid., p. 9.
151. Nakajima, *Bose of Nakamuraya*, pp. 178-9.
152. Rash Behari Bose, 'Japan's Budget Estimate for 1923-4: Notes from Japan', *The Standard Bearer* III, 20, 16-01-23, rpt. in *Rash Behari Bose. Collected works*, p. 211.
153. Bose, *Collected Works*, p. 195.
154. West Bengal State Archives, I.B., *Proposal to send Revolutionaries to the Far East in Connection with Arms Smuggling*, (3 April 1927, Sl. no. 164/1927).
155. Sareen, 'India and Japan in Historical Perspectives', p. 38.
156. 'Japan's annexation of Korea', *The Modern Review*, September 1910, p. 345.

157. Jyotirindranath Tagore, 'Adhunik Japan', *Bharati*, Ashin, (1315 BS, 1908), p. 269.
158. Ibid.
159. Tagore, *Nationalism*, rpt. in *Rabindranath Tagore Omnibus III* (New Delhi: Rupa & Co., 2011), p. 20.
160. Seven Saaler, 'Pan Asianism in Meiji and Taisho Japan: A Preliminary Framework', http://*www.dijtokyo.org*. (accessed on 31 November 2015), p. 7.
161. Sarala Devi, *Jiboner Jhora Pata*, p. 139.
162. Kenneth Scoutte Latourette, *The History of Japan*, p. 159.
163. 'Japanider Bharatbarshe Boudhdhormo Prochar Chestha', *Prabasi*, Poush (1343 BS, 1936), p. 473 (Anonymous text).
164. Uma Das Gupta, ed., *Rabindranath Tagore: My Life in My Words* (New Delhi: Penguin Books, 2006), p. 176.
165. Ibid.
166. *Gora*, trans., rpt. in Rabindranath Tagore *Omnibus I*, (New Delhi: Rupa & Co. 2011), p. 783.
167. Tagore, *The Message From India to Japan*, p. 268.
168. Tagore, *Nationalism*, p. 20.
169. Tagore, *The Message from India to Japan*, p. 271.
170. Tagore, *Nationalism*, p. 20.
171. Ibid., p. 18.
172. Tagore, *The Soul of the East*, April 1925, rpt. in *Japan Jatri*, Rabindranath Tagore (Kolkata: Visva-Bharati, 2007), p. 132.
173. Hay, *Asian Ideas of East and West*, p. 117.
174. Ibid., p. 117.
175. Kyoko Niwa, 'Rabindranath Tagore and Japan: On His Visit with His Message and its Results', *Tagore and Japan: Dialogue, Exchange and Encounter*, ed., Pratyay Banerjee and Anindya Kundu (New Delhi: Synergy Publishers), p. 71.
176. Ibid.
177. Ibid., p. 76.
178. Uma Mukherjee, *Two Great Revolutionaries* (Kolkata: Firma K.L. Mukhopadhyay, 1966), p. 148.
179. Niwa, 'Rabindranath Tagore and Japan: On His Visit with His Message and its Results', p. 51.
180. Ibid., p. 49.
181. Krishna Dutta and Andrew Robinson, ed., *Selected Letters of Rabindranath Tagore* (New Delhi: Cambridge University Press, 2005), p. 497.
182. Ibid., p. 502.

183. Benode Behari in his *Chitrakar* has mentioned that he visited Japan in 1938. However, from the editorial note provided in the *Binodebehari Mukherjee (1904-1980) Centenary Retrospective*, it has been noted that Benode Behari was in Japan during 1936-7. The mistake was due to lapse of memory.
184. Benodebehari Mukherjee, *Chitrakar* (Kolkata: Aruna Prokashoni, 2007), p. 37.
185. Ibid., p. 39.
186. Krishna Dutta & Andrew Robinson, ed., *Selected Letters of Rabindranath Tagore*, p. 498.
187. qtd. in *His Majesty's Opponent*, p. 122.
188. Bipan Chandra, *India's Struggle for Independence* (New Delhi: Penguin, 1989), p. 394.
189. qtd. in Nakajima, *Bose of Nakamuraya: An Indian Revolutionary in Japan*, p. 256.
190. Maulana Abdul Kalam Azad, *India Wins Freedom* (Madras: Orient Longman, 1988), p. 72.
191. J.G. Ohsawa, *Two Great Indian in Japan: Rash Behari Bose & Subhas Chandra Bose* (Kolkata: Kusa Publications, 1954), p. 42.
192. Rash Behari Bose, 'Letters', *Collected Works*, ed. Asitava Das (Kolkata: Kisholoy Prakashon, 2006), p. 379.
193. Nikki (Ryukan) Kimura, 'My Memory about the Late Rash Behari Bose', *Rash Behari Bose: His Struggle for India's Independence*, ed. Radhanath Rath (Kolkata: Biplabi Mahanayak Rash Behari Bose Smarok Samity, 1963), pp. 41-2.
194. Nakajima, *Bose of Nakamuraya: An Indian Revolutionary in Japan*, p. 247.
195. Ibid., p. 290.
196. K.K. Ghosh, *The Indian National Army* (Meerut: Meenakshi Prakashan, 1969), p. 177.
197. Takeshi Nakajima, 'The Tokyo Tribunal, Justice Pal and the Revisionist Distortion of History', *Asia-Pacific Journal/ Japan Focus*, https.//apjjf.org/2011/9/44/Nakajima-Takeshi/3627/article.html, (accessed on 12 December 2015).
198. Norimitsu Onishi, 'Decades After War Trials, Japan Still Honors a Dissenting Judge', *The New York Times*, 31 August 2007, http:// *mobile.nytimes.com* (accessed on 17 December 2015).
199. T.R. Sareen, 'India and Japan in Historical Perspctives', p. 48.
200. Japaner Netribrinder Bichar', *Prabasi*, Agrahan (1355 BS, 1948), p. 114.
201. https://en.wikipedia.org/wiki/Asia_Dialogue.

CHAPTER 3

Reception of Japanese Culture in Bengal during the Early Twentieth Century

The early twentieth century, which witnessed a vibrant transaction between two parts of Asia, Japan and India, also facilitated more specifically a long course of exchange in the arena of art and culture between Japan and undivided Bengal. We can well agree with T.R. Sareen that even during the 1930s, when Japan's militarism and her aggressive policies led to a strong disapproval and disillusionment among Indian nationalists, there was a regular flow of artists from both sides. The writer in support of his agreement has referred to the visit of two eminent Japanese artists, Kishi Kawai and Kosetsu Nosu[1] who came to India at that time, and during their stay, copied the Ajanta murals. Also, a close study of materials preserved in the Rabindra-Bhavana Archives reveals the fact that even during the 1930s there was frequent correspondence between Santiniketan and different art institutes of Japan,[2] also Tagore till the end of his life received many letters from his admirers in Japan; his own correspondence also shows that till the end of his life Tagore remained an admirer of Japanese aesthetics despite all the bitterness caused by the Japanese aggression on China.

Historically, the beginning of this exchange and interaction between artists and intellectuals of Japan and Bengal can be traced back to 1902, the year Okakura Tenshin came to Kolkata. The fact that Okakura Tenshin during his maiden visit to Kolkata (Calcutta then) received a warm reception among the Jorasanko circle has already been mentioned in the earlier chapters. O.C. Ganguly in two of his essays, 'Indo-Japanese Painting', published in the journal, *Rupam* (10) and 'A Group of Apsaras by a Japanese Artist', published in *Rupam* (8) has rightly pointed out that the Meiji Restoration of 1868 marks the renewal of contact between artists and intellectuals of these two cultural zones of Asia. In his essay, Ganguly has mentioned the arrival of Japanese pilgrims to rediscover ancient Indian relics of Buddhism which had influenced many splendid artistic relics of Japan in ancient times such as the art work of the Nara temple or the marvellous frescoes of the Horyuji temple. According to Ganguly, the first 'Japanese to visit India and the Buddhist shrines after the restoration was Rev. Mokuri Shimaji' and he came to India in 1872.[3] As mentioned by the author, this led to a series of pilgrimages on the part of Japanese artists and Buddhist scholars to rediscover one prime source of their cultural heritage. Needless to say, among these pilgrims, it was Okakura Tenshin's association with the intellectuals of Bengal which triggered the most fruitful result in the cultural scenario of Bengal of the early twentieth century. Okakura Tenshin came to Kolkata twice, once in 1902 and the last time in 1912. Abanindranath Tagore's recollection, as we come across in *Jorasankor Dhare*, also, other sources as, *Bharat Silpi Nandalal* by Panchanan Mandal, give an account of Okakura's association with the new artists of Bengal and his appreciation of the new art movement in Bengal that had been taking a concrete form in the hands of Abanindranath Tagore and his students. Abanindranath Tagore's recollection of Okakura's appreciation may be recalled in this regard: 'Ten years back when I had visited India, I failed to find anything remarkable of contemporary Indian art. Now I see, modern Indian art is becoming developed.'[4]

Responding to Abanindranath Tagore's invitation to visit the Government Art College in Kolkata, Okakura during his second visit to Kolkata visited the Art College and held discussions on art with the students. From Nandalal Bose's recollection, penned down by his biographer, Panchanan Mandal, we come to know Okakura's association with the budding painters who would come to him with their work for suggestions.[5] Also, Okakura himself took the initiative to send to Kolkata, young artists of the Nihon Bijutsu-in, the private art school, which he had founded after having compelled to resign from the Tokyo Bijutsu Gakko.[6] Thus, in 1903, a year after Okakura's first visit came two young Japanese artists, Taikan Yokohama and Shunshu Hishida. From Panchanan Mandal's biography of Nandalal Bose, we further learn that the Japanese artists boarded at Surendranath Tagore's house in Kolkata and spent a considerable time working at Abanindranath Tagore's studio, wielding their brushes to paint Indian mythological subjects.[7] In 1905, another Japanese of the Okakura circle, Shaokin Katsuta, came to India. From the short biographical sketch penned down by Kazuo Azuma in his book entitled, *Japan O Rabindranath: Satoborsher Binimoy*, we further learn that apart from visiting Jorasanko, an exposure, which led to an exchange of aesthetic ideals with Abanindranath and Gaganendranath Tagore, he also went to Tagore's Santiniketan and started teaching Japanese painting to the students.[8] A review of Katsuta's paintings on the life of Lord Buddha, based on his remembrance of the frescoes of Ajanta which he visited in 1907, was published by O.C. Ganguly in *Rupam* (10, 39), the quarterly journal of the Indian Society of Oriental Art. From Protima Devi's *Smriti Chitro*, another memoir of this period, we get a fascinating recounting of the presence of Japanese painters at Jorasanko, which initiated an enriching period of exchange in the world of art, engaging artists from both these two cultural spaces, Japan and Bengal. For Protima Devi this exposure to the art of Japan brought out a happy synthesis of Indian and Japanese art:

> The artistic creation of Gaganendranath Tagore and Abanindranath Tagore led to the commencement of a new era in the history of modern Indian art. The nuances of their art got fused with Japanese painting techniques. I can still remember a group of Japanese painters, who were painting while sitting on a mat (*Madur*). On the other end of that room, Gaganendranath and Abanindranath were busy finishing their work.[9]

During his first visit to Japan, Rabindranath Tagore consulted Taikan Yokohama with the objective of employing a Japanese art teacher at Vichitra in Jorasanko and also in Santiniketan, who would take the task of introducing the students to the practice of Japanese brush work. Thus, as recommended by Taikan, Arai

Kampo, another Japanese painter came to Kolkata and became engaged in teaching Japanese painting both at the Vichitra Club in Jorasanko and in Santiniketan. Tagore's letter to Gaganendranath Tagore from Japan dated, 13 August 1916, speaks of his initiative to employ Aria Kampo:

> Finally, after a great deal of deliberation and on the advice of Taikan, I am sending you an artist named Arai. He and his companion will live in India for a couple of years, buying of Indian art and painting pictures of India. If he can stay even six months in our house and provide you with some training that would be good. A new stimulus from outside reawakens our mind—the company of these artists will benefit you in this way. . . . Your boys must gain proficiency in the skills of Japanese brush work. This man is gentle and of good character—though he is not as good an artist as Taikan, he is by no means inferior.[10]

The long quotation mentioned above clearly shows Tagore's receptiveness to another culture of Asia. It also speaks his eagerness to derive an impetus from a foreign culture, which he believed would be helpful in bringing a development of Bengal art during that time. From Arai Kampo's diary translated by Kazuo Azuma, and also from other sources, such as the remembrances of Nandalal Bose and Mukul Dey, we get a lively depiction of Arai Kampo's association with the painters of Bengal, which led to a fruitful exchange of aesthetic ideals during this period. Thus, it would not be incorrect to sum up that it was Tagore and Okakura, the two mentors, whose initiative in bringing artists of Japan and Bengal to know each other's works, which initiated a new era of exchange in visual art in Bengal.

The impetus on the part of a creative artist, to look beyond his geographical region for assimilation of aesthetic ideals, which can play a contributory role in the development of his own literature, or art is no longer looked upon as a negative quality. It is not borrowing or sheer yielding to the aestheic ideals of another foreign culture. The idea has been emphatically voiced by Suryakant Tripati in 'Nirala'. In this text, the protagonist has brushed aside all charges of lack of purity of sources: 'If any form of creation is to remain progressive/dynamic, it is imperative that diverse thoughts and feelings intermingle within it to strengthen it. Diverse qualities alone lend strength to creation.'[11]

Nirala has put forward her argument in support of her receptivity to Bengali literature (her mother tongue is Hindi). Remembering her justification for her receptivity to Bengali literature, we can also say that Bengal's receptivity to the artistic tradition of Japan, also induced a spirit of synthesis of aesthetic ideals, rooted in different cultural spaces, Indian, Persian and that of the South-East Asia. Needless to say, a close study of art and art reviews of the period is essential to come to such a conclusion. In the previous chapters, we have already mentioned the fact that the Bangla journals of this period showed an eagerness to publish news items on Japan. The wide range of articles published on Japan is nothing less than a wonder. Among these essays there are quite a few writings on Japanese art. These reviews of Japanese art should also be considered an integral part of the reception of Japanese aesthetics, during the first two decades of twentieth century.

It would be wrong to suppose that fine art, chiefly, painting and sculpture were the only areas enriched by this cross-cultural experience; In the first two decades of the twentieth century, Bengal also showed a receptivity to many other cultural items associated with Japan as, *jujutsu* (Japanese martial art), Japanese tea-ceremony and flower arrangements, etc. It is widely known that Tagore developed his Visva-Bharati with a lofty aim, and his earnest desire was that Visva-Bharati would become no ordinary university but 'a great meeting place for individuals from all countries' believing in the spiritual unity of mankind; this message he himself voiced in one of the talks he had delivered in Japan.[12]

Tagore invited educators from all over the world, so as to provide his students an exposure to the new idea that flourished in various corners of the world. Interestingly, many Japanese teachers and students visited Santiniketan during the first few decades of the twentieth century; their involvement with the making of Visva-Bharati deserves mention in this context. Tagore, a great admirer of traditional Japanese culture, was an ardent admirer of *Jujutsu*. Responding to an invitation to teach *jujutsu* to the students of

Santiniketan, in 1905, Jinnosuke Sano came to Santiniketan and started imparting the skills of *jujutsu* to the students of the ashram.[13] Apart from imparting *jujutsu* lessons to the students, he also pioneered the introduction of Japanese language teaching in India. Nabin Panda, referring to sources such as *Indo oyubi Indojin* (India as well as Indians), the book which Sano wrote on his experiences in India, has touched upon Sano's contribution in starting Japanese language teaching in Santiniketan, in his article entitled, 'Tagore and Japanese Language: from the Writings of Sano Jinnosuke'. In 1929, on his way back from Canada, Tagore paid a short visit to Japan; there he contacted the Tokyo Kodaikan, the chief centre for Judo in Japan. Following Tagore's request to them to send a Judo teacher, Shinzo Takagaki, a renowned teacher of Judo, joined Santiniketan in November 1929.[14] Also, Makiko Hoshi, the sister-in-law of Rash Behari Bose, came to Santiniketan and started teaching Japanese floral arrangement and the art of tea-ceremony to the students. From Nandalal Bose's recollection as narrated by Panchanan Mandal, we come across a lively recounting of organizing Japanese tea-ceremonies in Santiniketan. From Nandalal Bose's recollection, and also from that of Amita Sen, we learn about Kintaro Kasahara and his art of carpentry and horticulture. The presence of so many Japanese students and teachers who became a part of the making of Visva-Bharati is indeed a unique aspect. Their culture and aesthetics melted into the environment of Santiniketan making a synthesis of a foreign culture and the aesthetic ideals of Tagore in creating his own school.

In the second chapter of this book, we have already referred to Priyambada Devi's translation of Okakura's English work, *The Book of Tea*, which shows the translator's receptivity to Okakura's Pan-Asian ideology. Like Priyambada Devi's translation of Okakura's work, some other texts written by Japanese writers were also translated during this period. Another translation that needs mentioning in this context of reception of Japanese culture through translations is Ekai Kawaguchi's travelogue, *Three Years in Tibet*, which was translated by Sri Hemlata Devi and was published serially in the Bangla magazine *Prabasi* under the title, 'Tibbot Rajye Tinbochor'. Similarly, Tagore played a pioneering role in introducing the Bengali reader to the world of *Haiku*, a Japanese poem of three lines, consisting of 5-7-5 syllabic pattern. However, we must remember the fact that the time when Tagore visited Japan, the term *Haiku* had not become fashionable. Tagore in his *Japanjatri* has described it as a short verse of three lines (tin liner kabo).[15] Though translated from English to Bangla language, these translation works initiate a transaction of two distinct cultures, those of Japan and Bengal. A close study of these translated texts with reference to the original can show how the translator, in dealing with the original texts, has dealt with culture-specific issues, or his endeavour to familiarize the original text to the readers of Bengal, through synthesis of ideas, which are intrinsically located in a foreign culture. Further, the translator's selection of certain portions, or his effort to emphasize certain elements of the original text to provide his reader the essence of the Target Language texts are significant aspects of this study of translated works. These, we are taking into account in this chapter. These issues will be dealt in details in the different sections of this chapter.

To conclude this introductory section, it should be remembered that this renewal of contact between Japan and Bengal that started during this period, also kindled a renewed interest in Buddhist studies. We can agree with O.C. Ganguly that the reception of Buddhism and Buddhist art in Japan, and also the visit of Indian missionaries to Japan in the eighth century (Ganguly has referred to the visit of Bodhisena, a Brahmin priest who reached Japan in AD 746), created another movement towards India. O.C. Ganguly has referred to Rev. Mokurai Shimaji, who came to India in 1872, and visited the Buddhist shrines in India. The early twentieth century, which witnessed the upholding of the Pan-Asian ideology of Asian unity, also contributed no less to this renewed interest in Buddhism, as Buddhism turns out to the one significant cultural linkage between India and the South-East Asia. In this context, it must also be remembered that in Okakura's Pan-Asian ideology, Buddhism occupies a central position as the source of Asia's spiritual unity. This aspect of Okakura's Pan-Asian ideology has already been discussed in details in the previous chapters. Okakura, during his stay in India, paid a visit to the Buddhist pilgrimage of Bodh Gaya. There, his mission was to set up a centre for Buddhist pilgrims which eventually did not materialize.[16] Also, Shitoku Hori, a Buddhist scholar and the first international student in Santiniketan, came along with Okakura during his first visit to India. From the translator's note included in the translation of Shitoko Hori's diary, by Kazuo Azuma, we further learn that Hori's prime objective was initiating the revival of Buddhism, which too had been witnessing a hard time since 1868, the year, in which the Japanese government had issued an act introducing a segregation of Buddhism from Shinto, the traditional religion of Japan, and showing a preference for the latter.[17] During his stay in Santiniketan, Shitoku Hori took up the task of studying ancient texts and Sanskrit grammar, as we come to know from his diary.[18] In 1897, another Buddhist pilgrim and scholar, Ekai Kawaguchi, left Japan and after spending a year at Sarat Chandra Das' residence in Darjeeling where he learnt Tibetan language, took a different route encompassing the Himalayan provinces of Nepal. He finally reached Lhasa, the capital of Tibet. Ekai Kawaguchi later on authored a travelogue entitled, *Three Years in Tibet.* The book recounts his experiences in Tibet. Another Buddhist scholar, Ryukan Kimura, first came to Chittagong in 1911 where he studied at a Sanskrit school, later on came to Kolkata and started teaching Pali language in Calcutta University from 1918 to1926.[19] From the preface of the publication of his doctoral thesis which he submitted to the Calcutta University, we further learn of how he had received encouragement from Sir Asutosh Mukhopadhyay, in continuing his research on the the history of Indian Buddhism. Thus, though initiated by Japanese scholars and pilgrims, this renewed interest in Buddhist study, received the attention of the intelligentsia of Bengal who encouraged and helped them to carry out their mission. In the following sections we will try to deal in details with the subjects that have been mentioned in this introductory section.

EXCHANGE IN THE ARENA OF ART: JAPAN AND BENGAL OF THE EARLY TWENTIETH CENTURY

The colonization of Bengal and other parts of British India, led to a superfluous taste of imitating western culture among educated minds during the late nineteenth and early twentieth century. We can agree with Benode Behari Mukherjee that in different fields of culture of this period in India as in 'painting, sculpture, architecture, house decoration and dress, a pseudo-European taste held full sway'.[20] In the following section, dealing with the history of artistic movements in Bengal of this period, we will try to take into account this issue, i.e. hegemonic influence of the West in the arena of culture during the period immediately following the establishment of the colonial control over a vast region of India.

Japan never came under foreign rule, yet, it could not escape the impact of western hegemony. Thus, within a few years after the Meiji Restoration in 1868, Japan showed an eagerness to mimic western food habit and customs. In the previous chapters, we have already tried to locate this growing taste for western customs in Japan during the first two decades of the twentieth century. Accounts of the traveller's exposure to the westernization of Japanese society of this period, as we have seen in Sureshchandra Bandyopadhyay's travelogue *Japan*, may once again be mentioned. According to Michiaki Kawakita, western painting was first introduced to Japan during the Momoyama period (1573-1614) by the Christian missionaries; in the nineteenth century of Japan, Kawakita in his study has pointed out, Japan witnessed a growing taste for western art during the Meiji period and import of western art like other cultural elements became quite in vogue during the Meiji period.[21] Okakura was also well aware of this changing scenario in Japan during his time. Satyajit Chowdhury in his essay entitled, 'Okakura Tensh in O Abanindranath', referring to Okakura's biographer Ellise Grrilli and an observation made in the Boston Museum Bulletin (vol. IX, no. 52, August 1911), has rightly pointed out that Okakura showed a dualism of interest regarding the westernization of Japan during his time. As an art connoisseur, he showed a respectful attitude towards his own tradition, but at the same time he was prepared to accept new ideas which were entering from the West.[22] The idea has been also voiced by Okakura in the *Ideals of the East*, in his own rhetorical manner:

> There are today two mighty chains of forces which enthral the Japanese mind, entwining dragon-like upon their own coils, each struggling to become sole master of the jewel of life, both lost now and again in an ocean of ferment. One is the Asiatic ideal, replete with grand visions of universal sweeping through the concrete and particular, and the other European science, with her organized culture, armed in all its array of differentiated knowledge, and keen with the edge of competitive energy.[23]

For Okakura, Japan of his time has to make a balance between these two mighty forces and in the arena of art, Okakura chose to steer a middle path, an idea he has advocated in the same book just after a few pages: 'Technique is thus but the weapon of the artistic warfare; scientific knowledge of anatomy and perspective, the commissariat that sustains the army. These Japanese arts may safely accept from the West, without detracting from its own nature.'[24]

The relevance of citing these two somewhat long quotations lies in the fact that the painters of Bengal of the late nineteenth and early twentieth century had to face a similar kind of situation prevailing in the art world of that time, owing to the impact of the west. The colonization of Bengal and the rest of India led to a complete ignorance and neglect of indigenous Indian art work. On the other hand, it led to a popular taste for western artefacts and encouraged the practice of copying nineteenth century realistic oil works of European painters. We have already referred to Benode Behari Mukherjee's opinion that during this period in different fields as in 'painting, sculpture, architecture, house decoration and dress, a pseudo-European style held full sway'.[25] Further, the colonial era brought out a sharp demarcation between fine art and the artisan craft of the pre-colonial world, which had been carried out by craftsmen in workshops under the close supervision of feudal masters, who had been their patrons. In contrast to the craftsmen, a new class of independent studio artists came into existence that took interest in oil paintings and could sell their paintings in the open market.[26] The Calcutta Art School was founded in 1854 and it came under the direct supervision of Director of Public Instruction in 1855. Also, counterparts of this Calcutta Art School were set up in Bombay and in Madras. From Sumit Sarkar's book entitled, *Modern Times*, we come to know the role of the colonial administration in providing opportunities of art education in India which according to Sarkar, started from the 1850s. As noted in Sarkar's book, the art training introduced by the British aimed at providing an acquaintance with European masterpieces chiefly by encouraging students to make copies of western form of painting; it also aimed at imparting training in applied art as in the field of draughtsmanship and drawing, learning which in government departments students could fetch jobs.[27] There was indeed no room for Indian painting in the art education introduced by the British and this inferior form of art training based on chiefly copying of Victorian paintings, has been severely criticized by Abanindranath Tagore, whose creativity found little satisfaction in the western art training that was prevalent during that time: 'The students are encouraged to copy from mediocre samples of western paintings and are trained to become an imitator of western oil painters and water colour painters. It is as if one is taking part in a stage show to enact the role of great western masters like Raphael and Titian.'[28]

It is interesting to note that Abanindranath Tagore had also been trained in western painting; he took lessons of oil painting from an Italian art teacher Gilbardi and an English painter C.S. Palmer. Thus we can agree with Margaret Richardson that though 'Abanindranath rejected academic naturalism, he did not abandon naturalistic details in his painting', and M. Richardson referring to artist Subramanyan's style has identified an eclecticism, a reconciliation of different cultural forms as the characteristic of Abanindranath's creative work.[29] From Abanindranth's biographies and also from his *Jorasankor Dhare*, we come to know how his interest in Mughal painting had been enkindled when he received a gift of a set of miniatures of Mughal painting from his brother-in-law Sheshendrabhusan Chattopadhyay,[30] the other inspiration from his family circle came from Rabindranath Tagore. Responding to Rabindranath's suggestion to read *Vaishnab Podaboli*,

Abanindranath took to the task of creating paintings based on these poetic subjects. Thus, the Krishna Lila series (1895) were portrayed where we come across a lyrical rendition of this mythological subject, as pointed out by Benode Behari Mukherjee in his essay 'Abanindranather Chobi':

> The Krishna Lila series of Abanindranath Tagore represent more of a modern mind than adhering to the artistic traditions of a by-gone time. Thus, the journey of the Modern Indian art may well be traced from that period. Needless to say, the historical value of the Krishna Lila series is due to this reason. Though, they are based on ancient mythological subjects, they have become successful in exploring the depth of human mind in a dramatic fashion.[31]

Another important aspect to be noted with reference to this work, is that it fuses European and Indian technique of painting into a happy synthesis; in the introductory essay included in the book *Abanindranath Tagore: His Early Work,* Benode Behari Mukherjee has drawn our attention to this aspect of the painting: 'But there his previous training in European technique had influenced the work and did not allow the Indian decorative to remain absolutely pure. As a result these pictures had become something which was neither a true European miniature nor an Indian decorative painting.'[32]

The third interesting aspect to be noted with reference to these Krishna Lila series is that the paintings were composed in 1895, prior to Abanindranth's meeting with Havell in 1897[33], whose interest in bringing about a revival of classical Indian art, and also his recognition of the latter, as the inheritor of the Indian tradition, led to a bond of friendship between the two. Abanindranath in many of his writings has described himself as a collaborator of Havell and has fondly described himsef as a 'chela'(follower) of Havell.[34]

The other significant impetus which led him to embark upon the mission of seeking artistic expression in coherence with Indian life and culture came from the nationalist sentiment of the early twentieth century. The Swadeshi and Boycott movement followed by Lord Curzon's decision to the partition of Bengal fanned a patriotic spirit. This spirit of patriotism proliferated in the arena of aristic activies of the time as well. From Abanindranath's rendition as recounted by Rani Chanda we come to learn how under the spell of the swadeshi age, Abanindranath took to the task of seeking indigenous expressions of art, free from the taint of western impact:

> We were prepared to paint and create compositions in a complete Indian way. Ravi Varma also strove to create paintings based on Indian subjects. However, he failed to come out of western influence. Thus, the posture of Ravi Varma's *Sita* resembles that of Venus of western paintings. I discarded the western portrait tradition and tried to explore the scroll techniques of the Bengal potters.[35]

It was during this period that Abanindranath painted his *Bharat Mata* which drew a good deal of appreciation from the nationalists' circle. It is interesting to note that Abanindranath created the picture in 1902 and named it *Bongo Mata* in 1905. The same picture was renamed *Bharat Mata*, which clearly shows Abanindranath's involvement with the Swadeshi movement of that time.[36] From Abanindranath Tagore's reminiscences, as written down by Rani Chanda in her *Ghorowa*, we learn how the tide of the Swadeshi age, bringing a new wave in the artistic activities of Bengal, incorporated the active participation of Japanese painters who had been staying in Kolkata (then Calcutta) at that time: 'I painted the *Bharat Mata.* Her fingers had the indication of offering assurance of food and clothing. A Japanese painter created a flag out of it. I do not know where I have lost it.'[37]

In Chapter II, we have already discussed that for Okakura and Nivedita, issues relating to art and nationalism were not watertight areas but overlapping subjects. For instance, in the introduction to the book, *The Ideals of the East* written by Nivedita, we find an acceptance of Okukura's belief in the supremacy of the Japanese nation for retaining her sovereignty and also becoming a repository of Asian culture: 'Art can only be developed by nations that are in a state of freedom.'[38]

The overwhelming response of Nivedita towards Abanindranath's *Bharat Mata* once again shows how Nivedita's appreciation of *Bharat*

Mata was motivated by her nationalist impulses. Needless to say, Nivedita found in *Bharat Mata* a befitting symbol of emerging nationalism, as described in her essay 'India the Mother': 'We see in Mr. Tagore's drawing, which is reproduced here, something for which Indian art has long been waiting, the birth of those new combinations which are to mark the modern age in India.'[39]

Thus, before we start looking into the range of cultural exchange facilitated by the visit of Okakura and the painters whom he had sent to Jorasanko following his own visit, it must be noted that by the time these Japanese people arrived in Kolkata, a new movement in the field of painting had already proliferated. Artists like Abanindranath had already been engaged in evolving an artistic expression through a happy synthesis of techniques of painting located in different cultures. In Chapter II, we have already discussed in details, the reception of Okakura's seminal text, *Ideals of the East,* among the reading public of Bengal of that time. *Ideals of the East,* with its detailed study of the history of Japanese art, speaks of the rich heritage of Asian culture, having derived its sustenance of two mighty civilizations of the East, India and China. The idea of Indian art and culture as one source of Asian culture, influenced many of that period, including Abanindranath, whose attention had already been drawn towards the rich cultural heritage of India. Abanindranath found in Okakura's Pan-Asian ideology a confirmation of his belief in the cultural supremacy of India. A passage from Okakura's obituary penned down by Abanindranath and published in the Bangla magazine *Bharati* can be cited as a testimony of this derivation: 'When I met Okakura for the first time, he had then completed his work in the realm of art. He was then experiencing a secluded life in India. He then took the task of propagating his lofty ideal of oneness of Asia. On the other hand, I had just then embarked upon my artistic career.'[40]

Thus, we can well agree with R. Siva Kumar that the importance given to India in Okakura's vision of Asia, specially its status as the fountainhead of Buddhism, Advaita philosophy and by extension of much Buddhist art, had a strong impact upon the Indian reader of that period. For R. Siva Kumar, the other important influence of Japanese aesthetics on Indian artists of that period had also been a derivation of Okakura's ideal of Asia's cultural unity which influenced the artists of Bengal to look upon Japanese art as an alien tradition and fostered a taste for delving deep into their cultural and artistic tradition.[41] Abanindranth and Okakura, the two mentors of the modern art movement in Japan and Bengal, also shared some common aesthetic ideals; an interesting article that provides us insights into the subject of common artistic notions shared by both Abanindranath and Okakura is 'Okakura Tenshin O Abanindranath' by Satyajit Chowdhury, published in the *Visva-Bharati Patrika* (Kartick 1383 BS). According to Chowdhury, both Okakura and Abanindranath upheld freedom as the essential quality of all creative work. As art teacher, Abanindranath never came up with direct suggestions for his students but encouraged them to paint according to their imagination. An interesting incident that can demonstrate how liberal a teacher Abanindranath was, has been recalled by many as Nandalal Bose did. Following is a passage from *Nandalal Bose and Indian Painting* by Ramyansyu Sekhar Das, that needs referring in this context:

> There is a story relating to his student Nandalal Bose who, in his early days, drew a picture of devoted Uma. It was indeed a picture of austere devotion for winning Siva and Nandalal did not decorate Uma with usual ornaments. When the latter showed the picture to Abanindranath, he advised decoration. Nandalal, however, left in a sceptical mood but Abanindranath had a second thought over the matter. He could not sleep properly thinking that the picture might be spoiled due to his wrong advice. Uma must not have ornaments as she was practicing austerity. So, he hurried to Nandalal in the early morning and was relieved to find him hesitating before undertaking the operation.[42]

Okakura's *Ideals of the East* also gives us a similar impression about Okakura as a liberal art-teacher. Okakura in this text has also pointed out that the Government Art School at Ueno, Tokyo, with which he had been associated, always upheld freedom as the greatest privilege of an artist.[43]

Again, freedom of artistic expression has a larger dimension; this, too, has been pointed out by Okakura in his *Ideals of the East*, where the writer has rightly pointed out that this freedom on the part of an artist plays an evolutionary role in the self development of the artist.[44]

It must be remembered that Abanindranath Tagore was an artist of rare creativity and his paintings show an unmistakable stamp of the individual expression of an artist. Thus, freedom on the part of the artist involves his conscious choice to be free from adhering to any particular artistic tendency and to carry out his creative work in the light of his own imagination. We come across a similar kind of advice to an artist in Okakura's *Ideals of the East*, where he has warned that imitation whether of nature or of the old masters or above all of the self, is suicidal to the realization of individuality.[45] Like the European Romantics, in Abanindranath's art, imagination of the artist and his subjective experience of a situation, play the most significant part. To substantiate this argument, a passage from *Jorasankor Dhare*, describing his own view about his painting *The Passing of Shah Jahan*, needs citing: 'After returning home I took to the task of painting *The Passing of Shah Jahan*. The agony I had undergone when my daughter passed away, stimulated me to depict this painting. That is why this work has become so successful.'[46]

It would not be inappropriate to agree with Satyajit Chowdhury that viewing from this aspect of freedom as an important part in the self development of an artist, we find some commonality in the aesthetic ideals of both Okakura and Abanindranath:

> Just as Tenshin has laid emphasis on the evolutionary self-development of the modern artist, Abanindranath also considered the self-realization of the painter to be the most coveted element in his creation. Both of them have emhasized on the self-consciousness of the artist to be the most significant aspect of the creative experiance of a modern artist.[47]

For Satyajit Chowdhury, Okakura's attempt to give equal emphasis on tradition and the requirement of the modern times is another artistic principle, which can also be associated with Abanindranath:

> At first both of them laid emphasis on adhering to ancient artistic traditions of their own country. This came as a reaction against the mimicry of western style of painting, which was then quite in vogue both in India and in Japan.

However, with matured understanding they came to the realization that mere revivalist attempts take away the freedom of artistic creation.[48]

We have earlier referred to Abaninandranath's association with Havell; the latter's interest in reviving the glory of ancient Indian art drew Abanindranath's attention. In his *Indian Sculpture and Painting,* Havell has observed that Indian art is essentially idealistic, mystic, symbolic and transcendental.[49]

It can be said that Havell's view of Indian art attributed to it an exclusive spiritual quality and for art critics like Tapati Guha Thakurta, this can be taken as an extension of the Orientalist discourse in the arena of Indian art. While Tapati Guha Thakurta is full of praise of the uniqueness of the style in which Abanindranath has expressed his views on Indian art, as for the subject of the text, and his preference for those European scholars who have tried to understand Indian art not from from the path of dry scholarship but with their heart and soul, Tapati Guha Thakurta in her book entitled, *Monuments, Objects, Histories,* has commented that, 'Bharat Shilpo is strewn with evidence of the close partnership between the author and his guru, Havell, in their joint crusade for Indian art'.[50]

However, what needs asking is that, should a painter be judged by one of his essays, or by the evaluation of the work, he has left behind? Again, not all of his writings endorse to the revivalist crusade; a passage from Satyajit Chowdhury's essay entitled, 'Abanindranath: Nandonik Nibondhomala', needs citation in this context:

> We must remember that the artist and his work come first, followed by the theoretical engagement of the art critic. Art is not meant for art-theories, on the other hand, art theories will ever try to explore art works'—how can this be taken as an idea of a revivalist? Abanindranath has further justified the importance of freedom on the part of an artist by quoting Kandinosky—'Efforts to revive the art principles of the past will at best produce an art that is still-born . . . such imitation is merely aping.[51]

A passage from Abanindranath's letter written to Dhirendra Krishna Deb Burman, dated, 29 April 1924, can also point out how Abanindranath distanced himself from this revivalist cult of that time:

Remember I have cautioned Nandalal before all of you, whether you take after Ajanta or Greek or Japan or China, it is nothing but taking to another man's way. Why should I berth my boat at an alien port when each one of us has our own? We have no option but to go alone. . . . You have no room in my boat nor have I in yours.

'No room, no room, the boat is too small.
Loaded with my own golden paddy, the boat is full'.[52]

We can agree with R. Siva Kumar that 'though Havell brought the whole issue under the umbrella of revivalism and Abanindranath called for a reverence to tradition this did not mean for him the repetition of old art.'[53] In contrast to this notion of viewing Abanindranath as a revivalist, what we find in his work is a synthesis of painting techniques belonging to different cultural spaces; R. Siva Kumar in his essay entitled, 'Abanindranath: From Cultural Nationalism to Modernism', has illuminated us this aspect of Abanindranath's creation:

As a cultural nationalist he valued the re-creation of the distinctive national culture but he tried to achieve it not by resurrecting the past but by re-reading it in the light of his sensibilities, and apprehending through sensibility is a fundamental modernist impulse as already noted and a source of much modernist individualism. Thus, in his paintings Western, Mughal and Far Eastern elements enter into an elective union to produce a personal style that is unlike anything traditionally Indian.[54]

We can well agree with Siva Kumar's opinion about Abanindranath's painting as a fine synthesis of the visual art of different cultures and not simply a repetition of traditional Hindu art. It must be remembered that Rabindranath Tagore's view on Indian art also emphasizes this receptivity to the art tradition of other cultural spaces: 'It is admitted that in Indian Art the Persian element found no obstacles, and there are signs of various other alien influences.'[55]

With reference to this power of assimilating artistic techniques of different geographical spaces in Abanindranath's painting, it would be worth paying attention to the artist's receptivity of Japanese painting, chiefly the wash technique, which he himself has acknowledged in his autobiographical work *Jorasankor Dhare*:

Taikan used to teach me line-drawing; I also learnt from him to master the brush. We usually draw a line hurriedly—I learnt from him the art of drawing a line with care and a great deal of patience. . . . I saw Taikan watering the surface of his painting, using wash technique. I also dipped my painting into water. After taking it out, I found that a new effect has come upon the picture. From then wash technique found its place in our painting.[56]

The technique of immersing a whole painting in water is known as wash or *morotai*. It must be noted that Abanindranath picked up this technique from Japanese painters like Taikan and Shunsho Hishida who had used this extremely experimental style for a rather short period of time in their artistic career. However, the wash technique that Abanindranath mastered, following his association with the Japanese painters, also fused with his own style, and also with the European training he had undertaken in his early life. Benode Behari Mukherjee's observations on Abanindranath's paintings produced under the Japanese influence may be referred to in this context: 'However, the ease of Abanindranath's style is neither comparable to the western painting, nor to those of Japanese or Mughal. The spontaneity of his style is his uniqueness.'[57]

The paintings of Abanindranath created between 1900 to 1911, a period during which he became acquainted with the wash technique of Japanese painters, show how Abanindranath Tagore in his attempt to explore different artistic techniques, was able to create a definite individual style. Thus, from Nandalal Bose's recountings, penned down by Panchanan Mandal, we get this impression of a fusion of artistic techniques in Abanindranath's paintings following his exposure to the wash techniques of Japanese painters:

Abanindranath started painting following the Japanese wash technique. However, it was more a fusion of his style and that of the Japanese painters. This expanded the horizon of modern Indian art. Abanindranath also brought out certain changes in the wash technique of water colour painting. During the Swadeshi age Abanindranath painted *Bango Mata* using the wash technique . . . Abanbabu in his early life had taken training in western painting. He had earned mastery in his use of mediums as pastel, water colour and oil painting. His training in western painting got fused with his own style. Japanese style and Persian styles were among those that he learnt also. All these painting techniques belonging to different cultural spaces got fused and created a unique expression in the way Abanindranath created his paintings.[58]

From Rani Chanda's biography of Abanindranath Tagore entitled, *Silpoguru Abanindranath*, we find a description of how Abanindranath Tagore, during his stay at Udayan in Santiniketan, drew a painting of a wild jasmine tree in full bloom using this wash technique. Rani Chanda has recounted that while having an evening stroll, Abanindranath Tagore for a few days watched a jasmine tree in full bloom. Behind the jasmine tree, the western horizon at that moment became illuminated by the rays of the setting sun. Finally, a student was asked to bring out a sketch of the tree; once, the sketch had been finished, Abanindranath remained busy in administering colour with every stroke of his brush. Then, with a flat brush, he started giving wash to it. The process of the creation of this painting finds an interesting description in Rani Chanda's biography entitled, *Silpoguru Abanindranath*:

> I watched how Abanindranath remained immersed in painting the picture; he kept on adding wash to it. He also used a dry brush to paint the sun, which had been hidden by the wash effect. At first, the sun was seen in the middle of the tree. The more he painted the sun with wash effect, the more the sun seemed to change its position and went lower. With every wash the painting seemed to reach its finished state. When Abanindranath drew the sun for the last time, the sun which was earlier visible through twigs came lower and was beside the stem of the tree. Abanindranath signed the painting and wiped the brush. He said, 'Finally the sun has set'.[59]

We can well agree with Jogen Chowdhury that Abanindranath, an artist gifted with a rare creativity was able to administer wash technique along with western form of use of colour. A passage from Jogen Chowdhury's interview taken by Agnimitra Ghosh, the correspondent of the Bangla magazine, *Paschimbanga* needs mentioning in this context: 'It is surprising how Abanindranath could easily use the Japanese wash technique along with European style of using of colour. I have tried to paint following Abanindranath's style; however, it is far from being an easy task.'[60]

To conclude this section on Abanindranath's use of wash technique, it must be remembered that the use of wash by painters of Abanindranath's followers mostly became flat and monotonous. Their works lacked the crispiness of Abanindranath's painting. Also, they lacked the brilliance of his use of colour. Thus, Nandalal Bose has rightly observed that Abanindranath's early training had been along the line of western painting; painters of the later generation, who lacked this knowledge of western anatomy, also lacked their sense of perspective in art. They failed to achieve the brilliance of wash painting, that Abanindranath had mastered:

> We must remember that the line drawings of Abanindranath's paintings are neither flat like those of Ajanta, Rajput paintings or Persian paintings, nor are they calligraphic. The drawings of his art show the influence of his early training in western painting. . . . Those who lack the knowledge of anatomy or have little sense of perspective in drawing should not try to follow Abanindranath's style of painting.[61]

Apart from the reception of wash technique, the visit of Japanese painters to Jorasanko in Kolkata (then Calcutta) provided an opportunity to view the works of these Japanese painters and to see how they worked with paint and brush. Abanindranath Tagore himself has recalled how a Japanese painter, before beginning to paint, would stare fixedly at the blank piece of paper, engrossed in a state of meditation like Zen master:

> I have seen how Taikan used to stare fixedly at a piece of paper with rapt attention before starting to draw a picture. During that time of meditation, he used to keep his colours, brushes beside him. Then, finally, he used to dip the brush into his paints and create a few line drawings on his paper. He could visualize the painting on the empty paper before creating it with the strokes of his brush.[62]

Interestingly, we get a similar kind of impression from Mukul Dey's recounting of Kampo Arai and other Japanese painters whom he met during his visit to Ajanta caves in 1917. Dey found them busy in copying frescoes of the Ajanta caves. From Mukul Dey's book entitled *My Pilgrimages to Ajanta and Bagh*, we further learn how Arai Kampo worked tirelessly to copy the fresco of Great Buddha and continued his painting with a lamp after darkness had descended. In his autobiography *Amar Kotha*, Mukul Dey is full of praise of the Japanese painters, chiefly, their dedication to their art: 'I have found one thing of the Japanese painters to be truly praiseworthy. They do not talk among themselves while working.'[63]

The interaction among artists of Bengal and Japan was not limited to the adoption of wash technique alone. Whereas, in the hands of Abanindranath Tagore, the wash technique of the Japanese painters found an extremely artistic treatment, in the case of his brother, Gaganendranath Tagore, it yielded the creation of another kind of painting, that of Chinese monochrome ink. Gaganandranath Tagore painted the picture of crows standing on railing, eagerly waiting to gobble leftovers, using this technique of ink painting.[64] From Krishna Chaitanya's book *History of Indian Painting: Modern Period,* we learn that Gaganendranath Tagore first learnt this technique from a demonstration by Taikan at an exhibition of Japanese paintings, organized by the Society of the Oriental Art, in 1910.[65] From his contact with the Japanese painters as, Yokohama Taikan, Gaganendranath received the impetus to take up ink and brush as his medium; however, what he started as an amateur, finally turned out to be a sophisticated and experimental work, assimilating and making synthesis of painting techniques belonging to different cultural spaces. Thus, Krishna Chaitanya's observation regarding the landscapes and cityscapes, painted by Gaganendranath Tagore needs citing in this context: 'In his landscapes and cityscapes Gaganendranath integrated the aesthetic quality of japanese ink painting and the impressionism of Whistler (*History of Indian Painting*).'[66]

Gaganendranath Tagore achieved remarkable maturity in deailing with the medium he had acquired from his association with Japanese painters. His creative temperament led him to make free experimentation with this medium. Thus, from Krishna Chaitanya, we further learn that Gaganendranath experimented with the form by sprinkling mica dust on the painting surface. The play of cast light and shadows, a unique feature of Gaganendranath's painting, received appreciation from Rabindranath, his uncle, and Gaganendranath also illustrated *Jeevan Smriti,* Rabindranath Tagore's autobiography. With reference to this Japanese connection, another interesting fact that needs to be mentioned is Gaganendranath's fascination for Japanese seals containing his name inscribed in Chinese letters (Kanji). From Kamal Sarkar's biography entitled *Rupodokho Gaganendranath*, we learn how Gaganendranath, with the help of Japanese painters, created a seal of his own; the imprint of the said seal can be found in the illustrations for Tagore's *Jeevan Smriti*: 'So far as my knowledge goes, Gaganendranath created this seal taking the help of Japanese painters who had been at Jorasanko during that time. The seal contained the artist's name engraved in Japanese character (Kanji).'[67]

Chintamoni Kar, in the introductory section of his souvenir on Gaganendranath Tagore, has rightly pointed out that though Gaganendranath, like his brother, is associated with the revivalist school of Bengal, Gaganendranath never allowed himself to be influenced by the tradition or styles of Indian art that had been influential among a large number of painters of his time.[68] A great amateur, as Benode Behari would love to describe him, Gaganendranath followed his own creative and experimental temperament and remained free from academic bias.[69] As he had freely experimented with cubism in his later period, his early adoption of Japanese brush-and-ink technique, was never been a meticulous following of the painting style of Japanese painters. It was his imaginative handling of the medium. Benode Behari Mukherjee's observation in his essay entitled, 'The Art of Gaganendranath', clearly points out this aspect of ink paintings of Gaganendranath Tagore:

> He was fascinated by the apparent ease and the inherent refinement of ink-work. But his inventive mind was too active to remain contented with this new material only. He wanted to create something new, something which would satisfy his creative urge. And when we look at his work in the so-called Japanese style (which is not really Japanese) we cannot say that Gaganendranath had over-estimated his powers.[70]

Gaganendranath Tagore painted quite a few pictures in this semi-Japanese style ('pseudo-Japanese', to quote Benod Behari's words), including paintings of birds, landscape, portrait, a series of twenty pictures on the life of Sri Chaitanya and also his illustrations for Tagore's *Jeevan Smriti.*

In the introductory section of this chapter, we have already mentioned that Okakura's second visit in 1912 turned out to be a more profitable one for the new artists of Bengal. From Nandalal Bose's recollections, that we come across in Dinkar Kowshik's book entitled, *Nandalal Bose: The Doyen of India Art*, we find a lively recounting of Okakura's association with the students of Government Art College in Kolkata:

> The young artists brought their work for his comments, and what he analyzed was clear, pointed and critical without being abrasive. In one instance he referred to a colour scheme as dirty: what he desired to say was probably that the colour lacked transparency and appears to be heavy. In another picture he described a figure as reptilineal and not human. He went on to explain that a human being was a complete self, whose parts could not be isolated without harming its oneness: while a reptile was able to suffer a division, each part assuming organic independence.[71]

Another text, which we have already mentioned, is *Bharatsilpi Nandalal*, by Panchanan Mandal. *Bharatsilpi Nandalal* gives us a prodigy of details regarding Nandalal Bose's artistic career, and also of his association with Japanese artists of that period. Panchanan Mandal, the biographer of Nandalal Bose, has recounted Bose's view of art education, as it was practiced at Kala Bahavana, during his time. Nandalal Bose was of the opinion that the perfect art training should aim at imparting to students three significant aspect of art education; these were, according to him, nature study, adherence to tradition and inculcating originality; the said aesthetic tradition of Kala Bhavan, according to Nandalal Bose, had been founded on Okakura's commentary that he delivered during his interaction with the students of Art School. Nandalal Bose recollected that Okakura held the view that the perfect artistic experience is like a triangle, the three sides of which stand for the three essential aspects of art, tradition, observation and originality. From Nandalal Bose's recollection as it has been penned down by his biographer, Panchanan Mandal, we come across Bose's own receptivity of Okakura's aesthetic ideals, which turned out to be the backbone art training in Santiniketan:

> The principle of art teaching that has been introduced in Kala Bhavana, Santiniketan, was based upon Okakura's opinion of art teaching, which Bose

had learnt from his interaction with Okakura. Okakura held the opinion that the perfect art training should aim at developing three aspects among the learners. These are inculcating originality, nature study and adherence to one's aesthetic tradition.[72]

Panchanan Mandal's recounting speaks of Nandalal Bose's observations on art, based on Okakura's comment that he had heard as a student of the Government Art College, in Kolkata:

> If one strives to be only original in his painting, it will be an insane attempt, full of flaws . . . only study work of nature and surroundings will make imitative drawings. As the inner eye of the artist has not been prepared, he will not be able to create compositions out of natural surroundings. Similarly, if one only tries to adhere to tradition, it will make stereotyped paintings, unimaginative repetitions of past works. Blindly following only one principle of art teaching, or exluding any of them, will deprive the beauty of their paintings.[73]

To sum up, after this long reference to Nandalal Bose's inheritance of Japanese aesthetics, it can be said that the contact and interaction between Japanese and Bengali painters of this period bore different artistic trends in accordance with the painter's temperament and artistic ideals. We have taken into account Abanindranath Tagore's brilliant use of wash technique, a painting technique that he learnt from Japanese painters; his brother Gaganendranath Tagore learnt and improvised the use of Japanese brush-and-ink technique and for Nandalal Bose, the prime architect of Kala Bhavana, the ideals of his art teaching were founded on his association with men like Okakura.

In 1916, Mukul Dey, a young art student then, accompanied RabindranathTagore during the bard's maiden voyage to Japan. A short unpublished article entitled, *Yokohama Taikan: A I Knew Him*, included in the webpage of the Mukul Dey Archives, speaks of Dey's recollections of his voyage to Japan, which among its many itineraries, included the prospect of meeting Japanese painters as, Taikan Yokohama: 'As a young artist pupil of the Tagore family, I was so fortunate as to be invited to join Gurudev's part on his lecture tour to America. On the way we decided to visit Japan in order to meet again the famous Japanese artist Yokohama Taikan, who had been to India soon after 1900'.

Dey's letters written from Tomitaro Hara's[74] residence, at Yokohama, Tokyo, also speak of his pleasure in learning painting from Taikan and also of his desire to learn art techniques from Kazan Shimamura, another eminent painter of Japan of that period: 'During the time I stayed in Tokyo, I took art training from Taikan. Shimamura lives in the city Yokohama, which is not also far from my dwelling. I have also decided to pay a visit to Shimamura's house and to learn painting from him.'[75]

Dey's autobiography, entitled *Amar Kotha*, gives us a lively account of his visit to a place, accompanied by Taikan, where he could see many ancient artifacts of Japan: 'One day, Taikan took me to a place called 'Nodamus'. There I could see ancient paintings of thousand years ago. I saw a picture of a huge golden pine tree.'[76]

Taikan, as Mukul Dey found him, nurtured an intense love for nature, this would make him wander about and take part in nature study. This close association with nature would provide the substance of his art, which he could transform into a masterpiece, with the gift of his imagination:

> Taikan told me that he never draws more than one or two paintings in a year. His works are scroll paintings. And have four-five folds. Most of the time, he wanders here and there and studies natural objects. These viewed objects mingled up with his own ideas turn out to be masterpieces, adorned with the colour of the artist.[77]

The abovementioned quotations reveal how Mukul Dey's exposure to the aesthetics of Japan contributed to develop his artistic vision in studying nature and representing it in accordance with his artistic temperament.

In the introductory section, we have already mentioned of Kampo Arai's visit to Jorasanko in Kolkata, following Tagore's maiden visit to Japan in 1916, a trip which played no less a role in forging a steady interaction between artists of Bengal and Japan. We have also referred to Tagore's letter to Gaganendranath Tagore from Japan, dated, 13 August 1916, which speaks of his initiative to employ Arai Kampo at the 'Vichitra' in Jorasanko mansion and also in Santiniketan. From an entry included in Kampo Arai's diary translated from the original Japanese text by Kazuo Azuma, we learn that Arai reached Jorasanko on 18 December 1916, where he received a warm welcome from the hosts including, Gaganendranath Tagore, Abanindranath Tagore, and Pratima Devi.[78]

From the diary, we also come across a lively description of his visit to Santiniketan and also about his involvement at the Vichitra, in Jorasanko, where he took up the task of training the students in mastering the Japanese style of painting.[79] Dinakar Kowshik, in his biography of Nandalal Bose, entitled *Nandalal Bose: The Doyen of Indian Art,* has recounted how during the Vichitra phase, association with Kampo Arai kindled a love for the art of China and Japan in Nandalal Bose. The companionship they developed while working at the Vichitra studio resulted in a long friendship between the two; also, Bose's own recollection gives us an idea of how Bose too learnt Japanese painting style during the time they worked together at the Vichitra studio in Jorasanko: 'A Japanese artist named Kampo Arai came here during this period. He joined the Vichitra studio and we strated practicing (correct) Japanese style of painting, under his direction' (*Bharatsilpi Nandalal* I: 400).

With reference to this Vichitra phase and Arai Kampo's association with the painters of Bengal, another interseting text that needs mentioning is Mukul Dey's unpublished diary of that period which was posthumously published along with Dey's letters from Japan, entitled *Japan Theke Jorasanko.* An entry in his diary on 7 October 1917, recounts how Kampo Arai helped him to get over the defects of one of his etchings that he had accomplished during that period:

> Today I made an etching, based on the drawing of the ferryghat. Gurudev selected the title and entitled it—'At the crossing'. Arai San found quite a few mistakes of the drawing. He advised me to draw from my memory while doing etching, which is carved on a plate of copper. He was of the view that if one attempts to do etching based on his sketch it will look like a copywork. Even if mistakes occur when one draws from his own mind it will not look bad. However, the mistakes of a copy work can spoil the picture. I have seen that at first the Japanese painters create a sketch, and then while doing an etching, they create it from their mind.[80]

Kampo Arai stayed in India for about two years; during this period he also visited the Ajanta caves with a group of Japanese painters and worked there tirelessly, copying the frescoes of Ajanta caves. From an entry included in this diary, we learn that Arai reached Ajanta on 30 January 1918. Incidentally, Mukul Dey, after returning from Japan, took a pilgrimage to the caves of Ajanta and Bagh during the same time. Mukul Dey's book entitled, *My Pilgrimages to Ajanta and Bagh*, has recounted how he was delighted to meet Aria at the entry point of Ajanta Caves and how he accompanied the Japanese painters during their copy work at the Ajanta caves. Dey has recollected how Arai took him to his bungalow and in the proper Japanese manner introduced him to Professor Sentaro Sawamura, the leader of the party. Mukul Dey received a shelter at that bunglow with other Japanese painters.[81] Every morning, after having finished their breakfast, they used to visit the caves, copying the frescoes. The artists used to scatter into different groups; however, the writer who had not yet received a formal permission from the Nizam government to take part in copy work, remained with his friend, Kampo Arai. In the book, Dey has recalled how even after darkness, Arai would continue his work, copying the fresco of Buddha, holding a lamp in his other hand.[82] Inga Shigemi, a Japanese art critic, in his article entitled, 'The Interaction of Bengali and Japanese Artstic Milieus in the First Half of the Twentieth Century (1901-45): Rabindranath Tagore, Arai Kampo and Nandalal Bose' has taken into account the works of Arai which were created just after his return to Japan from India. Shigemi is of the view that the paintings of Buddha he undertook just after returning to Japan show considerable influence of his experiences in India, chiefly, his visit to the Ajanta caves where he made copies of murals of Ajanta Further, his choice of pigment in portraying landscapes also shows his exposure to the beauty of Indian landscapes he witnessed during his visit to Ranchi. Shigemi's observation may be recalled in this regard:

> Arai applied a sophisticated palette and vivid primary colours without hesitation. He had stayed in Ranchi in the state of Bihar. The beauty of the landscape in the evening particularly attracted the artist. The painter audaciously applied the same combination of blue, green and orange in the iconography, realizing the mysteriously colourful divinities in meditation.[83]

Thus, the contact between the two parts of Asia led to a fruitful exchange among artists of Bengal and Japan, enriching each other through this interaction. It has been located in many biographical texts of this period that the painters of Japan, during their stay in Bengal, came to know about Indian mythology and had created paintings dealing with Indian mythological subjects. From Abanindranath Tagore's *Jorasankor Dhare,* we get to know about the visit of Taikan and other painters at Jorasanko which resulted in a mutual appreciation of each other's art:

> At first, I had difficulty in appreciating their paintings I shared with Suren my inability to enjoy Japanese paintings. Suren advised me to be patient and to view more of their works. Shortly thereafter, I started liking their works. They painted quite a few pictures. I had to explain them from Sanskrit texts in order to help them to paint on Hindu mythological subjects. Taikan composed two paintings of Kali and Saraswati. These were bought by Sarala Devi.[84]

Taikan during his stay, had also created a picture of *Rashlila*; Abanindranath's *Jorasankor Dhare* includes a brilliant recounting of the making of this painting. Taikan, wishing to depict a picture of *Rashlila*, received from the author, necessary details about the mythological issue, the style of wearing an Indian sari had also been shown. However, Taikan could not draw his picture to his full satisfaction. It was the time of blooming of jasmine flowers; a handful of jasmines in full bloom showed the artist what was indeed missing in the picture. His exposure to this Indian flower finally enabled him to finish the picture to his full satisfaction:

> It was the time for the blooming of the Sheuli flower. The women of the house have collected the flowers in the morning and have kept in a bowl in that room. A few of them were littered on the floor. Taikan collected those flowers and placed them on his palm. He took the covering of the painting then scattered the flowers on the surface of the canvas. After decorating with flowers, he then took them away and placed them on the bowl again. He took one single Sheuli flower in his left hand and started painting flowers on the canvas with white and orange colour. Soon the painting becme full of flowers, it appeared as if flowers were dropping from the sky. It seemed as if a gust of wind had carried the flowers and dropped them amidst the dance of

the festival of *Rashleela.* The white hue of the flowers created an impression of a moonlit night. He finished his painting and said that previously the painting lacked something which he was unable to provide.[85]

The long passage taken from *Jorasankor Dhare,* describes in details how Taikan, with his new exposure to Indian culture and environment that is intrinsically Indian in nature, created a masterpiece based on the mythological theme of *Rashleela,* a picture that would not have been created without his first-hand exposure to Indian life and culture.

The history of this interaction between Japanese and Bengali painters would remain unfinished without mentioning the role played by the Indian Society of Oriental Art which took the task of organizing successive art exhibitions on and from 1908.[86] As mentioned in Kamal Sarkar's book entitled *Rupodokho Gaganendranath,* the Indian Society of Oriental Art founded in 1907, at first organized an art exhibition at Gaganendranath Tagore's residence; there, silk prints of Taikan, Katsuta and Hishida were displayed along with the paintings of Bengali painters. The Society organised its first exhibition for the public on 29 January 1908. There also, specimens of Chinese and Japanese modern and ancient art were exhibitted along with the new artistic creations of the Tagore brothers and their students. The following excerpt from *The Englishman,* dated 30 January 1908, quoted in Kamal Sarkar's biography of Gaganendranath Tagore, gives us an idea about the patronizing role played by the Indo Oriental Society: 'A large number of very skilfull and pleasing paintings by Japanese artists, Yokohama Taikan, Yoshio Katsuta, Hunso and Otake Chikuha were shown.'[87]

Rupam, the journal of Oriental Art, edited by O.C. Gangoly, in its April edition of 1922, published an interesting article entitled, 'Indo-Japanese Painting', delineating in detail the works of Japanese painters Taikan, Hishida and Katsuta, created during their stay in India, dealing with traditional Indian mythological subjects, Hindu or Buddhist. In this article it has been noted that Mr. Katsuta visited the Ajanta caves in 1907 and according to the anonymous writer of this article 'Indo-Japanese Painting', the works of Katsuta, delineating with the life of Buddha, show considerable influence of his closeness to an Indian environment, chiefly, his memory of having witnessed the frescoes of the Ajanta caves. Another Japanese painter, Shunnso Hishida conceived a picture representing the Hindu goddess 'Saraswati' and Taikan Yokohama conceived another painting representing the Hindu Goddess of destruction 'Kali'. Both these paintings find reference in this article.[88] Commenting on this picture, the author has pointed out that, though Shiva or Rudra had travelled to Japan, in the guise of Fudo, his consort, 'Kali' has no Japanese parallel. Hence, according to the writer, Yokohama's interest in 'Kali' seems to be more original than the conception of 'Saraswati', which can be associated with the Japanese goddess, 'Benten'.[89] What really induced Taikan to depict the picture of 'Kali' has been pointed out by Inga Shigemi in his article entitled, 'The interaction of Bengali and Japanese Milieus in the First Half of the Twentieth Century', a well-written article where the writer has rightly associated the art movement of that time with the politics of that period. According to Shigemi's analysis, the worship of 'Kali' had already been popularized and internationalized by Sister Nivedita through her book *Kali the Mother*, published in the year 1901. Shigemi also has correctly mentioned how Nivedita's idealized representation of Kali, had an impact upon Okakura whose political manifesto, 'We are One', written in 1902, though posthumously published in 1938, begins with an invocation to Kali Goddess-'Om to the Steel of honour! Om to the Strong!' Shigemi has concluded that Nivedita's vision of Kali might have been transmitted to the Japanese painters through Okakura, prior to their visit in 1903.[90]

Thus, not only Indian mythological subjects of a bygone era, but also, the emergent cultural nationalism of Bengal of that period found a visual representation in the hands of Japanese painters such as Taikan Yokohama. Truly, the interaction between artists of both these parts of Asia, Bengal and Japan, did not result in a one-way traffic where artists of one part learnt and assimilated aesthetic ideals of a superior culture. Rather, it generated a lively exchange and interaction, enriching artists of both Bengal and Japan.

TRANSLATION OF JAPANESE WRITINGS OF THE EARLY TWENTIETH CENTURY

It is widely known that translation from one language to another is now viewed as a dialogue between cultures rather than an engagement between languages. This has been pointed out by Harish Trivedi in his article entitled 'Translating Culture vs. Cultural Translation', where the writer has rightly pointed out that in the past, translation was viewed as a sub-field of linguistics dealing with the transaction of two languages. Later on, Trivedi has argued, the awareness dawned among translators that literary texts are not merely rooted in languages, more so in different cultures. Thus, Trivedi is of the opinion that this change of attitude has caused a paradigmatic departure in which the translation of a literary text has become not merely a transaction between languages, but a complex negotiation of cultures.[91]

With reference to Trivedi's view on translation as an engagement of different cultures, it would be worth taking a look at the translation of Japanese writings into Bangla, which was started during the first few decades of twentieth century. The writings of Japanese writers were in almost all cases translated from English to Bangla. The translation was undertaken from a growing interest in Japanese life, culture and society. They demonstrate the yearning among the educated classes of Bengal and beyond, a desire to know more about another Asian country, which was at that time, determining the fate of many colonized races of Asian continent.

As mentioned earlier, the translation of Matthew Perry's travelogue by Madhusudhan Mukhopadhyay, published in the year 1863, seems to be the first Bangla writing dealing with the life of Japan and her people. Matthew C. Perry is usually credited for having opened Japan to the western world following the Kanagawa Treaty. In 1853, Perry arrived with his fleet of warships in Uraga Bay near Yedo and after successful negotiation compelled the Shugunate regime to come to terms with the West. Thus, following Perry's visit, two ports of Japan were kept open for American vessels. Matthew C. Perry's book, *Narrative of the Expedition of an American Squadron to the Chinese Seas andJapan* was translated into

Bangla language by Madhusudhan Mukhopadhyay and is titled *Jepan.* No doubt, the book seems to be the first of its kind to introduce Japan to the Bengali reader and deserves praise for that. Yet, the translated Bangla text does nothing more than view Japan from the perspective of the western world. The translator has tried to provide a faithful reproduction of the original text written in English and has dealt with most reverence as a specimen of 'superior culture'. There are, in fact, quite a few passages in this translated book which represent Japanese people as an inferior and savage race. This is a common stereotype that can be traced in many colonial narratives of that period. The book recounts many adventures of the western navigators to this island. We also learn that finally, Commodore Perry became successful in compelling the Japanese emperor to negotiate with the West. Needless to say, the rendition is from the western point of view and contains even frightful description of atrocities meted out to shipwrecked American sailors:

> Doibodurbipak boshoto voyonkor jhotika hetu oi jahaj Jepan somudrer choray giya lage. Japanira tahadigoke kararudho koriya bohu jontrona dey, kiyodin ordhoashone rakhe.tahadiger krishto dhormer prodhan chinyo Crush aniya tahadigoke kohe eti amader japaner vut, ihar upor tomra podhaghat koro, na korile amra tomader prandondo koribo.[92]
>
> Sixteen American mariners were sailing eastward in a vessel. Their ship met with a violent storm and they finally landed on a Japanese shore. They were imprisoned by the Japanese and were tortured. They were threatened to be executed if they refused to kick the Holy Cross.

Such descriptions of the hostile attitude of Japanese towards foreigners abound in the text. It is interesting to note how western dress and manner play an important part in imposing the domination over Japanese people, as mentioned in the book. Thus, as narrated in the book in this translated text, we come across a description of how American sailors putting on impressive attire and the soldiers with their aggressive attitude scared the Japanese ruler.[93] Recurrent stereotyping of the indigenous customs and culture of Japanese people are ample in this text. Madhusudhan

Mukhopadhyay, in his translated text, has given a narration of Sumo wrestling being presented by Japanese wrestlers, which the Americans found to be loathsome and barbaric. After having watched Sumo wrestling, the Americans viewed the railway and the telegraph system, which had been introduced in Japan by that time. These achievements in introducing western technology surprised the Americans as it was far from their idea of 'Japan', a hilly island, located in the midst of the Pacific:

> Sushikhito rakhoshdiger oi poshubot kormo sokol somapto hoile, Americanra Japanidiger railroad o telegraph dekhite gelen. Commodore Japanidigoke ordhosovho lok boliya janiten, pahariha lokdiger moto kodorjyachare lipto thakiyao tahara Podartho bidhyay je eto unnoti koribe kokhonoi tini emon bibechoa korenni.[94]
>
> After having seen the barbaric wrestling match (Sumo), the Americans went out to examine the achievements of the Japanese people in setting up railway and telegraph system. Commodore Perry considered the Japanese people to be a barbaric race. However, the fact that the Japanese people, even though they practice many vulgar customs like hilly people, were also capable of making astounding success in material science, was far from the expectations of Perry. He was surprised to see their achievements in science.

The translator has tried to remain as authentic as possible to the original text. He could have inserted his own view point by using footnotes in the text, which he did not. Still, the book is a pioneer in introducing the Bangla reader to the life of Japan. Only at the end of this text, it has been mentioned that Japan had made considerable progress since the time of Commodore Perry:

> Japaner ekhon se obostha nai, purbapekha sovhotar mohottota ebong oudarjo bridhi hoiyache. Purbe je japaner lokera onno deshe gele ekbare desh hoite bohishkrito hoito, tahara ekhon England o Americar prodhan prodhan bidyaloye bidyasikharte jaiteche, ar kichudin por aro koto hoibe.[95]

Since the time of Perry's visit, Japan has developed a lot, both in terms of the quality of their civilization, and also, in terms of considerate attitude towards foreigners. Previously, many Japanese were banished from their country for having visited foreign countries, now these people are going to England and America to take education from their academic institutions. In near future many other changes will also follow.

If in Madhusudhan Mukhopadhyay's translated text *Jepan*, we find a representation of Japan from the western point of view, a completely different picture of Japan comes up, once we go through Priyambada Devi's translation of Okakura's English text, *The Book of Tea*. Teasim, as Okakura has described it in his work, also as it has been described in the translated text entitled, 'Cha-Grontho', is not about the obscure rituals of the East. In contrast, the ceremonious preparations of the tea-ceremony represent the supremacy of Asian culture. In this text, Okakura has also talked about western prejudice, which for him does not allow the West to appreciate their culture properly.

'WHEN WILL THE WEST UNDERSTAND, OR TRY TO UNDERSTAND THE EAST?'

Okakura has raised this question. The text itself may be taken as a befitting literary response to E.M. Foster's *Passage to India*, or similar colonial texts, which upheld the stereotype that the relation between Orient and Occident is irreconcilable. In the translated text of *The Book of Tea*, by Priyambada Devi entitled, 'Cha-Grontho' (included in the *Sekaler Bangla Samoyikpotre Japan*), we notice how Okakura's ideas about this colonial politics, its supremacy and racial prejudice, have been aptly rendered for the Bengali readers:

> Kobe proticho prachoke bujhibe-kinba bojhar chesta koribe? Asiabashi amadigoke sombondhe je odvut ebong kolponar jal rochito hoy, taha dekhiya amra ekebare hotobudhi hoiya jai.hoy amra podmosugondho sonvoge othoba chuchundori ebong toilopayika vojone jibondharon koriya thaki, emon jonosruti suniya jai.[96]

When will the West understand, or try to understand the East? We Asiatics are often appalled by the curious web of facts and fancies which has been woven concerning us. We are pictured as living on the perfume of the lotus, if not on mice and cockroaches.[97]

Musing on the cult of Teasim, Okakura, in his *The Book of Tea,* has found a suitable occasion to express his views on the supremacy of Japan, For Okakura, the cult of tea ceremony is an Eastern attribute, representing the quality of mind to adore 'the beautiful among the sordid facts of everyday existence' (*The Book of Tea* 1). Priyambada Devi's 'Cha Grontho' also gives expression to Okakura's Pan-Asian ideal of Japanese supremacy for being a storehouse of Asian heritage: 'Iha pracho gonotontrer jotharto porikolpona, keno na ei upaye, cha-dhormo-dikhito protyek bektike suruchir avijatyo prodan kora hoy.'[98]

It represents the true spirit of Eastern democracy by making all its votaries aristocrats in taste.[99]

Interestingly, 'Cha Grontho' is only the translation of the first chapter of Okakura's book *The Book of Tea* entitled 'The Cup of Humanity'. The later chapters such as 'The Schools of Tea', 'Tao-ism and Zenism', dealing with long culture-specific subjects like the history of Tea-cult, and how it was transported and transplanted from China to Japan, are issues with which the common Bangla reader would have little association. Priyambada Devi's translation was published in the Bangla magazine *Manashi;* it has also been included in the book *Sekaler Bangla Samoyikpotre Japan*, edited by Subrata Kumar Das. The editor in his Introduction to the book has mentioned that though marked as 'continued', the translation of the later part of Okakura's *Book of Tea*, had not been serialized in the following edition of *Manashi.*

The prime objective of translation is communication and it also shares space with another communicative act, namely interpreta-tion. Priyambada Devi, an educated Bengali woman and poet of the early twentieth century, maintained her epistolary relation-ship with Okakura, the latter at that time had been residing in Boston.[100] Priyambada Devi's letter dated, 6 October 1912, in splendid poetical expression gives voice to her admiration for Okakura's book *The Book of Tea*: 'Dry shrunken tea leaves, who ever dreamt, held in them yet such green wealth of spring-tide beauty and poetry. . . . Beautifully hast thou, son of Japan, painted eternal life's smiles and tears.'[101]

Priyambada Devi's effort to reproduce in the Bangla language the message that Okakura has delivered through his English text, *The Book of Tea,* i.e. the cultural supremacy of the East and the failure on the part of the western world, can show how translation in itself is a complex work involving a synthesis of ideas, eliminating a portion of it and giving emphasis upon certain aspect of the original text, which the translator desired to communicate through his mother tongue.

As early as from the time of Russo-Japanese War in 1905, the magazines published from Bengal displayed an eagerness to print a variety of news items relating to Japanese life, culture and politics, a fact we have tried to locate earlier. Also, the contact of these two cultural zones that triggered a renewed interest in Buddhist studies, has already been mentioned in the introduction of this chapter. Ekai Kawaguchi, a Japanese monk, left Japan in June 1897, and came to India and after spending some time in Kolkata and in Darjeeling, finally managed to reach Tibet through a perilous route encompassing a mountaineous region of the Himalayas in Nepal. Kawaguchi returned to Japan in 1904 and as mentioned in the preface of his book entitled, *Three Years in Tibet,* penned down his travelogue of exploring Tibet that was published in a Japanese newspaper, *The Jiji.* Further, taking the assistance of two Japanese gentlemen, Kawaguchi also brought out an English translation of the travelogue. Kawaguchi during his sojourn in Kolkata (then Calcutta) had been well associated with the intelligentsia of Bengal, and his association with another Tibetologist Sarat Chandra Das, is well known. It is no wonder that Kawaguchi's exploration of Tibet had created some interest among the reading public of Bengal. The English translation of his book entitled, *Three Years in Tibet,* was later translated into Bangla by Hemlata Devi and was published in the Bangla magazine *Prabasi,* in successive serials on and from 1916 (1323 BS). Kawaguchi's *Three Years in Tibet* is a voluminous travelogue consisting of 102 chapters, describing in details of his solo exploration of Tibet. The book begins with a description of his farewell party at Tokyo given by his friends in May 1897, and then with each chapter, Kawaguchi has narrated his visit to Kolkata, following which he reached Darjeeling. He stayed a year in Darjeeling and studied Tibetan language;

and then he started for Tibet, taking a secret route via Nepal-Tibet border of that Himalayan province. Hemlata Devi's translation of *Three Years in Tibet,* published in the *Prabasi* under the title, 'Tibbot Rajye Tinbochor', can well illustrate how for a translator dealing with a text full of reference to a specific culture, is justified in taking liberty to make a synthesis of ideas presented in the target-language text. On the whole, the translator has tried to maintain authenticity in following the original text as much as possible.

Thus, each chapter describes what has been recounted in the corresponding chapter of the original text; the chapters in Bangla translation match with the original text. Moreover, almost in all cases, the names of the sections turn out to be a literal translation of the names in English text. Thus, 'A kind of old Dame' (Chapter 13), has been translated into 'Doyamoyi Briddho' in the Bangla translation. However, unnecessary details and also culture-specific coinages, with which the common Bangla reader would have little association, have been omitted in the translated chapters. A few examples from 'Tibbot Rajye Tinbochor' may be referred to in this context. The first Chapter of 'Tibbot Rajye Tinbochor' entitled, 'Biday-Upohar', begins with a description of farewell party given by Kawaguchi's friend, as it has been described in the corresponding chapter. Both the books give us a detailed description of the party, how many of his friends tried their best to dissuade Kawaguchi from taking part in his solo expedition to Tibet and also, how many of them moved by the noble cause of his expedition, namely studying original Buddhist scriptures in Tibet, were resolved to quit bad practices as smoking or angling. Such narratives occur both in the original and the translated text. Only, the names of the Japanese visitors have been omitted. Similarly, the fact, that Kawaguchi after reaching Kolkata left for Darjeeling on 2 August 1897, has been mentioned in Hemlata Devi's translation. However, his journey by toy train from Siliguri to Darjeeling finds no mention in the translated book. Such changes occur in almost all chapters and can reveal how the act of translation involves an interpretation of the original text by the translator. Hemlata Devi has emphasized and made a selection of certain issues and facts, which she wanted to reproduce in her own mother tongue. The following Bangla translation in accordance with the respective English chapters recount Kawaguchi's stay at Sarat Chandra Das' residence in Darjeeling, where he studied Tibetan language for a year and finally, his visit to Manassarovara and Lhasa in Tibet, through a secret passage located in the frontier regions of Nepal and Tibet. Chapter six and seven of both the texts recount Kawaguchi's journey from Kathmandu to Lhasa taking a perilous route located in the frontiers of Nepal. Unnecessary details, with which the Bangla reader would find little association, have been once again cut short, as in the sixth chapter of the translation dealing with details of Kawaguchi's tour to the surrounding villages of the Kasyapa Tower in Kathmandu. However, his real intention of befriending beggars in that area, i.e. finding out a secret passage of entering Tibet, finds mention in that translated portion:

> ami vabilam je-sokol doridrojatri nepal hoite tibbot jay, taharao prodhan prodhan giripothgulo diya jatayat korite pare na, karon bistor utkoch nadile, e sokol pothe rahadani mile na. Amar onuman thik hoilo. tokhon vabilam ei sob doridroloker sohit bondhuta koriya pother songbad valo koriya loite hoibe.[102]

It occurred to me that the Tibetan beggars, who go on pilgrimage in and out of their country, could not be in possession of the pass that gave them open passage through the numerous frontier gates. I rememembered also that no unprivileged person—even the natives—could obtain permission to pass through these gates, either way, unless he could bribe the guards heavily, and it was plain that these wanderers could not do this. Encouraged by these considerations, I took to befriending the Tibetan mendicants, of whom there was then a large number hanging about the Kasyapa Buddha tower, and my liberality soon made me very popular among them.[103]

Similarly, in the following translated chapter, entitled 'Tungo Himalay' (7th Chapter), we notice how the long description of his stay in Pokhara, that we come across in the corresponding English chapter, has been cut short. Not even the name of Mt. Fishtail, a renowned peak of Nepal, and mentioned in the English chapter, finds mention in this translated portion. Hemalata Devi has only mentioned the geographical significance of the city, as an entry point of Tibet: 'pordin ushakale uttor-poschim 'Pokhra'ovimukhe jatra korilam. E sthan hoite Tibbot-simante 'Kiring' panchdiner poth.'[104]

Early in the morning on the next day we started on the north-western path leading to Pokhra, although there is a short way, only five days' journey from the place to Kirong in Tibet.[105]

Kawaguchi's *Three Years in Tibet* is essentially the Japanese monk's narrative of his exploration of Tibet. Kawaguchi has never refrained from making judgement about life and culture of Tibetan people. In many cases his contemptuous attitude towards Tibetans for their lack of hygiene and cleanliness has been voiced explicitly. He has also never tried to conceal his contempt at the form of Buddhism that used to be in vogue there. For instance, in the 9th Chapter of the book entitled 'Beautiful Tsarang and Dirty Tsarangese', where Kawaguchi recounts his short stay at a place named Tsarang, located in the frontiers of Tibet, Kawaguchi's repulsive feeling for the lack of hygiene among Tibetans has been explicitly voiced. Further, he found among Tibetans a Buddhist sect that practiced and tried to justify polygamy. Interestingly, the translated text also reproduces a similar image of Tibet viewed through the lenses of the Japanese priest, too conscious of his own belonging to a superior society than the Tibetans: 'Ami kina Tibbotjatri, Sareng sohore bash koriya Tibbotider mlechho ritiniti sikhiya loilam. Oporichonnotay Tibbotira prithibir modhe ogrogonno. Sareng er lokera bodh kori oporichhonnotay tahaderoporasto koriyache.'[106]

The days I spent in Tsarang were, in a sense, the days of my tutelage in the art of living amidst filth and filthy habits. In point of uncleaniness, Tibetans stand very high among the inhabitants of the earth, but I think the natives of Tsarang go still higher in this respect.

The town Tsarang, as mentioned by Kawaguchi, was located in the Nepal-Tibet border region, as we move along with the narrative, we come across a similar contemptuous attitude towards Tibetans living in the mainland. The translated portion also creates a similar image about the Tibetans. For instance, Kawaguchi's experience in another small location on his way to Lhasa, described in the 29th Chapter of the translated text may be cited in this regard: 'Tibbotira jothatoi prêt. Ami vumimondole emon mlechhojati kothao dekhi nai. Je keho edeshe ashiben, ei joghonno kodorjo oporichonno lokeder pret boliya dakiya boshiben.'[107]

The Tibetans may indeed be regarded as devils that live on dung, being the filthiest race of all I have ever seen or heard of.[108]

Juxtaposing certain portions from the translated travelogue 'Tibbot Rajye Tin Bochor' and the English text *Three Years in Tibet*, we can find how the translator has yielded to even many racist remarks on the part of Kawaguchi about the Tibetans in order to maintain authenticity to the text. Had *Three Years in Tibet* been a travelogue written from an objective point of view, there would not have been the need to take into account of this translation in this section. However, contrasting the original and the translated one, we can locate certain instances, where Hemlata Devi's translation seems to surpass the original text in removing many of Kawaguchi's prejudiced observations, making the narrative more acceptable to the reader. Thus, in Chapter XII of the book *Three Years in Tibet*, Kawaguchi has narrated how trudging through snow he found shelter in the tents of Tibetan nomads. There an old woman welcomed her with a cup of tea and some baked flour. Kawaguchi accepted the beverage but declined the food, stating that he had been fasting. The explanation he provided had been translated in the Bangla translation. However, the fact that Kawaguchi also found the tea far removed from his taste, as it was brewed in a different manner in contrast to Japan, has been explicitly mentioned in the English text, though skipped in the translated portion. Did the translator omit such portion only for reducing the narration or did she find in Kawaguch's remarks an echo of the Englishmen's stereotyping of her own brethren? As a researcher, I feel the temptation to brood over this subject without coming to any conclusive answer. Leaving aside such rare instances, once again it is Tibet as viewed and narrated by a Japanese priest, that seemed to be the authentic representation of Tibet for the Bangla reader of that time. Nevertheless, Hemlata Devi's translation deserves praise for its treatment of so singular a subject, which is full of culture-specific issues and fascinating details.

The Bangla magazine's receptiveness to Japanese art and culture is a fact that has been mentioned earlier. In this context it would not be irrelevant to refer to a translation of a Noh play that was published in the Bangla magazine *Bharati* (Joistho, 1329 BS). The title of this play as mentioned in this magazine is 'Keu Noy'. Whether Subodh Chattopadhyay, the translator, translated from Japanese or from English translation, we do not know. Further, the presentation of a Noh play usually involves the use of visual appearances and choric accompaniments, of which no mention has been made in this translated piece. The brevity of the scene and the humorous situation this play presents can help us to identify it as belonging to a type of Noh play known as *Kyogen*, which are humorous sketches based on everyday situations. The plot of this humorous skit narrates how Taro and Giro, the two servants, are ordered by their master to take care of a box before leaving the house. The master tells them that the box contained a deadly poison named nothing ('Keu Noy'). Once the master leaves the place the servants cannot resist the temptation and opens the box, and finding nothing but sugar in it, devour it completely. Taro and Giro have to confess everything after the arrival of their master. The stage direction is bare and provides very little information which can help us to identify it as a Japanese Noh play. The scene begins with the presentation of a common Japanese room, with a picture hanging on the wall. The names of the servants, mentioned in this translated play, are Taro and Giro. With the exception of these two common Japanese names, there are indeed very little clues that can identify the translated piece as a Japanese play. Leaving aside these few details, no other culture-specific theatrical prop has been provided by the translator. The translated dramatic piece presents an ordinary humorous situation and is of little literary significance. Nevertheless, Subodh Chattopadhyay, the translator, deserves praise for taking interest in a type of Japanese drama regarding which the common Bangla reader of that time had little exposure.

Tagore was a pioneer in introducing the Bangla reader of his time to the appreciation of Haiku, a Japanese verse usually of 5-7-5 syllables. Before taking the task of rereading Tagore's translations of *Haiku*, it would be worth asking what really inspired the bard to translate them into Bangla language. A detailed reading of his travelogue entitled *Japan Jatri* can show us that Tagore found in *Haiku*, brevity and subtleness, a lack of ornamentation, which seemed to the poet a characteristic of Japanese culture, a unique feature which he could find in other cultural forms associated with Japan. It is reticence or the preference to exclude any unnecessary detail in case of Japanese verse, their preference for keeping empty spaces in visual art, that Tagore found to be an intrinsic merit of Japanese aesthetics and the bard praised it opulently. In this context, I feel the allure of referring to a passage from Rabindranath Tagore's speech entitled 'To Japanese Artists':

> You have the reticence in your nature, but look at Arabia, one monotonous stretch of desert. That is not what I call reticence, it is a negative, it has no content but in Japan where exuberance of life is accompanied by reticence, the sense of proportion becomes a symbol in your own life of a greater passion under control.[109]

Tagore in this lecture has also observed that Japanese masters as Taikan Yokohama were not afraid of leaving great spaces in their paintings. These spaces, according to Tagore, were not merely negative; on the contrary, they have the power to speak to our mind.[110]

It is this reticence or power to be suggestive, which Tagore located in Japanese poetry, a trait, he believed, to be an essential quality of Japanese culture:

> Ei je nijer prokashke ottonto songkhipto korte thaka, E Oder kobitateo dekha jay. Tin liner kabyo jogoter ar kothao nei. Ei tinline i oder kobi, pathok, uvoyer pokhe jothesto.[111]
>
> The great reserve of self-expression is also seen in their poetry. Nowhere else in the world are three lines poems written, yet for them—for both the poet and the reader—three lines are enough.[112]

We should remember that Tagore did not use the term 'Haiku' in describing this genre. He has called them verse of three lines. This is due to the fact that the time when Tagore visited Japan for the first time, i.e. 1916, the term 'Haiku' was yet to gain popularity. 'Haiku' as a verse form, apart from being unrhymed and consisting of three lines with a 5-7-5 syllabic pattern[113], also has certain distinctive features. These include brevity, juxtaposition of two contrasting images and also the use of 'Kigo', or seasonal images, in most of the cases. A close study of Tagore's translation with reference to some of the original pieces, and also their respective English translation, can be illuminating in showing us the uniqueness of Tagore's translation. Though translated from English, Tagore's translations render us the charm of this Japanese verse form. The first translation of 'Haiku' included in Tagore's *Japan Jatri* is based on the English translation of a well-known poem by Matsuo Basho (1644-94), *The Frog Haiku.* Following are the original poem and the Bangla translation which Tagore accomplished:

Furu- ike- ya 5
Kawa- zu- to-bi-ko-mu 7
Mi-zu-no-o-to 5[114]
Puruno pukur,
Banger laf,
Joler Sobdo.

Sujit Kumar Mandal, editor of the annotated anthology of poems translated by Tagore entitled, *Bideshi Fuler Gucho* has rightly identified the source of the translation, i.e. Basho's *Frog Haiku,* and has also suggested us an English translation which had inspired the poet to translate it into Bangla.[115] Tagore himself has not mentioned any source but has referred to the poems as an ancient poem of Japan (Purono kobita). The English translation that has been mentioned in the book entitled, *Bideshi Fuler Gucho* is as follows:

Old pond:
Frog Jump in
Water -sound.

With reference to this possible English source of the Bangla translated verse, we must also remember that *Frog Haiku,* being an ancient poem, there must have existed quite a few English translations of the same Japanese verse during the time Tagore visited Japan. For instance, in the article entitled, 'Matsu Basho's Frog Haiku', the anonymous writer has referred to 32 translations of this poem and has also added a commentary on the translations. Hence, Tagore's own Bangla translation seems to be a transcreation of possible sources he had gone through. Leaving aside this issue regarding sources, it is worth paying attention to the translated piece and to see how the Bangla translation effectively recreates in a different language some aspects of 'Haiku', a Japanese verse. The two juxtaposed images in the translation are the leaping of a frog into an old pond and the sound of water. The Japanese word 'furu ike' translates as old pond ('purono pukur' in Bangla) and 'kawazu tobikomu' means jumping of a frog ('Banger laaf' in Bangla). The other image, 'Joler sobdo' or sound of water is the translation of the Japanese expression 'mizu no oto'. The Japanese word, which does not find any equivalent expression in the Bangla translation is 'ya', which is a cutting word, joining and also segregating expressions before and after. According to an entry in the Oxford Japanese Mini dictionary, the Japanese 'ya' is a word that joins a list of nouns which is not complete and although translatable as 'and', it carries the meaning of 'among other things. It is evident that Tagore's translation was not based on the original Japanese text; hence we find such differences from the original one. While translating 'Haikus' into other languages, translators have often shown disregard for the strict prosodic pattern of 'Haiku' consisting of 5-7-5 syllabic structure. So also, Tagore's translation does not attempt to fulfil such criteria. Bangla prosodic structure differs from both Japanese and English rhyme pattern and Tagore's translation also shows obvious change in syllabic pattern of the verse. The following prosodic division of the poem 'Purono Pukur' can illuminate this issue:

Pu-ro-no pu-kur 6
baan-ger-laf 5
jo-ler-sho-bdo 6

On the whole, it can be said that it is the reticence of this verse; the implicit way of narrating a situation within the span of three lines in a verse form, which had appealed to the bard. While translating it, Tagore took care to represent the brevity of 'Haiku' as much possible. Tagore's observation on this particular translated piece also hammers home this idea:

> Bash! Ar dorkar nei! Japani pathoker monta chokhe vora! Ei purono pukurer chobita kivabe moner modhe eke nite hobe seituku kebol kobi ishara koredile.[116]
>
> That is all. Nothing more is required, for the Japanese mind is full of eyes. An old pond, abandoned by men, quiet and dark, a frog jumps and sound is heard. That it is heard at all is testament to the silence of the pond.[117]

Elsewhere, in a short essay on Japanese metres that was published in the journal *Bhandar* (Ashar, 1312 BS); Tagore has endeavoured to draw the attention of the Bangla reader to the uniqueness of this Japanese verse form. Following is an extract from the essay that has also been included as an appendage of the text *Japan Jatri*:

> Japani kobita sadharonoto ottonto sonkhipto hoyiya thake. tahate miler o kono lokhon dekhina, kebol ottonto sorol mitrar niyom ache . . . tobe iha nischoy je, erup songkhipto o sorol kabyorochonar riti onnotro dekha jay na. Ihader osoman matrar tinliner kobitakonagulike dekhile beder tristuv chonder shlok mone pore.[118]

Japanese poems are usually brief and concise. They are unrhymed, the rhythmic pattern of the verses are simple. Nowhere in the world can one come across so much brevity in poetic expression. These short verses of three lines and of uneven rhyme pattern remind us of the *Tristuv* rhymed verses of the Vedas.

The second 'Haiku' translated by Tagore and included in *Japan Jatri*, is also a Bangla translation of another renowned poem by Matsuo Basho. Following is the original Japanese poem and its Bangla translation Tagore created, based on English translations of the poem.

Kare eda ni
Karasu-no-tomari-keri
Aki no kure
Pocha dal,
ekti kak,
Saratkal.

Elin Sutiiste in an article entitled, 'A Crow on a Bare Branch: A Comparison of Matsuo Bashou's Haiku 'Kare-Eda-Ni' and its English translations' has referred to twenty-two English translations of the said 'Haiku', written down by translators during the last century. A few have been mentioned below:

On a withered branch
A crow is sitting
This autumn eve. Aston. 1899
On a withered branch
A crow has settled:
Autumn nightfall. Henderson. 1933

The two translations of the same 'Haiku' mentioned above shows us how translations of even so short a poem can differ from each other. It seems Tagore based his Bangla translation on the available English translations of the poem 'Kare Eda Ni'. Elin Sutiiste, in the article on English translations of the Japanese 'Haiku' 'Kare Eda Ni' has prepared a detailed analysis of the poem and has shown us how according to the translator's interpretation of a Japanese word, English translations have differed from each other. The Japanese expression 'kare-eda ni' means on a withered branch ('eda' means branch, 'kare' is a compressed form of the Japanese word 'kareru', meaning withered); the second line 'Karasu-no-tomari-keri' connotes the idea of a perching of a crow ('karasu' means crow and 'tomari' connotes perching) and finally in the last line a new idea has been introduced, i.e. the end of autumn, or an autumnal evening, by the Japanese expression 'akino kure'. Earlier, we have tried to locate how Tagore's Bangla translations of 'Haiku', though based on English translations of the respective verses, reveal certain features of 'Haiku' as a verse form. It is widely known that 'Haikus', which were composed on the beauty of season, often contain a seasonal image ('kigo') in Japanese. In this translated piece of Tagore, the 'kigo' is 'saratkal' (autumn). It is once again this brief depiction of the scene of a crow being perched upon a rotten branch in an autumnal evening, suggesting the consciousness of death and decay, which drew the bard's attention. His own observation on the poem also points out the same idea:

Shiter deshe saratkal hoche gacher pata jhore jabar, ful pore jabar, kuwashay mlan hobar kal-ei kalta mrittur vab mone ane. Pocha dale kalo kak bose ache, eitukutei pathok saratkaler somosto riktota o mlanotar chobi moner samne dekhte pay.[119]

And no more is said. Autumn, with no leaves on the tree, and a crow on one of the branches. In cold countries, autumn is the time when the leaves fall, when the flowers wither and the sky becomes dark with mists—it is a time that brings with it the feeling of death.[120]

The translation of the third 'Haiku', included in Tagore's *Japan Jatri* seems to be a tribute to Buddhism, the religion that binds India with China and Japan. Tagore's interest in Buddhism is well known. In his speech entitled, *To the Indian Community in Japan,* Tagore rightly pointed out how the heritage of Buddhism in Japan contributed to the nurturing of self-control and inner discipline among her citizens:

Buddhism is a religion which calls for medication and introspection, to self-control and self-emancipation, repression of passion and cultivation of sympathy. . . . These people have thus come to believe in a heroism which is not self-exaggeration, but in a resigned spirit that can quietly accept either action or inaction as honour or duty might dictate. Therein lies the beauty of their inner strength; it is in that detachment of mind, which does not forget the ideal of excellence in its greed and hurry for result.[121]

Tagore's own remark on this 'Haiku' also emphasizes how Buddhism turns out to be the cultural link between Japan and India. Following is Tagore's translation of the 'Haiku' and the bard's own commentary on the said verse:

Swargo ebong Morto hoche Ful,
Debotara ebong Buddha hochen Ful-
Manusher Hridoy hocheFuler Ontoratma[122]
Heaven and earth are flowers,
The Gods and Buddha are flowers,
Man's mind is the heart of flowers.[123]

For Tagore, the poem is far from being a pictorial representation and tends to suggest some deeper truth. He has further observed that the idea expressed in this short verse has constructed a bridge of harmony between India and Japan. Japan, according to the poet, has been capable of viewing both heaven and earth as a flower in full bloom; on the other hand, Tagore points out that in India, these two flowers, heaven and earth, God and Buddha are viewed as being inseparable flowers hanging from the same branch. Had there not been the human heart to perceive these ideals, the beauty of the flowers would have been external fancies.

In view of Tagore's interest in 'Haiku', an anecdote recollected by Parimal Goswami in his memoir entitled, *Smritichitra*, needs to be mentioned. The writer, recalling his student life in Santiniketan during the 1920s has recollected how Tagore, charmed by the beauty of this verse, took the pain of taking on a few classes on Japanese poetry for his students. Following is an extract from this memoir mentioned above:

> It was an evening of September 1921. Tagore was taking a class on Japanese poetry. We were a group of ten-twelve students and we gathered round him on the roof of our school. The place was dimly lit-up by the light of a single lantern. Tagore had been greatly moved by the uniqueness of *Haikai*, a kind of lyrical epigrammatic verse form of Japan. He could not find delight until he had shared with us his sense of wonder at the uniqueness of this poetic form. Though brief and compact in its form, yet, a few of these verses express a profound feeling in an implicit way.

The Bangla journal *Bhandar* (Ashar, 1312 BS), which published a short essay by Tagore on Japanese metres entitled, 'Japaner Proti', has already been referred to in this writing. The essay also includes three short verses in Bangla, composed by Tagore, making fine use of Japanese metres. Following are the verses, which Tagore composed in Bangla, based on Japanese metres:

1 Sedoko Chando (Sedoko rhyme)
Sagor tire
Shonito megh holo
nishith Oboshan.
Purob-Mohimare
Sonay joygan.
2 Choka Chondo(Choka rhyme)
Sahoshi Bir
Dekhechi koto ori

Koreche joy
Dekhini toma somo
Emon dhir-
Joyer dhoja dhori
Stobdho hoye roy.
3 Imaro Chando (Imaro rhyme)
Geruya bash pori
Dhormoguru
Sekhate giyechilo
Tomar deshe.
Aji se Shikibare
Kormoniti
Tomar dare dhay
Shishobeshe.[124]

Tagore's interest in the brevity of 'Haikus' may also be traced in the epigrammatic verses; he himself composed in Bangla. Tagore's verse selection entitled, *Sfulingo*, includes a few such epigrammatic verses. Following is a verse from *Sfulingo*:

Oshim Sunye Eka
Obak Chokhu
Dur-Rohosho-Dekha.[125]

RECREATING JAPANESE CULTURAL ITEMS IN TAGORE'S SANTINIKETAN

Tagore's fondness and admiration for Japanese culture did not end with his attempt to introduce the Bangla reader to the appreciation of Japanese poetry. In the introductory part of this section, we have already mentioned of Tagore's role in introducing some of the Japanese cultural items in his school at Bolpur. He invited Judo experts and experts of Ikebana (Japanese flower-arrangement), and Sadou (Japanese tea-ceremony), to his school. Tagore's vision of education was one of total activity. From its inception, one motivating ideal for Tagore's educational experiments in Santiniketan was universalism, as opposed to narrow national chauvinism. Commenting on this aspect of Tagore's educational ideal, Uma Das Gupta in an essay entitled, 'A Cultural Nationalism', has rightly pointed out that though Tagore at first conceived his own educational institution as 'A Centre of Indian Culture', he later termed it 'Visva-Bharati', as the translation of this word connotes the idea of a seat of learning of world culture.[126] Tagore invited educators from different parts of the world. He intended to imbibe into his pupils, the wisdom and new thinking that flourished in different corners of the world. It is not a mere coincidence, among the educators, who visited Santiniketan, quite a few were Japanese nationals. The first international student to join Tagore's school was Shitoku Hori. He arrived in India along with Okakura in 1902. Tagore's letters addressed to Jagadish Chandra Bose on June 1902, speak of Tagore's fondness for this particular student of his school: 'A Japanese student has joined our Santiniketan. He is nice and has become friendly with us. Your friend Mira, offers him everyday, a bowl full of flowers. Thus, she has become a friend of him. Mira has also picked up a few Japanese words while interacting with him.'[127]

There is no need to furnish biographical details of the Japanese students and teachers, who played an active part in the creation of Visva-Bharati, during Tagore's time. Earlier in the course of this chapter, we have already mentioned Japanese painters like Kampo Arai and Katsuta, who visited Santiniketan. They were engaged in teaching Japanese painting to the students there. In this section, we will try to take into account of the introduction of four cultural items in Santiniketan—Judu, Ikebana and Sadou (Japanese flower-decoration) and also Japanese carpentry.

JUDO/JUJUTSU

Tagore is credited with the introduction of Judo in India, a fact which is less talked about than his literary creation. However, the dawning of the interest of the Bengali middle class in mastering Judo (Jujutsu), can be traced some years before 1905[128] the year Sano Jinnosuke joined Santiniketan as a Judo expert, responding to Tagore's invitation. It is a well-known fact that the wake of a nationalist spirit in the late nineteenth and the early twentieth century popularized different forms of physical exercises. Apart from traditional games as wrestling, fencing and others, a new interest in Japanese martial art was also witnessed during this period. An interesting document, which needs citing, is a Home Political record of the West Bengal State Archives entitled, *History of Agitation against Bengal Partition.* Even before Sano Jinnosuke reached Santiniketan, an initiative had been taken by Saraladevi Ghosal at Ballygunj for instructing Bengali boys to learn fencing and *jujutsu.* In the record mentioned above, it has also been stated that Miss Ghosal (as mentioned in the document), employed a person named Murtaza, for the said purpose. Murtaza has been described in the document 'as a travelling acrobat and professional strong man'.[129] From another source, i.e. the autobiography of Pulin Behari Das, the founder member of Dacca Anushilan Samiti, and a revolutionary, who mastered in his life various forms of physical culture as jujutsu, fencing and others, we may get some useful information about Murtaza, whom Sarala Devi employed for teaching *jujutsu* and fencing. In *Amar Jiban Kahini,* the autobiography of Pulin Behari Das, it has been mentioned that Murtaza in his early life joined the Great Indian Circus, and soon became adept in various acrobatics. Further, as a practitioner of the circus party he visited America, China and Japan.[130] Whether Murtaza learnt *jujutsu* during when he toured in Japan is uncertain. Nothing has been stated in Das' biography. We also learn that during his later life, Murtaza took appointment as the bodyguard of the son of the deposed Nawab of Ayodh at Metiabruz in Kolkata. There, he used to teach *jujutsu* to young boys, residing in that area (Metiabruz). Das' own interst in *jujutsu* was kindled by watching some boys' demonstration of the art of *jujutsu.* A lively recounting of how as a young boy, he learnt *jujutsu* from boys, who had learnt from Murtaza, is narrated in his autobiography:

> Once, during my visit to Kolkata, I was charmed by the display of *jujutsu* by two boys. Being interested, I took their addresses and visited them at their residence in Metiabruz. In Metiabruz, there was also a branch of Anushilan Samity. I stayed there for two days and learnt their techniques. I also took extensive notes on their tricks. I watched them play with sticks, however, it failed to impress me.[131]

Pulin Behari Das in his autobiography, has also noted how during his frequent visit to Kolkata, he used to learn and take notes on different physical activities, such as playing with sticks, *jujutsu* and the art of mastering knife-play. Later on, he used to give training to the boys of Dacca, in these respective activities.[132] How far the art of *jujutsu*, which Das learnt, was a derivation of Japanese martial art, or it was a modification of indigenous physical exercise, is shrouded in mystery. His autobiography gives us little clue relating to these issues. Das has also mentioned that it is an Indianized form of *jujutsu* that he learnt from the boys, whom Murtaza had taught.[133] Nevertheless, the fact that this kindling of a patriotic spirit, also led to the popularization of Japanese martial art, can not be ruled out altogether. It seems two parallel efforts were taken to popularize *jujutsu*. For people like Das, the interest in *jujutsu* was from a nationalist point of of view, *jujutsu* became a symbol of Japanese supremacy, On the other hand, Tagore's interest in *jujutsu*, seems more from an educational point of view, he employed *jujutsu* experts from Japan, and took initiative in teaching his students the art of this game for the sake of moral and mental development of his pupils. In the following section, we will try to bring out a detailied discussion on this subject.

Tagore believed that physical exercises are an inseparable part of education. In his autobiographical work *Chelebela*, Tagore remembers his childhood experiences of taking lessons of wrestling from a wrestler, whom he describes as *Kana Palowan*, in the text. Similarly, young 'Rabi' was made to learn gymnastics under the guidance of a gymnastic instructor.[134] It is no wonder, Tagore, a great admirer of traditional Japanese culture, was an ardent admirer of Judo or *Jujutsu*. The difference of the meaning of the two terms will be discussed later. What evokes wonder is Tagore's endeavour to transplant it in an alien soil. He invited Judo instructors to his school, Santiniketan. The history of the introduction of *Jujutsu* in Santiniketan dates back to 1902, the year, which marks a historic meeting of two minds, Tagore and Tenshin in Kolkata. Tenshin Okakura (1862-1913), the eminent writer and art critic of Japan, was the founder of the renowned art school *'Nihon Bijutsuin'* (The Japan Art Institute). He came to Kolkata in 1902;

further, he also sent his disciple Shaokin Katsuta to join Santiniketan as an art teacher. Tagore also requested Okakura to send a *jujutsu* teacher for his school. Responding to his invitation, Sano Jinnosuke, who was a student of Keio University, was sent to Tagore's Ashram by Fukazawa of the Keio University. From Supriya Roy's *Makers of a Mission*, we come to know that, even before Sano's arrival, S. Kusumato, another Japanese teacher, whom Okakura had sent to teach carpentry in Santiniketan, was teaching the boys the basics of *Jujutsu.*[135] However, the introduction of formal teachings of *Jujutsu* in Santiniketan was surely a great contribution of Sano Jinnosuke. Sano Jinnosuke stayed in Santininiketan from 1905-8. During this period of time, he used to teach *Jujutsu* to the students of Santiniketan. Supriya Roy's short biographical sketch of Sano, the teacher, and his fostering role in the creation of Santiniketan, is worthy to be noted:

> A tin-roofed shed was built on the northern side of the mango-grove (*amrakunja*) for *jujutsu* classes. The students were enthusiastic about these classes. Rathindranath remembered, 'Father had bought a *jujutsu* expert from Japan. We took lessons from him in order to prepare ourselves to fight the British! Had not the spirit and training of judo helped the Japanese to win the war?[136]

We must remember that for Tagore and his generation, *Jujutsu* became an icon of Japanese nationalism. Japan succeeded to thwart the onward march of western imperialism. Japan's victory over Russia in the war of 1904-5, kindled the nationalistic impulses of Bengal's intelligentsia of the early twentieth century. This victory was celebrated in this part of the empire as an assertion of the power of Asians Also, Okakura's book *Ideals of the East*, with his famous phrase 'Asia is one', left an indelible impression on Tagore and his disciples. Thus this nationalist impulse played an important part in fostering Japanese martial art. Tagore's admiration for this traditional Japanese art and game is quite evident in his writing. While writing to Monoronjan Bandyopahyay, Tagore has praised Sano the teacher's skills in imparting lessons of Judo: 'A *Jujutsu* teacher has come from Japan—it is worth watching his capers!'[137]

It must be noted that Tagore's chosen word was 'Jujutsu', instead of Judo, though long before Tagore, the new coinage 'Judo' had already substituted the word 'Jujutsu'.

Judo, like *Kendo* or *Karate do*, rose out of the experiences of the Samuraies of medieval Japan. It belongs to the traditional Japanese cult known as, *Bushido.*

The Japanese character of 'Bushi' means Samurai, and the word '*Do*', connotes way of life.

With the passage of time the *Budo* or *Bushido*, culture in Japan underwent a change. It was cultivated for nurturing personal virtues. Self-control and respect are vital aspects of the Bushido culture. Kano Jigoro is considered as the founder of the modern Judo of the nineteenth century Japan. Kano Jigoro learnt traditional *Jujutsu* as a student of the Tokyo Imperial University. Kano Jigoro viewed Jujutsu from the perspective of education. Comparing Jujutsu to other forms of physical execrise he improvised *Jujustsu*; his purpose was to enable *Jujutsu* as an effective means of physical development (taiiku), spiritual development (shushin) and as combat and competition (Shobu). Kano Jigoro preferred to use the term Judo instead of 'Jujutsu'. He created his own school for teaching this martial art and named it 'Nihon-den Kodokan Judo'.[138] The character (Do) in Japanese connotes 'way', whereas, the character (Jutsu) denotes 'technique'. Kano Jigoro's choice probably emphasizes his purpose of popularizing Judo, not as a destructive means, but for the sake of moral and physical education.[139] It must also be noted that, he was a pioneer in introducing a system of progressive ranks (dan) and grades (kyo), which he did to encourage his students. Tagore's inclination for the older diction was perhaps due to his love for the traditional Japanese coinage. From a file of the National Archives entitled *Publication of a book entitled India and Indians by one J. Sano* (Foreign and Political 1918/21), we come to know that after Sano had left Santiniketan, he accepted an appointment in the Mysore State in 1910. Further, it has also been mentioned that the journal of the Indo-Japanese Association (no. 10/1917) published an advertisement of his book 'India and Indians'. The said advertisement drew the attention of the British authority, following which, all possible information regarding Sano was sought by the British government.

From this file of the National Archives, we come to know that after leaving Santiniketan, Sano took employment in the Mysore Darbar as a Japanese professor of *Jujutsu* and stayed there for a period of six months.[140] It has also been stated that Sano had been employed earlier as a *jujutsu* instructor to the officers and men of the 5th Fusiliers, Fort William, in Kolkata, and also to the members of the family of the Magharaja of Cooch Behar. As for the translation of the book 'India and the Indians', the then Foreign Secretary, Major A. M. Cardew has made his observation that he found the book to be interesting.[141] Further, referring to the translation of the text 'India and Indians' (*Indo oyobi Indojin*), A.M. Cardew has noted that he found nothing to be objectionable in the text. According to him, Sano has credited the colonial administration for the national prospects and safety of India.

Almost two decades after Sano had left Santiniketan; Tagore took another drive to bring another *Jujutsu* teacher from Japan. In 1929, on his way back from Canada, Tagore paid a short visit to Japan. There, he contacted the *Tokyo Kodaikan*, the chief centre for Judo in Japan. Following Tagore's request to them to send a Judo teacher, Shinzo Takagaki (1893-1977), a renowned teacher of Judo, came to Santiniketan. Shinzo Takagaki during his life time achieved the 9th *Dan* (9th Grade), one grade short of the highest grade awarded in Judo by the *Kodaikan*. Prior to Bengal, he had also taught *Jujutsu* in Canada. The news of Takagki's visit to Tagore's school was published in the Japanese daily *Ashai Shinbun*.[142] Tagore himself took the financial responsibility to bear the cost of employing Takagaki. He also appealed to Bidhanchandra Roy, Subhas Bose, and others, to support Takagaki's teaching of Judo in undivided Bengal.

In October 1929, Takagaki came to Santiniketan. It is said that Tagore himself took an important part in the welcome ceremony of Takagaki. Students of the Ashram greeted him with garlands and sandal wood. Tagore's famous song *Shonkocher o Biwuvolota nijer opoman* was composed during this time. Gurudev dedicated it for the cause of teaching of Judo in Santiniketan.[143] This time, in Santiniketan, a new gymnasium was built, fully equipped for the purpose of teaching *Jujutsu*. Shinzo Takagaki stayed in Santiniketan for two years. Within this period of time, he succeeded in popularizing *Jujutsu.* Professor Azuma in his biography of Takagaki has referred to a few memoirs of the period, which throw light upon how Takagaki used to involve his students in the practice of this game. As a teacher, he was extremely affectionate to his student; he used to prolong the practice of Judo, until the learners became adept in the crafts of Judo.

One significant aspect of this phase of Jujutsu training was that, girls took part along with boys. Those who were Takagaki Sensei's students, mention should be made of Amita Sen, Nibedita Ghosh, Yamuna Sen and others. Tagore believed that Judo could be useful for women from the perspective of self defense.[144] In Santiniketan, he succeeded in involving girls in *Jujutsu* classes at a time, when bringing a girl child to school was itself a challenge for educators.

Tagore wanted to popularize *Jujutsu.* Advised by Tagore, Takagaki with his students went to different places to demonstrate and to teach *Jujutsu.* Once, they went to Varanasi to display the craft of *Jujutsu* (Judo). Professor Azuma has referred to the travelogue of Maki Hoshi, sister-in law of Rash Behari Bose, in narrating this trip. Mrs. Indira Gandhi, our erstwhile Prime Minister, was among the audience that thronged at the field of Banaras Hindu University, to watch *Jujutsu.* It is said that, Takagaki and his team received tremendous appreciation in Varanasi.[145]

From its inception, the British government was sceptic and suspicious about Tagore's mission of setting up his school at Santiniketan. From time to time, they kept a keen watch upon the activities of this institution; and this time, the presence of a Japanese national teaching traditional Japanese martial art, did not escape the scrutiny of the British government. In a report of an I.B. officer dated Chandannagar, 11 February 1931, both the names of Mr. and Mrs. Takagaki, has been referred to. Also, the name of a Japanese carpentry teacher, who at that time lived at Surul, has also been mentioned. These archival documents of the Intelligence Branch, along with many other archival documents, have been published in the book entitled, A *Tribute to Rabindranath Tagore Glimpses from Archival Records.*

Tagore was extremely positive about Takagaki's involvement in

Santiniketan. He hoped that Takagaki's efforts would be helpful in popularizing the game. He also hoped to attain funding to support's Takagaki's teaching in Santiniketan. As noted earlier, Tagore appealed to Bidhan Chandra Roy and Subhas Chandra Bose, for this purpose. In this context, Tagore's letter to Dr. Bidhan Chandra Roy, dated 25 April 1931, needs citing:

> I wrote some time ago to Shrijukta Subhas Chandra Bose about our jiu-jitsu professor, Mr. Takagaki, but apparently he has not been able to reply to it as he is touring about in East Bengal. May I now put before you the case of Prof. Takagaki, whom as you know I brought from Japan specially for the purpose of giving a thorough training in the art of *jujutsu* to the students of Bengal. . . . When I found out that our countrymen did not properly realize the importance of the visit of Prof. Takagaki to our country I had to take up the entire financial responsibility of his travel and stay in this country.[146]

Tagore's hopes did not come true. He was probably ahead of his time.

Why was Tagore so keen on introducing *Jujutsu* in his school?

The possible answer to this question can be found in the kind of education, Tagore desired to impart to his students. For Tagore, the aim of education can never be confined to the needs of fulfilling the requirements of livelihood, but for him, education should unfold the 'the unity of truth'[147] a phrase, he coined in the lecture he delivered in America. In this lecture titled, 'My School', Tagore emphatically says: 'We devote our sole attention to giving children information, not knowing that by this emphasis we are accentuating a break between the intellectual, physical and the spiritual.'[148]

Tagore's vision of education was one of total activity. About Visva-Bharati, his dream vision was that 'it must be made into a centre for the spiritual endeavour of all mankind'.[149] It was also Tagore's desire to inculcate the spirit of universalism among his students.

Thus, it is no wonder, Tagore rightly perceived that Judo, or *Jujutsu* is not an ordinary game, the strength of it lies in the possibility of developing self-discipline, and spirituality, among the learners.

Although Tagore did not know Japanese, this never created an impediment to understand the essence of another culture. His efforts to introduce Judo or *Jujutsu* in Shatiniketan, was in accordance with his ideas about the making of Visva-Bharati, as an ideal seat of learning, where East would meet West, and all the wisdoms of the world would be available for his students.

IKEBANA (JAPANESE FLORAL ARRANGEMENT) AND *SADOU* (JAPANESE TEA-CEREMONY)

The adoration of flowers among the Japanese people and the extreme impotance to flowers, given in their culutaral life, as an inseparable part of the aesthetics of Japan, did not miss the attention of Tagore. In his travelogue on his maiden voyage to Japan (*Japan Jatri*), Tagore has rightly pointed out the difference that exists between their floral arrangement and that of ours:

> The same holds true in the arrangement of flowers. Elsewhere different flowers and leaves are gathered together and tied in a bunch—just as at the time of Baruni festival, all the travellers to the festival are crushed together in a third class compartment—but here the flowers are not tormented in that manner, a third class compartment is not allotted to them, but a private car is reserved.[150]

In Tagore's *Japan Jatri*, we also come across his experience in taking part in a Japanese tea-ceremony, another unique Japanese cultural item. For Tagore, the elaborate rituals of a tea-ceremony is marked by a religiosity, its objectives are to infuse self-restraint among the participants, and also to prepare them for the task of appreciating the beauty of this cultural practice: 'The self-restrain of the participant plays an important part in the the appreciation of this custom. There is not a dint of prodigy, the significance of the tea-ceremony lies in enabling the participants to attain a poise of mind, free from the mundane requirements of everday life.'

The receptiveness of Tagore in appreciating the uniqueness of Japanese culture, did not end up with these positive responses to Japan's culture, which we come across in his travelogue. Tagore also took some initiatives to recreate these cultural practices in his own school, Santiniketan.

During one of his visits to Japan, Tagore was introduced to Makiko Hoshi, the sister-in-law of Rash Behari Bose, whom he requested to join Santiniketan for providing training in flower arrangement, and also in tea-ceremony. An interesting document that is stored in the Rabindra Bhavana Archives, Santiniketan, is a letter written by Makiko Hoshi to Tagore, dated 14 October 1929, expressing her willingness to join Santiniketan for the sake of continuing further studies in Sanskrit, along which she would be dispensing the task of teaching the students, the art of tea-ceremony and flower arrangement.

From Kazuo Azuma's writings on Takagaki, included in his book *Ujjal Surjo*, we further come to know that Hoshi, accompanied by Takagaki's wife, reached Santiniketan on 6 November 1930. Nandalal Bose's recollection, penned down by his biographer Panchanan Mandal, recounts how Makiko Hoshi's presence in Santiniketan created an enthusiastic response among the residents to take part in the tea-ceremony regularly:

> Hoshi arranged the tea-ceremony. One has to become the host of this programme. We selected Mr. Khiti as the host. The host of this programme is supposed to prepare the tea and offer it to the guests. He took the task of preparing the tea with tea-powder, mixed with sherry, in the perfect Japanese fashion. And what is more surpising is that we noticed the similarity that exists between the rituals of Japanese tea-ceremony and that of the Tantric sect.[151]

In Chapter I, we have already noted the fact that the cultural traveller's encounter with the uniqueness of Japanese society and culture is in most cases, a reminder of some point of similarity with the culture of his homeland. Wherever the traveller goes, and whatever he sees, he own vision of 'home', never gets oblivious. It acts as a tool to find a comparison with the new experiences he gathers in a foreign land. Interestingly, for Nandalal Bose, the elaborate rituals of a Japanese tea-ceremony, finds resemblance with the tantric rituals that survived in India, and was transported to other countries in Asia, as Tibet and China: 'With reference to this topic, you can read the book *Tantravilashir Sadhusongo.* The rituals of the tea-ceremony bear resemblance with the rituals of the tantric community. Also, one can find similarity with those of China and of Tibet.'[152]

Apart from narrating Bose's experience in taking part in a Japanese tea-ceremony, Panchanan Mandal, the biographer of Nandalal Bose, has also included Bose's sketches of the tea-house and of utencils, used in a tea-ceremony.

JAPANESE HORTICULTURE AND CARPENTRY

During his visit to Japan, Tagore was fascinated by the beauty of the Japanese houses and gardens; his fondness for the uniqueness of the Japanese houses, and their interior designs, finds quite a few references in his travelogue. For Tagore, it is once again simplicity and an abundance of space in inner designing of the Japanese houses, which drew his attention. His observation in his travelogue *Japan Jatri,* needs mention: 'Another thing I noticed was that their houses are not very big—the walls, beams, doors, windows are as few as possible. This means that the house does not surpass the man but is entirely within his control—to maintain it and keep it clean is not difficult.'[153]

Tagore was also fascinated by the uniqueness of Japanese garden. Tagore's travelogue also speaks of his fondness for it:

> The Japanese know what a garden should be. Merely piling up earth and planting shrubs in geometrical patterns is not enough—as you will know if you have ever been in a Japanese garden. Both the eyes and the hands of the Japanese have learned their appreciation of beauty from nature itself as they can observe, so they can create.[154]

While writing to his son Rathindranath, Tagore has expressed his desire to transplant a whole Japanese wooden house, with its interiors, to his own place in Santiniketan.

Tagore's fondness for Japanese interior designing and gardening, did not end here. Arunendu Bandyopadhyay in his essay entitled, 'Santiniketan-Sthapothorup, Nirmito Paribesh ebong Rabindranath', has rightly pointed out that Tagore's admiration for the aesthetics of Japanese architecture can be witnessed in his experiments with space, the bard has given some concrete form in the creation of 'Udichi' and 'Punoscho'. Further, Tagore also engaged a Japanese horticulturalist, Kasahara, to create landscape gardening in Santiniketan.[155]

Tagore's admiration for Japanese carpentry can be traced back to the time, prior to Tagore's maiden voyage to Japan in 1916. From the diaries of Shitoku Hori, the first international student of Santiniketan, we learn that Shitoko was requested by Tagore to construct a handloom for his school.[156] Also, S. Kusumoto, another Japanese expert on carpentry, used to dispense service to Santiniketan, during its inception. From the biographical records included in Supriya Roy's book entitled *Makers of a Mission,* we come to know that Kusumoto joined Santiniketan Vidyalaya in March 1905. A portion from Roy' biographical sketch of Kusumoto may be referred to in this context:

> 'Kusumbabu' as he was called by all, was a friendly and cheerful person. He taught boys to make desks, shelves, clothes-horses and other items of utility. He had the habit of working silently and with concentration. He made two boats *Citra* and *Sonar Tari.* They were set afloat on the Bhuvandanga Lake. He had also built for Samindranath a model of Japanese war-ship and as a specimen it was kept on display by the *Vicitra* club at Jorasanko.[157]

The holdings of the Rabindra Bhavan Archives, Santiniketan includes a letter of S. Kusumoto to Tagore, dated, 31 March 1931, recalling the short duration he had dispensed his service to Santiniketan, almost 30 years back.[158]

However, it was in 1922, when Kintaro Kasahara joined Santiniketan as an expert on carpentry and horticulture, which helped Tagore to materialize his dream of experimentation with architecture and gardening, in Santiniketan. Kintaro Kasahara, the Japanese carpenter and horticulturalist came to Kolkata, during the first decades of twentieth century. Before he joined Santiniketan, he had been engaged as a carpenter at Abanindranath's residence in Jorasanko. From Mohanlal Gangopadhyay's recollection of his childhood days at Jorasanko, we learn that Kasahara came to Jorasanko as a carpenter. However, Abanindranath soon realized that Kasahara was not an ordinary carpenter. Rather, he was proficient in landscape gardening, according to the Japanese style. Mohanlal has also recollected how Kasahara's presence at Jorasanko, influenced Abanindranath to create bonsai trees. At first, three Japanese bonsai trees were imported from Japan. However, they failed to survive in Indian climate. Mohanlal has recounted how after this preliminary disaster, Abanindranath took up with a new gusto the task to create Indian bonsai of a tamarind tree, taking necessary help from Kasahara.[159] During the time, Kasahara stayed in Kolkata, he was also engaged as an expert in horticulture at Prodyutkumar Tagore's residence at Kasipore, in Calcutta. Kasahara created a landscape gardening there, which drew attention of many. Also, Jagadish Bose took his help to create a garden in his house.[160] Kasahara came to Santiniketan in 1922; Kasahara's presence in Santiniketan helped Tagore carry out his experiments with architectural forms in Santiniketan. Taking the help from Kasahara, Tagore brought newness to the house designings of Santiniketan. Kasahara created attractive gardens within the Udayan complex. The inclusion of rock-garden, bower, waterbodies and sculpturers, gave a new look to the Udayan Complex. From Arunendu Bandyopadhyay's essay, we further come to know that all wooden windows, doors and furnitures, inside the Udayan Complex, were furnished according to the Japanese fashion. A unique tree house was also created by Kasahara for Tagore's use.[161] We can agree with Arunendu Bandyopadhyay that the tree house created by Kasahara, was a remarkable experiment in the field of architecture. The experience to lodge in a wooden tree house turned out to be a delightful experience for Tagore. A few poems of his verse collection Purabi were composed there. Amita Sen in *Ananda Sarvokaje'* recounts the time; Tagore spent in the tree house that Kasahara constructed:

> Sometimes Rabindranath stays in Santiniketan.He also sometimes stays in the cottage of Surul. Japanese carpenter Kasahara has constructed a tree-house upon a great banyan tree. When the representatives of *Rabibashar* came to meet the poet, they met him at this poet's dwelling, i.e. the tree-house, which Kasahara prepared for the poet,[162]

To conclude, it can be said that as in the case of *jujutsu*, and other cultural items, transplantation of Japanese carpentry, and of horticulture, also included the subjective participation of the receptor; Tagore and his circle. Their own understanding, appreciation and likings for the Japanese architecture, played an inseparable part in the transplantation of this Japanese cultural item, in an alien soil—Santiniketan.

A RENEWED INTEREST IN BUDDHIST STUDIES

In the introductory section of this chapter, I have already mentioned of the fact that the renewal of contact between the two cultural zones of Asia, Bengal and Japan, also led to a renewed interest in Buddhist studies. This aspect also deserves mention, with reference to this subject of reception of Japanese culture in Bengal, during the early twentieth century. We have also referred to O.C. Ganguly's writings, who rightly pointed out that by the end of nineteenth century in Japan, a new wave of rediscovering the cultural roots in India, gained popularity in Japan. Pilgrims from Japan started to visit India, in search of paying their homage to the relics in India, associated with Lord Buddha. Buddhist missionaries in Japan were also facing a hard time, following the enactment of a new rule that brought a segregation of Buddhism from Shinto, the traditional religion of Japan. The Japanese government started showing preference for the latter. This in turn, gave rise to the cause of revival of Buddhism. This time, Buddhist missionaries in Japan took interest in rediscovering India, as the source of their religion. Zank Dinah in his article entitled, 'Painting the life of Buddha: Transculturality, Patronage and Artist's vision' has referred to the reconstruction of Buddhist temple at Sarnath, which received Japanese patronage. Zank Dinah in his article has also pointed out that the revivalist movement of Buddhism in Japan undertook the mission of creating an international network and spreading Japanese Buddhism to the West. Also, it strove to explore India, Nepal and Tibet as the root of Buddhism.[163] Thus, revival of Japanese Buddhism became intrinsically related to the notion of Pan-Asian doctrine of cultural unity of Asia. It is interesting to recall once again that in Okakura's vision of Asian unity, Buddhism occupies the central place, as it connects India with China and Japan: 'Or to turn again to Eastern Asia from the West, Buddhism—that great ocean of idealism, in which merge all the river-systems of Eastern Asiatic thought. . . .'[164]

It is worth noticing here, the similarity in thought, between Okakura's idea of Buddhism and that of Tagore. For Tagore also, it is Buddhism and the art that the mighty religion fostered in various places in Asia, which binds India with the rest of the continent:

'The barriers of race and country were swept away by the flood of truth, and India's message reached men of all races in every land. To that invitation came response from China and Burma and Japan, Tibet and Mongolia; the obstruction of seas and mountains gave way before that irresistible call.'[165]

Thus, the revivalist movement in Buddhism received a good deal of appreciation from the educated masses of Bengal, and other provinces of India. Japanese monks and scholars, who came to India, during the early twentieth century, in pursuit of studying ancient Buddhist texts, received cooperation and patronage from men like Rabindranath and Sir Asutosh Mukherjee. In the following section, we will try to account for the role played by Japanese scholars, who came to India during the early twentieth century, and how they received encouragement from the educated sections of Bengal.

We have earlier referred to *Three Years in Tibet*, the travelogue, Ekai Kawaguchi wrote on his experience of visiting Tibet. Among Japanese monks, who visited India during the late nineteenth century, in search of studying ancient texts on Buddhism, Ekai Kawaguchi's name deserves mention. As mentioned in his travelogue, Kawaguchi left Japan in June 1897. After spending some time in Kolkata, Darjeeling and Bodhgaya, he finally succeeded in entering Tibet, with a forged identity, through the frontier provinces of Nepal and Tibet. 'A Year in Darjeeling', the second chapter of his book, *Three Years in Tibet*, recounts his stay at Sarat Chandra Das' residence in Darjeeling, where he started learning Tibetan language for the purpose of entering Tibet, and to read Buddhist texts. We also come to know how Kawaguchi received help from Das, in continuing his learning of Tibetan language. Kawaguchi also enrolled himself in a government school of Darjeeling, where he studied Tibetan with children, during his one year stay in Darjeeling.[166] Determined to enter Tibet, Kawaguchi finally left Darjeeling. Through a different route that passes through Nepal, he was able to enter Tibet, by June 1898.[167] The book describes in details his visit to different monasteries in the frontier provinces, and also in Lhasa, the capital of Tibet. After reaching Lhasa, Kawaguchi took admission in a college, for persuing his study of Tibetan scriptures. It has been mentioned that

Kawaguchi had to sit for both written and oral tests, which he succeeded. He also received scholarship for continuing his study.[168] Among Japanese scholars, Kawaguchi was successful to meet the Dalai Lama of his time. In this context, the passage describing his meeting with Dalai Lama, needs mention:

> The Court Physician leading me a little to one side, in front of the Dalai Lama, saluted him. I saluted him three times, and taking my robe off one of my shoulders I stepped before him, when His Holiness streatched out his right hand to put it on my head. . . . The Dalai Lama then began by praising me for having healed many poor priests at Sera. He told me to stay at Sera and to do as I had done, and I answered that I would do with pleasure as he wished me.[169]

Kawaguchi's meeting with Dalai Lama of Tibet also finds reference in a document of the Foreign and Political Department of the National Archives. This document entitled, *Letters from his Holiness the Dalai Lama to Kawaguchi*, includes a letter that was written by the Dalai Lama to Kawaguchi, following the latter's departure from Tibet. In his letter, Dalai Lama enquired of a set of *Kagyur,* a book, which had been entrusted to Mr. Kawaguchi for delivering to Hongpa Hongaj Hosshu, after reaching Japan.[170]

Kawaguchi's *Three Years in Tibet* includes a chapter on Tibetan Buddhism. It is entitled 'Lamaism'. In this chapter, he has dealt in details his view about the form of Buddhism that he witnessed during his visit to Tibet. In short, there were two branches of Lamaism, during the time of his visit. The founder of the older sect, as mentioned by Kawaguchi, was a Tantric priest, named Lobon Padma Chunge, a priest, who according to Kawaguchi, advocated in favour of flesh-eating, marriage and drinking. Kawaguch has clearly observed that he found this form of Buddhism to be a gross deviation from the tenants of Buddhism: 'He ingeniously grafted carnal practices on to Buddhist doctrines, and declared that the only secret of perfection for priests consisted in leading a jovial life, and that by this means alone a man born into this world of five impurities can hope to attain quickly to Buddha-hood and salvation.'[171]

Earlier, Kawaguchi in the chapter entitled 'Beautiful Tsarang and Dirty Tsarangese', has expressed his disregard for this form of Buddhism:

> There is in existence to this day in Tibet a sect of Buddhists which believes in a teaching originated by a priest whose name may be translated into 'born of the lotus flower' (Padma Sambhava) or Padma Chungne in Tibetan, and whom they regard as their savior and as Buddha incarnate. His teaching is a sort of parody on Buddhism proper, and an attempt to sanctify the sexual relations of humankind, explaining and interpreting all the important passages and tenets in the sacred texts from a sensual standpoint.[172]

Kawaguchi has noted in his book that these degenerated doctrines advocated by Padma Chugne, the religious leader of the older sect remained widely popular until a reaction arose against it. Thus, in the eleventh century, Paldan Atisha, an Indian priest, gave the birth of a new sect of Tibetan Buddhism. However, Kawaguchi is of the opinion that during the time he visited Tibet, i.e. the early twentieth century, he found that the new sect too, had undergone considerable degeneration, and had incorporated much of the 'esoterism of the Old Sect'.[173] Kawaguchi's association with the educated cross-section of Bengal has already been mentioned. We have also taken into account Hemlata Devi's translation of his travelogue that was published serially in the Bengali magazine *Prabasi*, under the title 'Tibbot Rajye Tin Bochor'; a translated text, which clearly shows that Kawaguchi's vision of Tibet was accepted by the elites of Bengal.

Tenshin Okakura visited Kolkata in 1902. His association with the cultural leaders of Bengal needs no mention. It has already been discussed. From Surendranath Tagore's reminiscence of his visit to Bodh Gaya along with Okakura, we come to know that Okakura had a plan of reconstructing the temple complex at Bodh Gaya. He wanted to buy land from a Mohant, and set up a colony of devotees on that land:

> He had originally come, he told me, simply to make his offering of reverence to the Buddha, but far from being rewarded with peace of mind; he had been sorely distressed at the state of the temple and its ill-kept surroundings. There upon he had a vision of little colonies of devotees, hailing from all parts of the world, each housed according to the usage of its land, all clustering

round the temple grounds, contributing colourful variety of vesture and ceremonial to a common ideal of peace and good-will, inspired by the constant contemplation of the site of the Master's enlightment.[174]

The degradation of the temple at Bodh Gaya, and its vicinity, was a concern for the Buddhist communities of the world of that time. In this context, mention should be made of a news, published in the journal of the Maha Bodhi Society, of a mass protest meeting held at a Buddhist pagoda, denouncing the government's decision to decline the Buddhist community's appeal to hand over the mainintence of the temple to a Buddhist management. This news entitled 'Burman Buddhist Indignant at Transfer of Management to Hindu Mohant' was published in the *Maha Bodhi* (1937, 123); and almost three decades after Okakura's visit to Bodh Gaya, in 1902. From Surendranath Tagore's reminiscences of their visit to Bodh Gaya, we come to know that inspite of sincere wishes and efforts, Okakura's endeavour to set up a colony of Buddhist devotees at Bodh Gaya, did not materialize. The Mohant helplessly informed them that the British District Officer would not allow 'any transfer of land to an Asiatic alien'. Surendranath Tagore's concluding observation in this regard deserves remembering: 'So it was good-bye to Okakura's dream of high artistic collective worship, worthy of the Bodh Gaya shrine.'[175]

Shitoku Hori, the first international student of Santiniketan, was a Buddhist monk. He came to India in 1902; along with Okakura Tenshin. From the biographical notes given by Kazuo Azuma in his translation of Hori's diary entitled, *Shitoku Horir Dinoponji,* it has been explicitly mentioned that Hori's prime interest was his involvement with the revivalist movement in Buddhism. This led him to visit Bengal and other parts of India. During the period Hori stayed in Santiniketan, he took the task of learning Sanskrit language, and pursued his quest regarding Buddhism, and the revival of the religion.[176] The translation of Hori's diary also mentions of his visit to Bodh Gaya, and his stay at Tagore's ashram-school, where he started learning Sanskrit. He also made a copy of the Sanskrit text 'Amarkosh'.[177] Tagore's interest in Buddhism is well known, there are quite a few documents, stored in the Rabindra Bhavana Archives, Santiniketan, which are a testimony to this fact. There was a lively contact between Visva-Bharati of Tagore's time, and the various Buddhist organizations of Japan.[178] Tagore's epistolary exchanges with his friend Jagadish Chandra Bose, speak of their ambitious project of sending Hori to Japan and China, and to make copy of Sanskrit texts, that had been preserved in temples there:

> My plan is that at first we have to find out a student proficient in Sanskrit and in English language. He has to visit the Asiatic Society and to learn the scripts of Tibet. Then, the boy will accompany Hori to China and Japan. There, they will visit the monasteries, and will devote themselves in copying the ancient manuscripts (Bangla and Sanskrit), which have been stored there. We have to bear their expenses. I hope Hori will take interest in this work. Also, we have to develop our acquaintance with eminent persons of both China and Japan.[179]

However, this grand project to copy ancient texts from Japan and China did not materialize. This is owing to the fact that Shitoku Hori could not to stay in India for a long duration of time. From the biographical note provided by Azuma, in his translation entitled, *Shitoku Horir Dinoponji*, we learn that Hori found it difficult to accommodate with the climate of Bengal. He finally left Santiniketan on 24 January 1903.[180]

Two other Japanese scholars, who spent a considerable time in studying Buddhist texts in India, during the early twentieth century, are Ryukan Kimura and Tsusho Byodo. Ryukan Kimura has remembered his visit to Kolkata (then Calcutta), while recollecting his memories about Rash Behari in the article 'My Memories about the Late Rashbehari Bose', included in the book entitled *Rashbehari Bose his Struggle for India's Independence*. From this source, we come to learn that in 1907, Kimura first came to India. As a resident student to study Buddhism, he started staying at Chittagong, as during that time, Chittagong was the sole center for studying the Southern Buddhism (Hinayana). During his stay at Chittagong, he started learning Pali and Sanskrit. From Chittagong, Kimura came to Kolkata, and took admission in the Sanskrit College, where he continued his study on various subjects of ancient culture, under the guidance of Indian scholars.[181] Kimura in his recollection of

Rash Behari Bose has also mentioned that following a short break, he once again came to India in 1917, for continuing further studies in Indian philosophy. This time, he received guidance from H.P. Shastri. In 1918, Sir Asutosh Mukherjee, the then Vice-Chancellor of Calcutta University, appointed him as a lecturer. R. Kimura continued his service as a lecturer for about 15 years, giving lectures on subjects relating to Buddhist philosophy and history.[182] Kimura received encouragement from Sir Asutosh Mukherjee to write a whole book on the history of Indian Buddhism, as it has been mentioned in the preface of his book entitled, *A Historical Study of the Terms Hinayana and Mahayana Buddhism.* The book was published by Calcutta University in 1927. It is dedicated to the memory of Late Sir Asutosh Mukherjee. Following is an excerpt from the preface of the book:

> Since my appointment as a Post Graduate teacher in the Departments of Arts of the Calcutta University, it has been my intention to write a proper history of Indian Buddhism from the time of its founder up to the Pala dynasty, or more properly speaking, up to the Muhammadan conquest of Eastern India and also a history of Buddhist philosophy bearing on the original and developed forms of Buddhism. The genius of the late Sir Asutosh, the then Vice-Chancellor and the President of the Post Graduate Council of the University, was not slow to perceive the bright prospects of a protracted study and research on the chosen subject.[183]

The preface of his book entitled, A *Historical Study of the Terms Hinayana and Mahayana and the Origin of Mahayayana Buddhism*, also contains a brief description of his research arena, which includes the following subheadings:

What is Buddhism?
Shifting of the centres of Buddhism
Early history of the original Buddhist schools
Historical discussion on Buddhalogy
Original and developed Buddhism in charts

It has also been stated that his research on the history of Buddhism, was first published in the journals of Calcutta University (vol. 4). It was also published in the *Sir Asutosh Commemoration* journal (vol. I, part 2). The book is divided into two parts; the first part is mainly devoted to a full discussion of the terms 'Hinayana' and 'Mahayana' points of view. In the second part, the author has discussed the different applications of the terms 'Hinayana', and 'Mahayana', and also has narrated the history of the making of the Mahayana Buddhism.[184] Professor Kimura has also expressed thanks to his colleague Babu Sailendranath Mitra, for assisting him to translate some Pali passages, which he has cited in his books. The preface of his book dates 31 March 1927.[185]

Tsusho Byodho, scholar of Sanskrit and Buddhist literature, visited Santiniketan, during the 1930s. Professor Kazuo Azuma in his biographical study of Byodho, included in his book *Ujjal Surjo*, has translated a portion of Professor Byodho's reminiscence, describing the beginning of his research tenure in Santiniketan. Following is the excerpt from Professor Azuma's book entitled, *Ujjal Surjo*:

> In 1933, I boarded the ship Harunamaru of the Nihon-Yusen-Shipping company and left the port-city Yokohama. From Singapore, I boarded another ship named Tottori-Maru, and after crossing Penang and Rangoon, I finally reached the Khidirpur port of Kolkata. After reaching Kolkata, I sent my application along with the certificate of Tokyo University, and a letter from my mentor, Professor Takakusur. During my stay in Kolkata, I visited the Indian Museum. I got the reply from Visva-Bharati very soon. The reply from Visva-Bharati, welcomed me. I was told that Professor Bidusekhar Bhattacharya would personally assist me to continue my research. I was also given the permission to continue my research in my preferred area, i.e. Sanskrit Rhetoric.[186]

Kazuo Azuma's article entitled, 'Rabindranath O Rahul Sannidhe Bharattottobid Byodo', gives an account of Professor Byodo's research tenure in Santiniketan. Everyday, he used to attend Professor Shastri's lectures on Sanskrit Almkara (grammar). His tenure ended after the summer break in 1934, following which he returned to Japan.

We have earlier mentioned the reconstruction works of Buddhist sites, which started with the beginning of twentieth century. One such reconstruction work, that drew Japanese experts, and turned to be a joint venture of Japan and the Buddhist associations of the British India, was the rebuilding of the temple of Sarnath

(Mulagandhakuti Vihara). In 1932, the Mahabodhi Society of India initiated the reconstruction work at Sarnath; and commissioned Kosetsu Nousu, a Japanese painter, to portray the walls of the newly built temple at Sarnath. Zank Dinah in her article entitled, 'Paintings the Life of Buddha in Sarnath' has observed that the main donation for this reconstruction work came from Japanese sponsorers, such as the *Nichiren-shu, Jodoshin-shu* and the *Nippon Ginko* (Central Bank of Japan). Needless to say, this reconstruction work being headed by Japanese and Indian organizations, should be looked upon as an integral part of the Buddhist movement, that took an interesting form in the early twentieth century, as we have so far been discussing in this chapter. Interestingly, the story of this reconstruction work at Sarnath was described in detail in articles, published in *The Maha Bodhi*, the journals of the Maha Bodhi Society of India of the 1930s. Devapriya Valisingha delivered a welcome address note on the occasion of the inauguration of the frescoes at Sarnath, held on 18 May 1936. The lecture has been published in the journal *The Maha Bodhi*, (vol. 44, 1936). Devapriya Valisingha, in his welcome speech, thanked Mr. Yonezawa, the Consul General of Japan, who attended the inauguration ceremony, and also expressed his thanks to Mr. Kosetsu Nosu, and his assistant Mr. S. Kawai, for the stupendous work, which they carried out for three-and-a-half years, depicting the frescoes on the wall of the temple at Sarnath. He also expressed his firm belief that the beautiful frescoes that were set open on that day would further increase the bond of friendship between Japan and India.[187] Mr. Nousu, in his speech, thanked heartily to those who had helped them to complete the work. He also expressed his firm belief that the frescoes would help people to know about Lord Buddha's life, and would strengthen the friendship between India and Japan.[188] Zank Dinah, whose article we have already referred to, has rightly pointed that at first, the Japanese involvement in this preservation of a heritage structure, was not favourably taken by the Indian public. However, Dinah has pointed out that 'during Nosu's working period in India, these public reservations changed and inter-national newspapers described Sarnath, as a role model of Japanese Indian collaboration and friendship'. Further, Dinah is of the view that the Bengali intellectuals including Tagore, and the Government Art School in Kolkata, also played a significant part in creating a favourable evaluation of Nosu's work.[189] It would not be irrelevant to cite the news of the farewell ceremony of Nosu, and S. Kawaii, which was also published in the news section of the same journal, i.e. *The Maha Bodhi* (vol. 44, 1936). On 13 September 1936, just before the departure of Nousu and Kawai, a farewell party was organized jointly by the Mahabodhi Society, and the International University Association, at the Maha Bodhi Society Hall. As mentioned in the report, the programme was attended by many distinguished persons of Kolkata.[190]

It must be remembered that the involvement of Japanese artists in restoring a heritage structure of India took place at a time, when the Japanese ideology of uniting races of Asia, had already lost all its previous impacts. In the introduction of this chapter, and also in the previous chapters, we have already discussed how Japan's aggressive militarism created disillusionment among the educated people of Bengal, and in other parts of India. In this context, it would be apt referring to the strong criticism of Japanese aggression on China, which was published in the same Maha Bodhi Society's journal, the journal that had earlier celebrated and published the news of Nousu's involvement in restoring and beautifying the temple of Sarnath. The 45th volume of the *Maha Bodhi* brought out news on Japan's war against China. This clearly shows that Japan's aggressive foreign policies created a strong disapproval in all quarters. This news on the course of the war denounced Japan's invasion of China and described the war as a 'result of a campaign of hate', and had expressed sympathy for the aggrieved party, the Chinese, whose territories were invaded.[191] The case of Japanese artists' involvement in India, during the war time, and its acceptance among Indian multitude, leads us to ponder over a subject, we have mentioned in the introduction of this chapter. Once again, we can remember of T.R. Sareen's remark that though during the 1930s, politically Japan remained alienated from the rest of Asian races; there remained a steady contact between the artists of Bengal and Japan. We have also mentioned of many documents stored in the Rabindra Bhavana Archives, which also testify how there was a sustained contact between Tagore's Santiniketan, and the different cultural institutes of Japan. Even when the Japanese Pan-Asian ideology of forging an alliance of Asian races had lost its former reception among colonized races of Asia, the attractiveness of her unique culture, did not wither away. The destructiveness of Second World War could not also obliterate it. Among several correspondences between Visva-Bharati and different cultural bodies of Japan, that have been preserved in the Rabindra Bhavana Archives, I would like to refer to a letter written by Rathindranath Tagore to Professor Kizow Inazu, of Tanagawa University. The letter was written in 1945, the year the war ended. It can illumine the fact that the cultural linkage between Japan and Bengal did not wither away following the turmoils of the Second World War, and the alteration of global politics, which occurred after the Japanese army unconditionally surrendered to the Allied Force in 1945. In reply to Professor Inazu's letter, Rathindranath Tagore has expressed that he has been deeply touched by Professor Inazu's endeavour to prepare a translation of Debendranth Tagore's autobiography into Japanese. According to Rathindranath Tagore, the choice of Professor Inazu's book shows a 'genuine interest in promoting cultural exchange between Japan and India'.[192] Rathindranath in his reply, has fondly remembered the time, when Japanese artists like Katsuta and Taikan used to stay at their Jorasanko residence in Kolkata, also, has recollected how during their student life, the news of Japanese victory against the Russian, was a glorifying one for Asians. Though not connected with Visva-Bharati, as Rathindranath at that time was living a retired life in Dehra Dun, Rathindranath in his letter has welcomed Professor Inazu's proposal of writing a book on Tagore.

Thus, coming to the end of this chapter, we can come to the conclusion that reception of Japanese politics and culture, on the part of the intelligentsia of Bengal, though having some shared spaces, were not identical to each other. It is true that the ideology of Japanese leadership in uniting colonized races of Asia, kindled our interest in variegated elements of Japanese culture. However, it would be another oversimplification to hold that the ebb and flow of cultural movements were solely controlled by the role Japan played in the global politics, during that period.

NOTES

1. An entry on Kosetsu Nosu, included in the webpage of *Mukul Dey Archives*, contains a reproduction *Our Magazine*, vol. 1, no. 4 (December 1932). From this document, we learn that a reception to welcome Mr. Nosu, and his assistant, was organized by Mr. Hara, the then Consul of Japan, at the Nippon Club, 225, Lower Circular Road, on 12 December 1932. The reception party was attended by prominent persons of Calcutta.
2. There are indeed quite a few relevant documents stored in the Rabindra Bhavana Archives (Correspondence File 176). Among these, one that deserves mention, is a letter written by Setsuchi Aoki, the General Secretary of *Kokusai Bunka Shinoka* (The Society for the International Cultural Relation), Maruniuchi, Tokyo, in which the writer mentioned that the organization had sent in a separate cover, a book entitled *Japanese Woodblock Printing*, by Hiroshi Yoshida. The date of the letter, as mentioned in the document is 1 July 1939, the time, when the Pacific War was already continuing.
3. Anonymous, 'Indo-Japanese Painting', *Rupam* (10) (April 1922), *https://archive.org/* (accessed on 15 July 2014).
4. Abanindranath Tagore, *Jorasankor Dhare* (Kolkata: Visva Bharati, 1418 BS, 2011), p. 137.
5. Panchanan Mandal, *Bharatsilpi Nandalal*, vol. 4. (Santiniketan: Rar-Gabeshona Parshod, 1982), p. 178.
6. Kazuo Azuma, *Japan O Rabindranath: Satoborsher Binimoy* (Kolkata: N.E Publishers, 2004), p. 66.
7. Panchanan Mandal, *Bharatsilpi Nandalal*, vol. 1 , p. 137.
8. Kazuo Azuma, *Japan O Rabindranath: Satoborsher Binimoy* , p. 66.
9. Protima Devi, *Smriti Chitro* (Kolkata: Signet Press, 1359 BS, 1952), p. 58.
10. Krishna Dutta & Andrew Robinson, *Selected Letters of Rabindranath Tagore*, p. 176.
11. qtd. in Ipsita Chanda, *Reception of the Received* (Kolkata: Jadavpur University, 2006), p. 12.
12. Rabindranath Tagore, *Talks in Japan*, ed. Supriya Roy (Kolkata: Shizen, 2014), p. 14.
13. Azuma, *Japan O Rabindranath*, p. 18.
14. Supriya Roy, *Makers of a Mission 1901-41* (Santiniketan: Rabindra Bhavana, 2001), p. 1.
15. Tagore, *Japan Jatri*, p. 74.

16. Surendranath Tagore's reminiscences of Okakura, included in Dinkar Kowshik's biography entitled *Okakura*, p. 93.
17. Kazuo Azuma, tr., *Shitoku Horir Dinoponji*, p. 13.
18. Ibid., p. 71.
19. Kazuo Azuma, *Japan O Rabindranath: Satoborsher Binimoy*, p. 42.
20. Benode Behari Mukherjee, 'E.B. Havell', *Visva Bharati Quarterly*, 25.3 & 4, (1960), p. 70.
21. Michiaki Kawakita. *Modern Japanese Painting: The Force of the Tradition*, (Tokyo: Toto Bunka Company, 1957), https://archive.org/ (accessed on 10 February 2014), p. 66.
22. Satyajit. Chowdhury, 'Okakura Tenshin O Abanindranath', *Visva-Bharati Patrika*, Kartick (1384 BS, 1977), rpt. in *Visva Bharati Patrika: Nirbachito Probondho Sangraho (1942-2006)*, ed., Amitrosudhan Bhattacharya, (Kolkata: Visva-Bharati, 2007), p. 259.
23. Okakura, *Ideals of the East*, p. 126.
24. Ibid., p. 137.
25. Benode Behari Mukherjee, 'Havell', p. 69.
26. Sumit Sarkar, *Modern Times: India 1880s to 1950s* (New Delhi: Permanent Black, 2015), pp. 406-9.
27. Ibid., p. 412.
28. Abanindranath Tagore, 'E.B. Havell', *Abanindra Rachanaboli*, vol. 9, (Kolkata: Prakash Bhavan, 2011), p. 450.
29. Margaret Richardson, 'Understanding the Importance of Eclecticism: K.G. Subramanyan and Twentieth-Century Indian Art', *Southeast Review of Asian Studies*, vol. 29 (2007), http:// *www.highbeam.com*, (accessed on 18 August 2015).
30. Abanindranath Tagore, *Jorasankor Dhare*, p. 157.
31. Benode Behari Mukherjee, 'Abanindranather Chobi', *Visva Bharati Patrika*, Kartick-Choitro (1383 BS, 1976), p. 292.
32. Benode Behari Mukherjee, 'Introduction', *Abanindranath Tagore: His Early Work* (Kolkata: Indian Museum, 2006), p. 18.
33. Ibid., p. 17.
34. A portion from his letter written to Havell, dated, 2 November 1911, included in the Abanindra Sankha of the magazine *Baishaki*, can be referred to in this context. Following is the excerpt from the letter: 'Many thanks for your valuable book, I shall keep it always as a valued present from my 'Guru'.
35. Rani Chanda, *Ghorowa* (Kolkata: Visva-Bharati [1417 BS, 2007]), p. 32.
36. Panchanan Mandal, *Bharatsilpi Nandalal*, part I, p. 65.

37. Rani Chanda, *Ghorowa*, p. 26.
38. Nivedita, 'Introduction', *Ideals of the East*, p. 3.
39. Sister Nivedita, 'India the Mother', *Selected Essays of Sister Nivedita* (Madras: Ganesh, 1911), http://archive.org, (12 July 2013), p. 1.
40. Abanindranath Tagore, 'Okakura: Obitury', *Bharati*, Kartick 1320 BS (1913), p. 103.
41. R. Siva Kumar, 'Intra-Asian Transactions in Art (India and Japan Some Preliminary Thoughts)', *Nandan*, vol. XXVI, 2006, p. 49-68.
42. Ramyansyu Sekhar Das, *Nandalal Bose and Indian Painting* (Kolkata: Tower Publishers, 1958), p. 15.
43. Okakura *Ideals of the East*, p. 136.
44. Ibid.
45. Ibid.
46. Abanindranath Tagore, *Jorasankor Dhare* (Kolkata: Visva Bharati, 1418 BS, 2011), p. 163.
47. Satyajit Chowdhury, 'Okakura Tenshin O Abanindranath', *Visva Bharati Patrika: Nirbachito Probondho Sangraho (1942-2006)*, ed. Amitrosudhan Bhattacharya (Kolkata: Visva-Bharati, 2007), p. 272.
48. Ibid., p. 271.
49. qtd. in, R. Siva Kumar, 'Abanindranath: From Cultural Nationlism to Modernism', *Nandan*, vol. XVI, 1996, p. 51.
50. T.G. Thakurta, *Monuments, Objects, Histories* (New York: Columbia University Press, 2004), p. 161.
51. Satyajit Chowdhury, 'Abanindranath: Nandonik Nibondhomala', *Gabeshanar Rakampher* (Kolkata: Karigor, 2014), p. 126.
52. Abanindranath Tagore, 'Letter to Krishna Deb Burman', *Nandan*, December 1986, p. 22.
53. R. Siva Kumar, 'Abanindranath: From Cultural Nationalism to Modernism', p. 51.
54. Ibid., p. 66.
55. Rabindranath Tagore, 'Art and Tradition', *Rabindranath Tagore: Philosophy of Education and Painting*, ed. Devi Prasad (New Delhi: National Book Trust, 2008), p. 106.
56. Abanindranath Tagore, *Jorasankor Dhare*, p. 134.
57. Benode Behari Mukherjee, 'Abanindranath', *Paschimbongo: Abanindra Sankha* (1995), p. 31.
58. Panchanan Mandal, 'Bharatsilpe Nabojuger Vumikay Abanindranath', *Visva-Bharati Patrika*, Kartick-Choitro (1383 BS, 1976), p. 24.
59. Chanda Rani, *Silpoguru Abanindranath* (Kolkata: Visva-Bharati, 1406 BS, 1999), p. 99.

60. Jogen Chowdhury, 'An interview on Abanindranath's paintings', ed. Agnimitra Ghosh, Paschimbongo: Abanindra Sankha (1402 BS, 1995), p. 95.
61. Panchanan Mandal, *Bharatsilpi Nandalal*, vol. 4, p. 640.
62. Abanindranath Tagore, *Jorasankor Dhare*, p. 130.
63. Mukulchandra Dey, *Amar Kotha* (Kolkata: Visva Bharati, 1995), p. 77.
64. Kamal Sarkar, *Rupodokho Gaganendranath* (Kolkata: Rabindra Bharati Society, 1986), p. 11.
65. Kishna Chaitanya, *History of Indian Painting: Modern Period* (New Delhi: Abhinav Publication, 1994), http://google Book Search, (Accessed on 20 October 2015), p. 194.
66. Ibid., p. 194.
67. Kamal Sarkar, *Rupodokho Gaganendranath* (Kolkata: Rabindra Bharati Society, 1986), p. 16.
68. Chintamoni Kar, 'Introduction', in *Souvenir on Gaganendranath Tagore*, Kolkata: Academy of Fine Arts, 1957, p. 10.
69. Benode Behari Mukherjee, The Art of Gaganendranath Tagore', *Visva-Bharati Quarterly*, May-July (1949), p. 6.
70. Benode Behari Mukherjee, 'The Art of Gaganendranath Tagore', *Visva-Bharati Quarterly*, May-July 1949, http:// digital library india (Accessed on 20 October 2015), p. 7.
71. Dinkar Kowshik, *Nandalal Bose: The Doyen of Indian Art* (New Delhi: National Book Trust, 2001), p. 14.
72. Nandalal Bose, *Bharatsilpi Nandalal*, vol. III, p. 3.
73. Ibid.
74. Mukul Dey in his letter has called him 'a millionaire', who used to spend prodigally for the promotion of art. He was also Taikan's chief patron. For details see, *Mukulchandra Dey: Japan Theke Jorasanko*, ed. Satyasri, Kolkata: New Age, 2005, p. 31.
75. Satyasri Ukil, ed., *Mukulchandra Dey: Japan Theke Jorasanko*, Kolkata: New Age, 2005, p. 32.
76. Mukul Dey, *Amar Kotha*, p. 58.
77. Ibid.
78. Arai Kampo, *Bharat Bhromon Dinopanji*, tr. Kazuo Azuma (Kolkata, Rabindrabharati University, 1993), p. 15. Pratima Devi was Rabindranath Tagore's grand-daughter.
79. Ibid., pp. 15-21.
80. Dey, *Japan Theke Jorasanko*, p. 98.
81. Dey, *My Pilgrimages to Ajanta and Bagh* (London: Thornton Butterworth, 1925), p. 44. At that time Dey had little preparation for visiting Ajanta,

which was under the jurisdiction of the Nizam government. Thus, his earlier association with Kampo Arai enabled him to get a suitable lodging and also an opportunity to work with the Japanese painters, who stayed there to copy the frescoes.

82. Ibid., p. 47.
83. Inaga Shigemi, 'The Interaction of Bengali and Japanese Artistic Milieus in the First Half of the Twentieth Century (1901-45): Rabindranath Tagore, Arai Kampo and Nandalal Bose', *Japan Review*, 2009 (Accessed on 26 May 2015), p. 164.
84. Abanindranath Tagore, *Jorasankor Dhare*, p. 132.
85. Ibid., p. 133.
86. Kamal Sarkar, *Rupodokho Gaganendranath*, pp. 60-2.
87. Ibid., p. 62.
88. Anonymous 'Indo-Japanese Painting', *Rupam* (10) (April 1922), pp. 39-42, https://archive.org/ (Accessed on 15 July 2014), p. 41.
89. Ibid.
90. Shigemi, 'The Interaction of Bengali and Japanese Artistic Milieus in the First Half of the Twentieth Century (1901-45), p. 152.
91. Harish Trivedi, 'Translating Culture vs Cultural Translation', *Translation and Culture: Indian Perspective*, ed. G.J.V. Prasad (New Delhi: Pencraft International, 2010), p. 191.
92. Madhusudhan Mukhopadhyay, *Jepan* , pp. 59-60.
93. Ibid., p. 66.
94. Ibid., p. 142.
95. Ibid., p. 230.
96. Priyambada Devi, 'Cha Grontho', *Manashi*, 1321(1914), rpt. in *Sekaler Bangla Samoyikpotre Japan*, ed. Subrata Kumar Das (Dhaka: Nabajuga Prokashoni, 2012), p. 147.
97. Okakura, *The Book of Tea*, p. 3.
98. Priyambadi Devi, 'Cha Grontho', p. 146.
99. Okakura, *The Book of Tea*, p. 1.
100. Dinkar Kowshik, *Okakura*, pp. 103-17.
101. Ibid., p. 110.
102. Hemlata Devi, 'Tibbot Rajye Tinbochor', *Prabasi*, Poush (1323 BS, 1916), p. 253.
103. Ekai Kawaguchi, *Three Years in Tibet* (Benares & London: Theosophical Publishing Society, 1909), http://archive.org , (Accessed on 13 April 2012), p. 37.
104. Hemlata Devi, 'Tibbot Rajye Tinbochor', p. 253.
105. Kawaguchi, *Three Years in Tibet*, p. 41.

106. Hemlata Devi, 'Tibbot Rajye Tinbochor', *Prabasi*, Magh 1323 BS, p. 386.
107. Ibid., p. 52.
108. Kawaguchi, *Three Years in Tibet*, p. 161.
109. Tagore, *Talks in Japan*, p. 117.
110. Ibid.
111. Tagore, *Japan Jatri*, p. 74.
112. Shakuntala Rao Sastri, *A Visit to Japan by Rabindranath Tagore*, p. 69.
113. With reference to the syllabic pattern of 'Haiku', it should be remembered that modern English translations of 'Haiku' often show disregard for this 5-7-5 syllabic pattern. In this context, a portion from Elin Sutiiste's essay entitled 'A Crow On A Bare Branch: A Comparison Of Matsuo Basho's Haiku 'Kare Eda Ni' and its English Translations', needs citing: Still not all the features of the original Japanese 'haiku' are considered necessary for the 'western', or translated 'haiku'. For example, where as original 'haikus' composed in the West, seem to follow the requirement of 17 syllables rather keenly, the translations, often disregard the exact syllables .
114. Matsuo Basho: Frog Haiku, http://www.bopsecrets.org.
115. Sujit Kumar Mandal, ed., *Bideshi Fuler Gucho* (Kolkata: Papyrus, 2011), p. 519.
116. Tagore, *Japan Jatri*, p. 75.
117. Sastri, p. 70.
118. Tagore, *Japan Jatri*, p. 144.
119. *Japan Jatri*, p. 75.
120. Sastri, p. 70.
121. Rabindranath Tagore, 'To The Indian Community in Japan', April 1925, rpt. in *Japan Jatri*, (Kolkata: Visva Bharati, 2007), p. 124.
122. *Japan Jatri*, p. 75.
123. Sastri, p. 71.
124. Rpt. in Rabindranath Tagore's *Japan Jatri*, p. 145.
125. Rabindranath Tagore, *Sfulingo* (Kolkata: Visva Bharati, 1397 BS, 1992), p. 23.
126. Uma Das Gupta, 'A Cultural Nationalism', *Visva-Bharati Quarterly*, 49, 1-4, May 1983-April 1984, p. 376.
127. Tagore Letters to Jagadish Chandra B., *Dui Bondhur Chithi* (Kolkata: Monfakira, 2008), p. 30.
128. Supriya Roy, *Makers of a Mission*, p. 58.
129. Records of the State Archives, Govt. of West Bengal, Home Political,

History of Agitation against Bengal Partition, Calcutta, dated the 25 January 1906, F.N. 25/1906, p. 9.

130. Pulin Behari Das, *Amar Jiban Kahini* (Kolkata: Anushilan Samity, 1987), p. 51.
131. Ibid., p. 111.
132. Ibid., p. 112.
133. Ibid.
134. Tagore, *Chelebela* (Kolkata: Visva-Bharati, 1396 BS, 1986), pp. 722-23.
135. Sano Jinnosuke apart from instructing *jujutsu* to the boys of Santiniketan, also, took regular classes on Japanese language to the students. According to Nabin Panda, a Japanese language expert, and the author of the essay 'Tagore and Japanese Language: From the Writings of Sano Jinnosuke', Sano was invited to India, both as an expert of Japanese language and *jujutsu*. The writer in this essay has referred to old texts written by Sano Junosuke on his experience in India— *Tagore Sensei to jibun (Tagore Sensei and I) &Indo oyobi Indojin (India and its people)*.
136. Supriya Roy, *Makers of a Mission 1901-41* (Santiniketan: Rabindra Bhavana, 2001), p. 58.
137. qtd. Supriya Roy, *Makers of a Mission*, p. 58.
138. *Budo: The Martial Ways of Japan* (Tokyo: Nippon Budokan Foundation, 2009), p. 126.
139. Ibid., p. 40.
140. Records of the National Archives, Govt. of India, Foreign and Political Department, Publication of a book entitled *India and Indians by One J. Sano, a Japanese Professor of Ju-jutsu*, F.N.21/1918.3.
141. Ibid., p. 11.
142. Kazuo Azuma , *Ujjal Surjo* (Kolkata: Subarnarekha, 1996), p. 3.
143. Ibid., p. 4.
144. Ibid., *Ujjal Surjo* , p. 6.
145. Ibid., p. 10.
146. Krishna Dutta & Andrew Robinson, *Selected Letters of Rabindranath Tagore* (New Delhi: Cambridge University Press, 2005), p. 400.
147. Rabindranath Tagore, 'My School', *Lectures & Addresses by Rabindranath Tagore* (Delhi: Macmillan, 2001), p. 47.
148. Ibid.
149. qtd. in Uma Das Gupta, *Santiniketan and Sriniketan* (Kolkata: Visva-Bharati, October 2009), p. 13.
150. Sastri, *A Visit to Japan by Rabindranath Tagore*, p. 80.
151. Panchanan Mandal, *Bharatsilpi Nandalal*, 2nd vol., p. 245.
152. Ibid., p. 245.

153. Sastri, *A Visit to Japan by Rabindranath Tagore*, p. 79.
154. Ibid., pp. 72-3.
155. Arunenduv Bandyopadhyay, 'Santiniketan-Sthapothorup, Nirmito Paribesh Ebong Rabindranath', *Visva-Bharati Patrika* Kartick-Poush (1403 BS, 1996), pp. 103-4.
156. Kazuo Azuma, *Shitoku Horir Dinoponji*, p. 65.
157. Roy, *Makers of a Mission*, p. 38.
158. Rabindra Bhavana Archives, Santiniketan, S. Kusumoto, *A Letter to Rabindranath Tagore*, dated 31 March 1931, F.N. 176.1.21.
159. Mohanlal Gangopadhyay, *Dakhiner Baranda* (Kolkata: Visva-Bharati, 1414 BS, 2007), p. 99.
160. Ibid., p. 98.
161. Arunendu Bandyopadhyay, 'Stapothorup, Nirmito Poribesh Ebong Rabindranath', *Bharati*, Kartick-Poush 1403 BS (1996), p. 104.
162. Amita Sen, *Ananda Sarvokaje* (Kolkata: Tagore Reserch Institute, Rabindra Charcha Bhavan, March 1983), p. 120.
163. Zank Dinah, 'Painting the Life of Buddha: Trans-culturality, Patronage and Artist's vision', http://www.academia.edu, (Accessed on 27 December 2015), pp. 2-3.
164. Okakura, *Ideals of the East*, p. 10.
165. Tagore, 'Buddhadeva', *Visva-Bharati Quarterly*, 22.3 (1956-7), p. 172.
166. Ekai Kawaguchi, *Three Years in Tibet*, pp. 11-14.
167. Ibid., 68-72.
168. Ekai Kawaguchi, *Three Years in Tibet*, p. 303.
169. Ibid., p. 315.
170. Records of the National Archives, Govt. of India, *Letters from his Holiness the Dalai Lama to Kawaguchi*, Foreign and Political Department, F.N. 10/1918, p. 6.
171. Ekai Kawaguchi, *Three Years in Tibet*, p. 411.
172. Ibid., p. 53.
173. Idıd., p. 415.
174. Surendranath Tagore, 'Kakuzu Okakura', *Visva-Bharati Quarterly*, 25.3 & 4 (1960), http://digital library of India, (25 December 2013), p. 53.
175. Ibid., p. 54.
176. Kazuo Azuma, trans, *Shitoko Horir Dinoponji* (Kolkata:Visva-Bharati. 1996), p. 15.
177. Ibid., pp. 36-8.
178. There are infact quite a few documents that deserve mention in this context. Among these, I would like to mention of a letter, written by Rabindranath Tagore to Dr. Takakusu, dated 31 August 1929, included

in the Rabindra Bhavana Archives (File-Eng.176/1). Tagore in his letter has requeseted Dr. Takakusu to make a purchase of books relating to Buddhism and Japanese Arts & Literature. He has also requested Dr. Takakusu to make arrangements for donating a complete set of Chinese Tripitakas, edited by Professot Takakusu, which at that time could not be purchased, due to lack of funds.

179. Jagadish Chandra Bose, 'Letters to Rabindranath Tagore', *Dui Bondhur Chithi Parasparik O Paramparik* (Kolkata: Monfakira, 2008), p. 112.
180. Kazuo Azuma, trans., *Shitoko Horir Dinoponji*, p. 17.
181. Nikki (Ryukan) Kimura, 'My Memory about the Late Rash Behari Bose', *Rash Behari Bose: His Struggle for India's Independence*, ed. Radhanath Rath (Kolkata: Biplabi Mahanayak Rash Behari Bose Smarok Samity, 1963), p. 39.
182. Ibid., p. 40.
183. Nikki Kimura, 'Preface', *A Historical Study of the Terms Hinayana and Mahayana Buddhism* (Kolkata: Calcutta University, 1927), p. vii.
184. Ibid., p. vii.
185. Ibid., p. xi.
186. Kazuo Azuma, *Ujjal Surjo* (Kolkata: Subarnarekha, 1996), pp. 22-3.
187. 'Mulagandhakuti Frescoes Declared Open', *The Maha Bodhi*, 44 (1936), pp. 273-6.
188. Ibid., p. 279.
189. Zank Dinah, 'Painting the Life of Buddha: Trans-Culturality, Patronage and Artist's Vision', ttp://academia.edu, (Accessed on 27 December 2015), p. 7.
190. 'Farewell Ceremony of Nosu and S. Kawai', *The Maha Bodhi*, 44 (1936), pp. 527-8.
191. 'Japan's War Against China', *The Maha Bodhi*, 45 (1937), pp. 428-9.
192. Rabindra Bhavana Archives, Santiniketan, *A Letter from Rathindranath Tagore to Kizow Inazu of Tanagawa University*, F.N. 176.2.

Conclusion

A one-day seminar on Tagore's association with Japan took place in Jadavpur University in 2011.[1] Apart from Tagore's writings on Japan, the seminar, of which I was a participant, motivated me to explore some other relevant texts, which also shed light upon Bengal's cultural and ideological association with Japan, of the early twentieth century. My association with the subject of my research, i.e. *Reception of Japanese Culture and Politics in Bengal* (1893-1938), began from that time. It is regrettable that though India was one of the few countries to develop bilateral ties with Japan just after the end of the Second World War[2], the relations between India and Japan during the cold-war period became strained, owing to different reasons. The 1990s, with its change in the global scenario, once again saw these two countries, engaging themselves in many diplomatic alliances.[3] Diplomatic heads of both India and Japan, have also visited each other's country, during the last two decades. Is it not a befitting time to look back into the past, and to remember a phase in our cultural history, which is marked by a vibrant exchange and interaction with another Asian nation?

It is indeed sad that many significant aspects of this cross-cultural exchange between Japan and Bengal, of that period have disappeared from public memory. The three chapters of this research entitled, *Reception of Japanese Culture and Politics in Bengal (1893-1938),* have tried to refer to diverse literary materials, such as travelogues on Japan, articles published in different magazines, also archival sources, in order to explore Bengal's response to Japanese culture and politics of that time. It is true that Japan's drastic progress in different fields, following the historical event of Meiji Restoration of 1868, attracted the attention of our national leaders of the early twentieth century. I have tried to explore texts of this period, in which Japan occupies an important place. It is well-known that, Japan's emergence as a modern nation of early twentieth century drew the attention of the Bengali intelligentsia of that period. This finds mention in many other texts also. We can well agree with Sugata Bose, that the 'Swadeshi cultural milieu of the early twentieth century India, despite its interest in rejuvenating indigenous traditions, was not wholly inwardly looking'. Bose mentions the acceptance of the idea of Asian universalism, by the intellectuals of Bengal of that period. A new idea of constructing Asia was brought to India by Tenshin Okakura and Sister Nivedita.[4] In this book, referring to many a writings from Bengal of this period, I have tried to analyse the different response of the Bengali receptor, we notice towards the politics and culture of Japan, of the period mentioned above.

In the first Chapter, I have tried to explore the Bengali travel writer's response to variegated issues of Japanese society, such as the modernization of Japan during this time, the perpetuation of residual culture in Japan during this period, and also gender politics in Japanese society, as viewed by the travellers from Bengal. The first significant aspect to be noted is that the delineation of these issues, give us the idea of a cultural space, which is rapidly changing, and is capable of evoking various and even contrary responses among the viewers. Truly, the Japan, which we encounter in these writings, is a cultural space subjected to rapid social and economic changes. Hence, it is far removed from the colonist's depiction of the Orient, as a fixed space, to be discovered by the travellers. The 45 years of time span, from 1893 to 1938, has also given us a scope to study the reception on the part of the travellers, both horizontally and vertically. This is chiefly because, during the time Vivekananda visited Japan (1893), and the time, when Tagore visited Japan for the last time (1925), Japan had changed considerably. Similarly, we have also noticed how the reception of Japanese culture and politics on the part the visitors, could differ from each other, in accordance with their ideological position, which they had imbibed from their native land.

It is well-known that in many colonial narratives of that period, we come across stereotyped representation of the 'Other'. In some travelogues on Japan authored by Bengali writers also, we can locate how indigenous Japanese customs and practices have been represented according to western perception. As noted earlier, stereotyped representation of Japanese system of communal bathing, or of a Japanese cuisine of raw fish, as uncivilized practices bear testimony to this fact. Needless to say, this kind of a representation on the part of the traveller, which we notice in some cases, may be attributed to a lack of preparedness on the part of the traveller, venturing into a new cultural zone, markedly different from their familiar spaces. However, such stereotyped representation of Japan, according to the western perspective, can only be located in a few cases. Thus, as discussed earlier, more than the hegemonic influence of the West, we can trace in these writings, a reception of another dominant ideology, i.e. the Pan-Asian ideology, which solicited the clustering of all Asian nations. We have seen in the course of the analysis, how from the time of the Russo-Japanese War of 1905, the Pan-Asian ideology that spoke of clustering of Asian nations, under the leadership of Japan, gained confidence among the educated sections of Bengal. Thus, the reliance on Japan as a source of gaining technology and of new knowledge, the keenness to learn about Japan's educational and industrial achievements, as we have seen in the first Chapter, were certainly from this point of view. In the travelogues on Japan, and also in the articles of different magazines, we have tried to locate how the trope of the 'industrialized Japan', finds an important place. Further, the account of the modernization of Japan is, almost in all cases, a sad reminder of the poor condition prevailing in Bengal, and in other parts of colonial India. The depiction of a society, which is disciplined, developed, and is starkly in contrast to that of British India, shows an acceptance of this ideology, which projects Japan as the leader of the East.

A third and more ambivalent position, so far as representation of Japan is concerned, we witness in Tagore's writings on Japan. As mentioned earlier, Tagore seems to be extremely reticent in describing the process of the modernization, which Japan underwent during this time. For Tagore, Japan is 'the child of the ancient East'; a phrase, he coined in his lecture entitled, *India and Japan.*

Both Okakura and Tagore have stressed on Japan's legacy of the culture and civilization of East. It is true that such exaltation of Japan as an Eastern civilization, and rooted in the spiritual glory of a dim past, comes close to the Orientalist's representation of East, as a timeless zone. Needless to say, this can be located in many European narratives of the colonial period. However, to locate Tagore's representation, only within the trope of Orientalism, will be another mistake. We can agree with Bharucha that Tagore was not 'directly implicated in the academic institutionalization of Orientalism'.[5] Also, though Tagore was a bitter critic of nationalism, he did not dismiss modernity altogether, which is another aspect of his ambivalent attitude towards Japan, and also towards Asia. In this context, it would not be irrelevant to remember again that in Tagore's *Nationalism*, there is the admittance of the fact that, East 'has a great deal to learn from Europe' and the endowments of the European enlightenment have been fully acknowledged: 'Above all thing Europe has held high before our minds the banner of liberty of conscience, liberty of thought and action, liberty in the ideals of art and literature.'[6]

To conclude this section, it can be said that the writings on Japan of this time, with its manifold representation of Japan, according to the travel writer's ideological position, form a discourse, in which the writers of Bengal have tried to represent another Asian nation, in varying terms, which is also related to the role of the Empire, and its overpowering impact upon people of Asia.

The ideology of Pan-Asianism, which solicited the unity of Asian nations, and gained an acceptance both in Japan and beyond, should be viewed as an integral part of Japan's expansionist policy of the early twentieth century. This aspect has been discussed in details in the second chapter. The paradoxical nature of this ideology lies in the fact that Japan's hegemonic domination formed the axis of this ideology, despite its advocacy to unite colonized nations of Asia. Further, the idea of the supremacy of Japan, occupies a pivotal position in Okakura's ideology of Asian unity. This has also been examined in this book. With reference to this Japanese version of *Asian unity*, Bengal's response to this politics of Japan, as we have tried to locate, referring to Bangla and English writings of that period, is certainly one of accord and discord.

Japan's military success against a European nation (Russia) in the Russo-Japanese War (1905) kindled the nationalist aspiration of many. In the second chapter of this book entitled, 'Pan-Asianism and Bengal', I have tried to refer to texts like travelogues on Japan, reminiscences, and also Bangla articles published in different magazines, in which this historical event finds a glorious rendition. In this context, we can once again remember how the political significance of this war, has been emphatically mentioned in Hemchandra Kanungoe's book *Banglai Biplab Prachesta*:

> The proposal to partition Bengal was taken in December 1903. However, agitation against the partition of Bengal took its shape by the end of 1904. War between Russia and Japan also broke out on 4 February 1904. The military victory of Japan played an important part in exploding the myth of white men's superiority. It resurrected among us, the hope of freeing our country from colonial rule.[7] (Translation mine)

Another important event of the early twentieth century, which led to a series of exchange of ideas among the Bengali intellectuals, and that of Japan of the early twentieth century, is Okakura Tenshin's visit to Kolkata (known as Calcutta before 2001) in 1902. The overwhelming reception that Okakura received in Bengal during his stay, writings from this part of the country as the Introduction of the book *Ideals of the East* that Nivedita also authored, some other texts that we have cited, may well be taken as a testimony of the hegemony of Okakura's Pan-Asian ideology upon the Bengali literate section. However, Nivedita, who in her early writings expressed similarity with Okakura's belief in the supremacy of Japanese culture, did not take much time to be disillusioned with Okakura's political ideas. Without any hesitation, she denounced Japan's invasion on Korea in her essay 'Japan and Korea'. In the beginning of this concluding chapter, we have mentioned of Sugata Bose's book *The Nation as Mother*. In this book, Bose mentions of Nivedita and Okakura, as the forerunner of a new idea of constructing Asia, which held a significant influence among the literate society of that time. A close study of their writings, as I have attempted in the second chapter of this book, certainly reveals the fact that there existed discordant aspects in their political ideology. Thus, with reference to Bengal's reception of the politics of Japan during the early twentieth century, we can also identify another large group of writings, which seem to challenge this hegemonic domination of Japan over the idea of Pan-Asianism. To sum up this argument, let us once again remember an interview given by Tagore to *The Manchestor Guardian* (20 July 1916), where we come across Tagore's vision of *Asian unity*. Tagore in his interview, categorically pointed out that Japan alone could not stand for the fulfillment of this dream. Only by forging association with 'a free China, Siam, and perhaps, in the ultimate course of things a free India', this grand vision of unifying Asia can be materialized.[8]

The vision of unity of Asia, which we find in the above-mentioned interview of Tagore, puts emphasis on giving equal status and positions to different nations of Asia, some of them were yet to taste the freedom from colonial rule. Needless to say, Tagore's idea of Asian unity was just the opposite of the Japanese ideology of unifying Asia, which desired to substitute a European master by another Asian master. Tagore in his lectures, which he delivered in Japan during his several visits, denounced Japanese imperialism. Also, the fact that his message of pacifism left little impact upon Japanese intellectuals of that time has also been mentioned earlier. From 1910, the year Japan annexed Korea, to 1937, the year of Japanese aggression on China, Japanese government remained busy in asserting its military power over several parts of its neighbouring nation, a fact we have already taken into account. The news of Japanese exploitation of the people of Korea, and other parts of Asia, was known by the educated section of Bengal. We have already referred to a few texts, such as Nivedita's essay 'Korea and Japan', published in the *Modern Review,* also, Jyotindranath Tagore's 'Adhunik Japan', and Sarala Devi's memoir *Jiboner Jhora Pata.* These writings clearly show disillusionment with Japan's political role, during the first three decades of twentieth century. We have also tried to see how the sudden attack of Japan on China in 1937, caused a sharp reaction among Indian nationalists. The fact that the Congress called for a boycott of Japanese goods, following the aggression on China, must be remembered in this connection. Thus during the 1930s, a skepticism about Japan's political role substituted the earlier jubilant acceptance of Japan as the saviour of the East, which had been strong during the first decades of the twentieth century. Again, the beginning of the Second World War, with Japan having declared war against Great Britain, saw the recurrence of the acceptance of Pan-Asian ideal to liberate Asia under the leadership of Japan, among a section of our national leaders. We have already stated that the history of the formation of the I.N.A., under the leadership of Rash Behari Bose, will include a detailed study of numerous documents. We have refrained from bringing out a detailed study of Bengal's war-time response to Japan's politics of that period. Needless to say, this remains beyond the scope of the time span of this book, which restricts to roughly 45 years (1893-1938). However, in the concluding part of the second Chapter, I have tried to locate a few texts, dealing with the I.N.A., and its mission of liberating India from British rule.

In short, Bengal's response to Japanese-Asianism, as we have seen earlier, incorporated both acceptance and negation. It is true that the Pan-Asian ideology turned out to be the hegemonic tool in the hands of Japanese politicians of the early twentieth century. It was closely associated with Japan's empire building process. Yet, it must also be acknowledged that the ideologues of the Pan-Asianism pioneered addressing the issue of Asian unity. The idea of Asian unity did not wither away with Japan's unconditional surrender after the end of the Second World War. We can agree with T.A. Keenleyside that the theme of Asian unity had a lingering effect upon Indian leaders, several years after India attained freedom. The writer, in his essay entitled, 'Nationalist Indian Attitudes Towards Asia', has referred to the Jaipur session of Indian National Congress in 1948, which declared that close cooperation would be developed among Asian nations. According to T.A. Keenleyside, 'Nehru himself was responsible for keeping the Pan-Asian idea alive, during the 1950s'.[9] It must be noted that in comparison to many other Asian nations, India took a considerate attitude towards Japan, after the end of the war. As a testimony to this fact Indian judge Radhabinod Pal's dissenting note at the Tokyo Tribunal, and some documents relating to Pal's role at the tribunal, have already been mentioned.

Just after the end of the Second World War, an effort to give shape to this idea of Asian unity was taken under the leadership of Nehru. In 1947, the Asian Relations Conference took place in New Delhi, the first conference of Asian nations.[10] Nehru in his inaugural speech in the First Asian Relations Conference in New Delhi described the conference as an 'expression of deeper urge of the mind and spirit of Asia which has persisted in spite of the isolationism which grew up during the years of European domination'.[11] From T.R. Sareen's article entitled, 'India and Japan in Historical Perspective', we further learn that Nehru wanted Japan's participation in the Asian Relations Conference. However, this could not happen, due to the change of Japan's status after the end of the war, from a sovereign nation to a nation under the occupation of the Allies.[12] Thus, we can well agree with Ramchandra Guha that 'Nehru's foreign policy was shaped by two central (and interconnected) beliefs: Pan-Asianism and nonalignment.[13]

In June 1952, India entered into a bilateral treaty with Japan; the first bilateral treaty Japan signed with an Asian nation after the end of the Second World War.[14] This treaty should also be viewed as an important step with reference to the concept of Asian solidarity. The concept of Asian solidarity has been addressed at different platforms, by Asian leaders, during the post-war phase. Whereas nationalism was the key ideology that attracted people of different zones of Asia to come together, and to forge a unity based on common heritage, we can hope that in future, Asian nations will be able to give a concrete shape to the ideal of Asian unity, in terms of issues of peace, development and maintaining ecological balance in this region.

Bengal of the early twentieth century was extremely receptive to the art and culture of Japan, an aspect that has been dealt in details in the concluding chapter of this book entitled 'Reception of Japanese Culture in Bengal during the early twentieth century'. We have also seen how the interaction between these two parts of Asia, Bengal and Japan, led to a vibrant exchange of cultures, which encompassed various kinds of cultural items, such as fine arts, physical culture, etc. We have mentioned the Japanese painters, who visited Bengal during this time, and have noted how their association with the painters like Abanindranath Tagore and

Gaganendranath Tagore, led to a new age in the arena of Indian art. It must be noted that presently the Japan Foundation, New Delhi, organizes various Japanese cultural activities all over the country, as its sister organizations take initiatives to popularize Japanese culture in other countries. Also, every year the Japan Foundation organizes the Japanese Language Proficiency Test; in the chief metropolitan cities of India. Recent reviews in Japanese Language Studies have ascertained a steady growth in the Japanese language study in India. With reference to this new trend in the popularization of Japanese language and cultural studies, in the present-day India, it should be remembered that, a cross-section of the Bengali literate society of the early twentieth century, pioneered in taking interest in the unique culture of Japan. We have already referred to Nabin Panda's study of the history of Japanese language teaching in India. Referring to Jinnosuke Sano's *Tagore Sensei to Jibun* (Tagore Sensei and I), and *Indo oyobi Indojin* (India and its people)[15], the two articles, Sano wrote on his experience in teaching *Jujutsu* and Japanese language in Santiniketan, Nabin Panda in his article entitled 'Tagore and Japanese Language: from the writings of Sano Jinnosuke', has rightly illuminated upon the fact that without any government support, Tagore introduced Japanese language teaching in Santiniketan, by employing Jinnosuke Sano, both as a *Jujutsu* expert, and a Japanese language teacher in his school in 1905.[16]

Thus, in the absence of any central body, like the Japan Foundation of today, it was chiefly individual patrons, whose initiative and interest, led to the nurturing of certain Japanese cultural practices in Bengal of that time. As in the study of Bengal's response to the politics of Japan of that time, where we have already located multiple responses, Bengali intellectuals' reception of Japanese art and culture, as we have tried to notice in the third Chapter, was certainly full of diversity, depending upon the receptor's aesthetic ideal. We have seen in this chapter that the contact between Japanese painters, and the painters of the Bengal School, led to the nurturing of different aspects of Japanese aesthetics, depending upon the personal choice and the aesthetic ideal of the receptor. Abanindranath Tagore's interest in the use of wash technique, which he learnt from his association with Japanese painters, has been mentioned in this chapter. His brother, Gaganendranath, attained mastery on the use of brush and Chinese ink that he learnt from the Japanese painters. Also, we have seen that Nandalal Bose's ideals of art teaching, which he introduced in Kala Bhavana, Santiniketan, was derived from the aesthetic vision of Okakura. In Bengal, this phase witnessed a new movement in visual art, in which painters like Abanindranath Tagore and Gaganendranath Tagore, and their students, discarding imitative practice of European art, looked for indigenous expressions in art. Indeed, this is a significant aspect relating to the history of modern Indian art, we have already tried to touch upon. Thus, it is *synthesis of culture*, which can be accepted as one distinctive aspect of this exchange in the arena of art, which involved painters of Bengal and Japan. This blending of culture, as an important aspect of Bengal's receptivity to Japanese culture of the early twentieth century, can also be traced in Tagore's initiative in relocating certain Japanese cultural practices, such as *Jujutsu*, tea-ceremony, and Japanese flower-arrangement, in his school in Santiniketan. We have already discussed in details that Tagore's appreciation for certain Japanese cultural items, led to his employment of Japanese masters in Santiniketan. Once again, we can remember Kintaro Kasahara's role in Santiniketan and how his craftsmanship enabled Tagore to carry out his experiments with Japanese house-designing and in gardening. We have also tried to locate how Tagore's approach towards *Jujutsu*, which for him, was more an educational tool for the development of his students, differed from those belonging to the nationalist circle, like Pulin Behari Das. Pulin Behari Das' chief interest in *Jujutsu* came from the urge to empower the Bengali race, and to wipe out the stigma of being labelled as a non-martial race. Thus, it is the receptor's personal choice, his ideology, and his aesthetic value, which stimulated multiple and variegated response towards Japanese culture in Bengal, during this period.

To conclude, it can be said that one can draw a distinction between Bengal's receptivity towards Japanese culture, and that towards politics of that period, an aspect we have tried to touch upon in the concluding section of the last chapter. By the end of

1930s, as we have seen, Japanese political mission to unify Asia, under its leadership, had lost its earlier significance. With Japan's defeat in the Second World War, Japan's political role as a leading Asian nation, lost its relevance. However, as mentioned earlier, even during the war time, and also beyond, the interaction between artists and cultural activists of these two parts of Asia, was not disrupted. We have mentioned of Kosetsu Nosu's involvement in the reconstruction at Sarnath that took place on the eve of the war. We have also referred to some documents, stored in the Rabindra Bhavana Archives, Santiniketan, which can be taken as a testimony of this derivation. In our times, sponsored by the Japan Foundation, Japanese cultural activities are taking place in all metropolitan cities of India. Recent surveys in Japanese Language Studies have noted a significant growth of Japanese language learners all over India. It can be hoped that the uniqueness of Japanese culture, with its aesthetic appeal, will also attract people of the future generations of this subcontinent.

NOTES

1. Pratyay Banerjee and Anindya Kundu, *Tagore and Japan: Dialogue, Exchange and Encounter* (Kolkata: Synergy, 2016), Introduction, p. vii.
2. Sareen, 'India and Japan in Historical Perspective', p. 49.
3. K.D. Kapur, 'India and Japan Strategic Partnership in the Emerging Global Scenario', in *India and Japan in Search of Global Roles,* ed. Rajaram Panda and Yoo Fukazawa (New Delhi: Promilla & Co. 2007), pp. 53-97.
4. Sugata Bose, *The Nation as Mother and other Visions of Nationhood,* (Gurgaon: Penguin Random House India, 2017), p. 115.
5. Rustom Bharucha, *Another Asia* (Kolkata: Oxford University Press, 2006), p. 72.
6. Tagore, *Nationalism*, p. 28.
7. Kanungoe, *Banglai Biplab Prachesta*, p. 50.
8. Hay, *Asian Ideas of East and West*, p. 67.
9. T.A. Keenleyside, 'Nationalist Indian Attitudes Towards Asia', *Pacific Affairs,* 55.2, Summer, 1982, p. 224, http://www.jstor.org (Accessed on 23 June 2014).
10. Amitava Acharya, 'Asia is not One', *The Journal of Asian Studies,* 69.4,

November 2010, p. 1006, http://www.jstor.org, (Accessed on 23 June 2014).

11. Acharya, 'Asia is Not One', p. 1008.
12. Sareen, 'India and Japan in Historical Perspective', p. 46.
13. Ramchandra Guha, 'Jawaharlal Nehru: A Romantic in Politics', *Makers of Modern Asia* (Cambridge: Harvard University Press, 2014), p. 134.
14. Sareen, 'India and Japan in Historical Perspective', p. 49.
15. Nabin Panda, 'Tagore and Japanese Language: From the Writings of Sano Jinnosuke', *Tagore and Japan: Dialogue, Exchange and Encounter*, ed. Pratyay Banerjee and Anindya Kundu (New Delhi: Synergy Publishers, 2016), pp. 20-1.
16. Ibid., p. 30.

Annexure

Year	Event
1868	Meiji Restoration.
1893	Swami Vivekananda visits Japan.
1902	Tenshin Okakura visits Calcutta.
1905	Russo-Japanese War.
1905	Jinnosuke Sano came to Santiniketan.
1906	Manmatha Nath Ghosh visits Japan.
1906	Sureshchandra Bandyopadhyay visits Japan.
1912	Hariprobha Takeda visits Japan for the first time.
1914	Komagata Maru incident.
1915	Rash Behari Bose reaches Japan.
1915	Singapore Mutiny.
1916	Rabindranath Tagore visits Japan for the first time.
1926	Pan-Asiatic Conference held at Nagasaki in Japan.
1929	Shinzo Takagaki came to Santiniketan as a *Jujutsu* (uniformly used) expert.
1937	Japanese aggression on China begins.
1938	Noguchi-Tagore epistolary debate.

Bibliography

A Tribute to Rabindranath Tagore: Glimpses from Archival Records, Kolkata: Directorate of State Archives, 2011.

Acharya, Amitava, 'Asia is Not One', *The Journal of Asian Studies*, 69, 4 November 2010, http://www.jstor.org (Acceessed on 23 June 2014).

Althusser, Louis, 'Ideology and Ideological State Apparatuses', *Mapping Ideology*, ed. Slovaj Zizek, London: Verso, 1994.

Arai, Kampo, *Bharat Bhramon Dinopanji* (*Indo Nikki*) [Indian Diary;], trans. Kazuo Azuma, Kolkata: Rabindrabharati University, 1993.

Asia Cooperation Dialogue, http://www.acd.dialogue.org, (Accessed on 12 January 2016).

Atmaprana, Pravajika, *Sister Nivedita*, Kolkata: Sister Nivedita Girls' School, 2007.

'Autobiography', trans. Asitava Das, rpt. in *Rash Behari Bose: Collected Works*, ed. Asitava Das, Kolkata: Kisholoy Prakashon, 2006.

——, 'Japan's Budget Estimate for 1923-4: Notes from Japan', *The Standard Bearer*, III, 20, 16-01-23, rpt. in *Rash Behari Bose: Collected Works*, ed. Asitava Das, Kolkata: Kisholoy Prakashan, 2006.

——, 'Japan's Pariah Problem: Notes from Japan', *The Standard Bearer*, III.15, 5-12-1922, rpt. in *Rash Behari Bose: Collected Works*, ed. Asitava Das, Kolkata: Kisholoy Prakashan, 2006.

——, 'Notes from Japan', *The Standard Bearer*, III. 20. 16-1-23, rpt. in *Rash Behari Bose: Collected Works*, ed. Asitava Das, Kolkata: Kisholoy Prakashan, 2006.

——, 'Russo-Japan Relations: Notes from Japan', *The Standard Bearer*, III.15, 15-12-22, rpt. in *Rash Behari Bose: Collected Works*, ed. Asitava Das, Kolkata: Kisholoy Prakashon, 2006.

Azad, Maulana Abdul Kalam, *India Wins Freedom*, Madras: Orient Longman, 1988.

Azuma, Kazuo, *Japan O Rabindranath: Satoborsher Binimoy* (Japan and Rabindranath: An Exchange of a Century), Kolkata: N.E. Publishers, 2004.

——, *Prasango Rabindranath O Japan* (Rabindranath & Japan), Kolkata: Punoscho, 2010.

——, trans, *Shitoko Horir Dinoponji* (Diary of Shitoku Hori), Kolkata: Visva-Bharati, 1996.

——, *Ujjal Surjo* (The Bright Sun), Kolkata: Subarnarekha, 1996.

Bandyopadhyay, Arunendu, 'Santiniketan-Sthapothorup, Nirmito Paribesh Ebong Rabindranath' (Tagore and the Architectures of Santiniketan), *Visva-Bharati Patrika*, Kartick-Poush 1403 BS (1996), pp. 88-103.

Bandyopadhyay, Sekhar, 'Caste, Widow Remarriage and the Reform of Popular Culture in Colonial Bengal', in *Women and Social Reform in Modern India: A Reader*, ed. Sumit Sarkar &Tanika Sarkar, Bloomington: Indiana: Indiana University Press, 2008.

Bandyopadhyay, Sureshchandra, 'Japaner Naboborsho', (The New Year's Commemoration in Japan), *Bharati*, Boishak (1320 BS,1913), pp. 33-40.

——, *Japan* (Japan), Kolkata: Chatterjee & Co., 1317 (1910). http://dspace.wbpublibnet.gov.in:8080/jspui/, (Accessed on 28 July 2012).

Bassnett, Susan, 'The Empire Travel Writing and British Studies', in *Travel Writing and the Empire*, ed. Sachindra Mohanty, New Delhi: Katha, 2003.

Basu, Sankari Prasad, *Nivedita Lokmata* (Nivedita: The Mother of the Masses), vol. 2, Kolkata: Ananda, 2007.

Benett, Alexander, ed. and trs., *Budo: The Martial Ways of Japan*, Tokyo: Nippon Budokan Foundation, 2009.

Bhargava, Rajul, 'The Psychological Perspective in Translation Studies', in *Literary Translation*, ed. R.S. Gupta, New Delhi: Creative Books, 1999.

'Bharotbashir Japane Shilposhikha', (The Prospect of Attaining Technical Education in Japan for Indians), *Bharati*, Bhadro (1309 BS, 1902), pp. 483-6.

Bharucha, Rustom, *Another Asia*, Kolkata: Oxford University Press, 2006.

Bhattacharya, Amit, *Swadshi Enterprise in Bengal*, Kolkata: Readers Service, 2008.

——, *Transformation of Japan 1600-1945*, Kolkata: Setu Prakashani, 2009.

Bhattacharya, Buddhadev and Niharranjan Roy, *Freedom Struggle and Anushilan Samity*, Kolkata: Anushilan Samity, 1979.

Blanton, Casey, 'Preface', *Travel Writing: The Self and the World*, London: Routledge, 2002.

Bose, Arun Coomer, *Indian Revolutionaries Abroad, 1905-1922: In the Background of International Developments*, Patna: Bharati Bhawan, 1971.

Bose, Jagadish Chandra, 'Letters to Rabindranath Tagore', *Dui Bondhur Chithi Parasparik O Paramparik* (Epistolary Exchange Between Two Friends), Kolkata: Monfakira, 2008.

Bose, Nandalal, 'Bharatsilpe Nobojuger Vumikay Abanindranath' (Abanindranath: The Harbinjer of a New Era in Indian Art), *Paschimbongo: Abanindra Sankha* (1402 BS, 1995), pp. 24-7.

Bose, Rash Behari, 'Autobiography', tr. Asitava Das, rpt. in *Rash Behari Bose: Collected Works*, ed. Asitava Das, Kolkata: Kisholoy Prakashon, 2006.

——, 'Japan's Budget Estimate for 1923-1924: Notes from Japan', *The Standard Bearer*, III.20, 16-1-23, rpt. in *Rash Behari Bose: Collected Works*, ed. Asitava Das, Kolkata: Kisholoy Prakashon, 2006.

——, 'Japan's Pariah Problem: Notes from Japan', *The Standard Bearer*, III.15, 5-12-1922, rpt. in *Rash Behari Bose: Collected Works*, ed. Asitava Das, Kolkata: Kisholoy Prakashon, 2006.

——, 'Notes from Japan', *The Standard Bearer*, III.20, 16-1-23, rpt. in *Rash Behari Bose: Collected Works*, ed. Asitava Das, Kolkata: Kisholoy Prakashon, 2006.

——, 'Russo-Japan Relations: Notes from Japan', *The Standard Bearer*, III.15, 15-12-22, rpt. in *Rash Behari Bose: Collected Works*, ed. Asitava Das, Kolkata: Kisholoy Prakashon, 2006.

——, 'Atmokotha'(Autobiography), rpt. in *Rash Behari Basur Jibankatha O Rachanasangraha*, ed. Asitava Das, Kolkata: Patrolekha, 2014.

Bose, Sugata, *His Majesty's Opponent*, New Delhi: Penguin Books, 2011.

——, *The Nation as Mother and other Visions of Nationhood*, Gurgaon: Penguin Random House India, 2017.

'Burman Buddhist Indignant at Transfer of Management to Hindu Mohant', *Maha Bodhi*, 1937, p. 123 (Anonymous text).

Chaitanya, Krishna, *History of Indian Painting: Modern Period*, New Delhi: Abhinav Publication, 1994, https://books.google.co.in/books/, (Accessed on 20 October 2015).

Chanda, Ipsita, *Reception of the Received*, Kolkata: Jadavpur University, 2006.

Chanda, Rani, *Ghorowa* (Informal Conversations), Kolkata: Visva-Bharati, 1417 BS, 2007.

——, *Silpoguru Abanindranath* (Abanindranath: The Art Maestro), Kolkata: Visva-Bharati, 1406 BS, 1999.

Chandra, Bipan, *India's Struggle for Independence*, New Delhi: Penguin, 1989.

Chattopadhdhya, Kamaladevi, *Japan: Its Weakness and Strength*, Bombay: Padma Publishers, 1944.

Chattopadhyay, Gautam, *Abani Mukherjee: A Dauntless Revolutionary and Pioneering Communist*, Kolkata: People's Publishing House, 1976.

Chattopadhyay, Subodh, trans., 'Keu Noy' (No One), *Bharati*, Joistho 1329 BS, 1922, pp. 189-93.

Chattopadhyay, Suchetana, *Family Papers*, 'Summery of Educational Career and Govt. Service of Dr. N. Gupta; Correspondence of Relatives of Dr. N. Gupta Related to Him', Message to Pratyay Banerjee, (Accessed on 4 March 2018), e-mail.

Chowdhury, Satyajit, 'Okakura Tenshin O Abanindranath', (Okakura Tenshin & Abanindranath), *Visva-Bharati Patrika*, Kartick, 1384 BS, 1977, rpt. in *Visva Bharati Patrika: Nirbachito Probondho Sangraho (1942-2006)*, ed. Amitrosudhan Bhattacharya, Kolkata: Visva-Bharati, 2007.

——, 'Abanindranath: Nandonik Nibondhomala', *Gabeshanar Rakampher* (Abanindranath: Essays on Aesthetics), Kolkata: Karigor, 2014.

Chowdhury, Jogen, 'An Interview on Abanindranath's Paintings', ed. Agnimitra Ghosh, *Paschimbongo: Abanindra Sankha*, 1402 BS, 1995, pp. 93-8.

Clifford, James, *Writing Culture: The Poetics and Politics of Ethnography*, California: University of California, 1986.

Das Gupta, Uma, 'A Cultural Nationalism', *Visva-Bharati Quarterly*, 49, 1-4 May 1983-April 1984, pp. 378-85.

——, ed. *Rabindranath Tagore: My Life in My Words*, New Delhi: Penguin Books, 2006.

——, *Santiniketan and Sriniketan*, Kolkata: Visva-Bharati, October 2009.

Das, Pulin Behari, *Amar Jiban Kahini* (The Story of My Life), Kolkata: Anushilan Samity, 1987.

Das, Ramyansyu Sekhar, *Nandalal Bose and Indian Painting*, Kolkata: Tower Publishers, 1958.

Das, Sarat Chandra, 'Lecture at the Meeting of Indo- Japanese Association', rpt. in *Japan Theke Jorasanko*, ed. Satyasri Ukil, 257-8, Kolkata: New Age, 2005.

'Declaration taken by the Thirty Seven Societies of Japan', *The Modern Review*, May 1919, pp. 558-9 (Anonymous text).

Devi, Hemlata, 'Tibbot Rajye Tinbochor' (Three Years in Tibet), *Prabasi*, Kartick, 1321 BS, 1916, pp. 17-20; Agrahon 178-80; Poush 253-4; Magh 385-9; Joistho 1324 BS, 1917, pp. 140-4; Ashar 300-3; Srabon 408-12; Bhadro 473-7; Ashin 600-6; Kartick 52-7; Agrahon 137-41; Poush 300-6; Magh 340-8; Falgun 482-6; Choitro 531-6 .

Devi, Priyambada, 'Cha Grontho' (The Book of Tea), *Manashi*, 1321 BS, 1914, rpt. in *Sekaler Bangla Samoyikpotre Japan*, ed. Subrata Kumar Das, 145-51, Dhaka: Nabajuga Prokashoni, 2012.

Devi, Protima, *Smriti Chitro* (Reminiscence), Kolkata: Signet Press, 1359 BS, 1952.

Devi, Sarala, *Jiboner Jhora Pata* (The Fallen Leaves), Kolkata: Deys Publishers, 1975.

Dey, Mukulchandra, 'Mukulchandrar Lekha Chithi' (The Letters of Mukulchandra), *Mukulchandra Dey: Japan Theke Jorasanko*, ed. Satyasri Ukil, 3-200, Kolkata: New Age, 2005.

——, *Amar Kotha* (My Life), Kolkata: Visva Bharati, 1995.

——, *My Pilgrimages to Ajanta and Bagh*, London: Thornton Butterworth Limited, 1925.

Dinah, Zank, 'Painting the Life of Buddha: Trans-Culturality, Patronage and Artist's Vision', Ttp://www.academia.edu, (Accessed on 27 December 2015).

Dutta, Bhupendranath, *Oprokashito Rajnoitik Itihash* (Unpublished Political History), Kolkata: Nabobharat Publishers, 1959.

Dutta, Charuchandra, *Purano Kotha* (*Old Tales*), Kolkata: SIB, 2013.

Dutta, Krishna and Andrew Robinson, *Selected Letters of Rabindranath Tagore*, New Delhi: Cambridge University Press, 2005.

'Farewell Ceremony of Nosu and S. Kawaii', *The Maha Bodhi*, 44, 1936, pp. 527-8 (Anonymous text).

Gaikawad, Sampatro, 'A Glimpse of Japan', *Indian Magazine*, 284, August 1894, pp. 389-96.

Gangopadhyay, Manilal, 'Japaner Jhorna' (The Fountains of Japan), *Bharati* Srabon 1320 BS, 1913, pp. 417-21.

Gangopadhyay, Mohanlal, *Dakhiner Baranda* (The Veranda on the South), Kolkata: Visva-Bharati, 1414 BS, 2007.

Ganguly, O.C., 'A Group of Apsaras by a Japanese Artist', *Rupam* (8), October 1921, pp. 6-7, http://archive.org (Accessed on 15 July 2014).

'Geishar Swadhinota' (The Freedom of Geishas), *Bharati*, Poush 1329 BS, 1922, p. 875 (Anonymous text).

Ghosh, Aurobindo, 'Asiatic Democracy', *Bande Mataram*, 1 April 1908, rpt. in *Bande Mataram: Political Writings and Speeches (1890-1908)*, vol. 6 & 7 *The Complete Works of Sri Aurobindo*, Pondichery: Aurobindo Ashram Press, 2002, http://www.aurobindo.ru, (Accessed on 15 June 2015).

——, 'India and Mongolian', *Bande Mataram*, 1 April 1908, rpt. in *Bande Mataram: Political Writings and Speeches (1890-1908)*, vol. 6 & 7.

Ghosh, K.K., *The Indian National Army*, Meerut: Meenakshi Prakashan, 1969.

Ghosh, Manmatha Nath, *Japan Probash* (Japan Expatriation), Dhaka: Dibya Prokash, 2012.

——, *Nabyo Japan* (The New Japan), Kolkata: Sri Devaki Press, 1322 BS, 1915, http://dspace.wbpublibnet.gov.in:8080/ (Accessed on 17 July 2012).

——, *Supto Japan (The Eternal Japan)*, Kolkata: Sri Devaki Press, 1322 BS, 1915.

Glotefelty, Cheryll and Harold Fromm, *The Ecocriticism Reader*, Athens: University of Georgia Press, 1996.

Goldstein, Gidoni Olfa, 'Kimono and the Construction of Gendered and Cultural Identities', http://people.socsci.tau.ac.il, 2001 (Accessed on 17 July 2013).

Goswami, Parimal, *Smritichitra* (Memoirs), Kolkata: Protikhon, 1400 BS, 1993.

Govt. of India, Records of the National Archive, Foreign and Political Department, *Letters from his Holiness the Dalai Lama to Kawaguchi.*, F.N. 10/1918.

Govt. of India, Records of the National Archives, Foreign and Political Department, *Proceedings of the Pan-Asiatic Conference Held at Nagasaki*, F.N.526/1926.

Govt. of India, Records of the National Archives, Foreign and Political Department, publication of an article in the Japanese newspaper, *'Keijo Simpo'*, F.N.41-42/1911.

Govt. of India, Records of the National Archives, Foreign and Political Department, publication of a book entitled *'India and Indians by one J. Sano, a Japanese Professor of Jujutsu'.* F.N.21/1918.

Govt. of West Bengal, Records of the State Archives, Home Political, *History of Agitation Against Bengal Partition*, Calcutta, Dated the 25 January 1906, F.N. 25/1906.

Govt. of West Bengal, Records of the State Archives, Home Political, *Memorandum on the History of Terrorism in India (1905-1933)*, F.N. 172/1905.

Govt. of West Bengal, Home Political, Records of the State Archives, *Trade after the War: Japanese Activities*, F.N. 36/1919.

Govt. of West Bengal, Records of the State Archives, Home Political, *Report on the Indian Newspapers and Periodical*, January-March 1906.

Govt. of West Bengal, I.B. Records of the State Archives, *Proposal to Send Revolutionaries to the Far East in Connection with Arms Smuggling*, F.N. 164/1927.

Govt. of West Bengal, I.B. Records of the State Archives, *Proscription of a Bengali Book Entitled Sun Yat-sen by Sri Narendranth Roy*, F.N. 350/1925.

Govt. of West Bengal. I.B. Records of the State Archives, *Proscription of the Book Entitled, Biplabi Abani Mukherjee*, F.N. 11/1930.

Govt. of West Bengal, Records of the State Archives, *Riot by Passengers of the S.S. 'Komagata Maru' at Budge Budge, Home Political*, F.N. 322/1914.

Govt. of West Bengal, I.B. Records of the State Archives, *Visit of Two Japanese Employees of the South Manchurian Railway Company to India*, F.N. 137/1923.

Gupta, H.R., *Life and Letters of Sir Jadunath Sarkar*, Hoshiarpur: University of Punjab, 1958.

Guha, Ramchandra, *Makers of Modern Asia*, Cambridge: Harvard University Press, 2014.

Guha Thakurta, Tapati, *Monuments, Objects, Histories*, New York: Columbia University Press, 2004.

Halder, Jibantara, *Anushilan Samitir Itihash* (The History of Anushilan Samiti), Kolkata: Sutradhar, 2009.

Hay, Stephen, *Asian Ideas of East and West*, Bombay: Oxford University Press, 1970.

Hearn, Lafcadio and Basil Hall, 'Some Characteristics of Modern Japanese Life and Character', *Dawn*, May 1903, rpt. in *The Dawn*, ed. Madhabendra Nath Mitra, vol.VI, pp. 284-8, Kolkata: National Council of Education, 2005.

Heehs, Peter, *The Bomb in Bengal*, Oxford: Oxford University Press, 2004.

Hori, Shitoku, 'Japaner Sanaton Adorsho' (The Heritage of Japan), *Bharati*, Baishak 1310 BS, 1903, pp. 90-4.

Horioka, Yasuko, 'Okakura and Swami Vivekananda', *Prabuddha Bharata*, January1975, pp. 30-4; March 1975, pp. 140-4.

Hotta, Eri, *Pan-Asianism and Japan's War (1931-1945)*, New York: Palgrave Macmillan, 2007.

Iida, Yumiko, 'Fleeing the West, Making Asia Home: Transposition of Otherness in Japanese Pan-Asianism, 1905-30', *Alternatives: Global, Local, Political*, 32, 3 July to September 1997, http://*www.jstor.org*, (Accessed on 23 May 2014.)

'Indo-Japanese Painting', *Rupam* (10), April 1922, pp. 39-42 (Anonymous text), *https://archive.org/* (Accessed on 15 July 2014).

'Japan O Bharotborsho' (Japan and India), *Prabasi* Chaitro 1310 BS, 1903, pp. 509-15 (Anonymous text).

'Japan's Annexation of Korea', *The Modern Review*, September 1910, p. 345 (Anonymous text).

'Japan''s War Against China', *The Maha Bodhi*, 45, 1937, pp. 428-9 (Anonymous text).

'Japane Bharatiyo Chatro (The Indian Student in Japan), Poush 1309 BS, 1902, pp. 893-903 (Anonymous text).

'Japane Sikhar Obostha' (Japanese Education System), *Prabasi* Agrahon 1343 BS, 1936, pp. 297-8 (Anonymous text).

'Japaner Netribrinder Bichar' (The Trial of Japanese Leaders), *Prabasi* Agrahan 1355 BS, 1948, p. 114 (Anonymous text).

'Japanese Demands: Stronger Garrison in North China', *The Statesman*, 11 January 1936. 'Japanider Bharatbarshe Boudhdhormo Prochar Chestha', (Japanese Mission of Popularising Buddhism in India), *Prabasi*. Poush 1343 BS, 1936, p. 473 (Anonymous text).

Kanungoe, Hemchandra, *Banglai Biplab Prachesta* (The Efforts to Create a Revolution in Bengal), Kolkata: Radical Impression, 2016.

Kapur, K.D., 'India and Japan Strategic Partnership in the Emerging Global

Scenario', *India and Japan in Search of Global Roles*, ed. Rajaram Panda and Yoo Fukazawa, New Delhi: Promilla & Co., 2007.

Kar, Chintamoni, 'Introduction', *Souveneir on Gaganendranath Tagore*, Kolkata: Academy of Fine Arts, 1957.

Kawaguchi, Ekai, *Three Years in Tibet*, Benares and London: Theosophical Publishing Society, 1909, http://archive.org, (Acceesseed on 13 April 2012).

Kawakita, Michiaki, *Modern Japanese Painting: the Force of the Tradition*, Tokyo: Toto Bunka Company, 1957, https://archive.org/, (Accessed on 10 February 2014).

Keenleyside, T.A., 'Nationalist Indian Attitudes Towards Asia', *Pacific Affairs*, 55.2, Summer, 1982, http://www.jstor.org (Accessed on 23 June 2014).

Kenichi, Matsumoto, 'Okakura Tenshin and the Ideal of Pan-Asianism', in *Shadows of the Past: Of Okakura Tenshin and Pan-Asianism*, ed. Brij Tankha, Kolkata: Sampark, 2007.

Kiguchi, Junko, 'Japanese Women's Rights at the Miji Era', http://www.soka.ac.jp, (Accessed on 12 December 2012).

Kimura, Nikki (Ryukan), 'My Memory about the Late Rash Behari Bose', *Rash Behari Bose: His Struggle for India's Independence*, ed. Radhanath Rath, Kolkata: Biplabi Mahanayak Rash Behari Bose Smarok Samity, 1963.

——, *A Historical Study of the Terms Hinayana and Mahayana and the Origin of Mahayayana Buddhism*, Kolkata: Calcutta University, 1927.

Kowshik, Dinkar, *Nandalal Bose: The Doyen of Indian Art*, New Delhi: National Book Trust, 2001.

——, *Okakura*, Kolkata: Patralekha, 2011.

Kumar, R. Siva, 'Abanindranath: From Cultural Nationlism to Modernism', *Nandan*, XVI, 1996: 49-68.

——, 'Some Intra-Asian Transactions in Art India and Japan' *Nandan*, XXVI, 2006: 23-30.

Kuwajima, Sho, *Indian Mutiny in Singapore*, Kolkata: Ratna Prakashan, 1991.

Lala, R.M., *For the Love of India*, New Delhi: Penguin, 2004.

Latourette, Kenneth Scott, *The History of Japan*, New York: Macmillan Co., 1968.

Lockard, Lauren, *Geisha: Behind the Painted Smile*, http://www.scribd.com. (Accessed on 27 April 2013).

Mandal, Panchanan, *Bharatsilpi Nandalal* (Nandalal: The Indian Artist), 4 vols., Santiniketan: Rar-Gabeshona Parshod, 1982.

——, 'Bharatsilpe Nabojuger Vumikay Abanindranath' (Abanindranath and the New Era in Indian Art), *Visva-Bharati Patrika*, Kartick-Choitro 1383 BS, 1976, pp. 23-32.

Mandal, Sujit Kumar, ed., *Bideshi Fuler Gucho* (Bouquet of Foreign Flowers), Kolkata: Papyrus, 2011.

Mayo, Marlene J., 'Introduction', *The Emergance of Imperial Japan,* ed. Marlene J. Mayo, Massachusetts: D.C. Health and Co., 1970, pp. vii-xiv.

Mohanty, Sachindra, 'Introduction: Beyond the Imperial Eye', *Travel Writing and the Empire,* ed. Sachindra Mohanty, pp. x-xxi, New Delhi: Katha, 2003.

Mukherjee, Abhijit, 'Tagore's First Visit', *Tagore and Japan: Dialogue, Exchange and Encounter,* ed. Pratyay Banerjee, Anindya Kundu, New Delhi: Synergy Publishers, 2016.

Mukherjee, Benode Behari, 'Abanindranath', *Paschimbongo: Abanindra Sankha,* 1402 BS, 1995, pp. 27-32.

——, 'Abanindranather Chobi' (The Paintings of Abanindranath), *Visva Bharati Patrika,* Kartick-Choitro 1383 BS, 1976, pp. 291-301.

——, 'E.B.Havell', *Visva- Bharati Quarterly,* 25.3 & 4, 1960, pp. 61-76.

——, 'Introduction', *Abanindranath Tagore: His Early Work,* Kolkata: Indian Museum, 2006.

——, 'The Art of Gaganendranath Tagore', *Visva-Bharati Quarterly,* May-July 1949, pp. 6-12, http://dspace.wbpublibnet.gov.in:8080/ (Accessed on 20 October 2015).

Mukherjee, Benodebehari, *Chitrakar* (The Painter), Kolkata: Aruna Prokashoni, 1414 BS, 2007.

Mukherjee, Uma, *Two Great Revolutionaries,* Kolkata: Firma K.L. Mukhopadhyay, 1966.

Mukhopadhyay, Dhirendranath, 'Japan', *Bharatbarsa,* 1346BS, 1939, Bhadro, pp. 395-403.

Mukhopadhyay, Girindrachandra, 'Japan', *Bharatbarsa,* 1344 BS, 1937, Ashin, pp. 611-13.

Mukhopadhyay, Madhusudhan, *Jepan* (Japan), Kolkata: Calcutta School Book and Vernacular Literature Society, 1863, http://dspace.wbpublibnet. gov.in: 8080, (Accessed on 12 May 2012).

'Mulagandhakuti Frescoes Declared Open', *The Mahu Bodhii,* 44. 1936, pp. 2/8-82 (Anonymous writing).

Nakajima, Takeshi, 'The Tokyo Tribunal, Justice Pal and the Revisionist Distortion of History', *Asia-Pacific Journal/Japan Focus,* https://apjjf.org/2011/9/44/Nakajima-Takeshi/3627/article.html (Accessed on 12 December 2015).

——, *Bose of Nakamuraya: An Indian Revolutionary in Japan,* New Delhi: Promilla & Co., 2009.

Narashimhan, Sushila, 'India and Japan: Historical and Cultural Linkages', *India and Japan in Search of Global Roles,* ed. Rajaram Panda, Yoo Fukazawa, New Delhi: Promilla & Co., 2007.

Nath, Gourchandra, 'Japaner Sikhaniti' (The Education Policy of Japan), *Bharatbarsa*, Srabon 1346 BS, 1939, pp. 258-62.

Niwa, Kyoko, 'Rabindranath Tagore and Japan: On His Visit with His Message and its Results', *Tagore and Japan: Dialogue,Exchange and Encounter*, ed. Pratyay Banerjee and Anindya Kundu, New Delhi: Synergy Publishers, 2016.

——, 'Rabindranath Tagore and Noguchi Yonejiro', *Tagore and Japan: Dialogue, Exchange and Encounter*, ed. Pratyay Banerjee, Anindya Kundu, New Delhi: Synergy Publishers, 2016.

——, 'Rabindranath Tagore and Japan', Thesis, Jadavpur University, 1987.

Nosu, Kosetsu, http://www.chitralekha.org/the-archives, Web (Accessed on 18 June 2014.

Ohsawa, J.G., *Two Great Indian in Japan: Rash Behari Bose & Subhas Chandra Bose*, Kolkata: Kusa Publications, 1954.

Okakura, Kakuzo, 'Letters to a Friend', *Visva-Bharati Quarterly*, 21.2 Autumn 1955, pp. 181-208.

——, *Awakening of Japan*, New York: The Century Co., 1905, https://www.gutenberg.org/ (Accessed on 31 December 2012).

——, *The Book of Tea*, U.S.A.: Dreamsymth, 1906, https://www.tug.org (Accessed on 12 June 2012).

——, *The Ideals of the East, with Special Reference to the Art of Japan*, California: Stone Bridge Press, 2012.

Onishi, Norimitsu, 'Decades After War Trials, Japan Still Honours a Dissenting Judge', *The New York Times*, 31 August 2007, http://mobile.nytimes.com, (Accessed on 17 December 2015).

Palit, Chittabrata, and Subrata Pahri, ed., *Satish Chandra Mukherje: The Dawn Society and National Science*, Kolkata: Readers Service, 2002.

Panda, Nabin, 'Tagore and Japanese Language: From the Writings of Sano Jinnosuke', *Tagore and Japan: Dialogue, Exchange and Encounter*, ed. Pratyay Banerjee and Anindya Kundu, Kolkata: Synergy, 2016.

——, 'Language Learning Transcending Boundaries: The Japanese Language in India and Indian Languages in Japan', *India and Japan in Search of Global Roles*, ed. Rajaram Panda and Yoo Fukazawa, New Delhi: Promilla & Co., 2007.

Pearson, W.W., 'On an Indian Image Found in Japan', *The Modern Review* September 1917, pp. 260-1.

Pizer, John, 'Goethe's, "World Literature", Paradigm and Contemporary Cultural Globalization', *Comparative Literature*, vol. 52, no. 2, Summer 2000, pp. 213-27, http://www.jstor.org/stable/1771407 (Accessed on 26 October 2014).

Plumptre, Constance, 'Progress in Japan', *Indian Magazine*, 1886, pp. 226-36.

——, 'The Education in Japan', *Indian Magazine* 187, July 1886, pp. 327-47.

Pratt, Mary Louise, *Imperial Eyes: Travel Writing and Transculturation*, London: Routledge, 2008.

Rabindra Bhavana Archives, Santiniketan, *Letter from Rathindranath Tagore to Kizow Inazu of Tanagawa University*, F.N. 176.2.

Rabindra Bhavana Archives, Santiniketan, S. Kusumoto, *A Letter to Rabindranath Tagore*, dated 31 March 1931, F.N. 176.1.21.

Rai, Lajpat, 'Education in Japan', *The Modern Review*, September 1910, pp. 296-305.

Richardson, Margaret, 'Understanding the Importance of Eclecticism: K.G. Subramanyan and Twentieth-Century Indian Art', *Southeast Review of Asian Studies*, vol. 29, 2007, pp. 240-7, http://*www.highbeam.com*, (Accessed on 18 August 2015).

Roy, Ganapati, 'Japaner Sikha' (The Education System of Japan), *Bharati*, Bhadro1317 BS, 1910, pp. 374-8.

Roy, M.N., *M.N. Roy's Memoir*, Bombay: Allied Publishers, 1964.

Roy, Supriya, *Makers of a Mission: 1901-41*, Santiniketan: Rabindra Bhavana, 2001.

Saaler, Seven, 'Pan Asianism in Meiji and Taisho Japan-A Preliminary Framework', http://www.dijtokyo.org (Accessed on 30 November 2015).

Sankrityayana, Rahul, *Meri Jeevan Yatra* (*Amar Jibon Jatra/The Journey of My Life)*, trans. & ed. Satish Mashro, Saikat Rakhit, vol. 2, Kolkata: Rahul Sankrityayana Jonmosotoborso Committee, 1993.

Sanyal, Brajosundor, 'Japane Stri Sikha' (Women's Education in Japan), *Prabasi*, Agrahan 1315 BS, 1908, pp. 435-40.

Sareen, T.R., 'India and Japan in Historical Perspectives', *India and Japan in Search of Global Roles*, ed. Rajaram Panda and Yoo Fukazawa, New Delhi: Promilla & Co., 2007.

Sarkar, Anathbandhu, 'Japane Bharatiyo Chatrer Koto Bay Hoy' (How Much Does an Indian Student Have to Pay in Japan?), *Prabasi*, Chaitro 1315 BS, 1908, pp. 709-710.

Sarkar, Binoy Kumar, 'Markine Japani Mlecho' (Japanese People: The Outcaste in the United States), *Bharati* Magh 1322 BS, 1915, pp. 953-6.

——, 'Japaner Dilli' (The Delhi of Japan), *Bharatbarsa*, Jaistho 1317 BS, 1910, *Sekaler Bangla Samoyikpotre Japan*, ed. Subrata Kumar Das, Dhaka: Nabajuga Prokashoni, 2012, pp. 112-30.

Sarkar, Jadunath, 'Japaner Sikha O Banijyo', (Education & Commerce in Japan), *Bharati*, Joistho 1321 BS, 1914, pp. 145-51.

——, 'Daidokoro', (Kitchen in Japan), *Bharati*, Magh 1320 BS, 1913, pp. 1065-70.

——, 'Japaner Rail O Tram' (Japanese Railway and Trams), *Bharati*, Falgun 1319 BS, 1912, pp. 1131-8.

——, 'Japaner Rajniti' (Japanese Politics), *Bharati*, Joistho 1313 BS, 1906, pp. 176-207.

——, 'Japaner Sena O Nau Bahini' (Japanese Army and Navy), *Bharati*, Falgun 1318 BS, 1911, pp. 1061-70.

——, 'Japaner Sohit Bharater Sombondho' (India's Relation with Japan), *Bharati*, Jaistho 1319 BS, 1912, pp. 125-32.

——, 'Japaner Songbadpotro' (The Newspapers of Japan), *Bharati*, Magh 1317 BS, 1912, pp. 870-4.

——, 'Mikado', *Bharati*, Ashin 1319 BS, 1912, pp. 660-8.

——, 'Japani Akriti Prokriti' (Japanese People: Their Look and Features), *Bharati*, Boishak 1318 BS, 1911, pp. 41-9.

Sarkar, Kamal, *Rupodokho Gaganendranath* (Gaganendranath: The Master of Art), Kolkata: Rabindra Bharati Society, 1986.

Sarkar, Prabir Bikash, *Jana Ojana Japan* (Known and Unknown Facts about Japan), Tokyo, Manchitro, 2007.

Sarkar, Sumit, *Modern India*, New Delhi: Macmillan India Limited, 1983.

——, *Modern Times: India 1880s to 1950s*, New Delhi: Permanent Black, 2015.

Sastri, Shakuntala Rao, trans., *A Visit to Japan by Rabindranath Tagore*, New York: East West Institute, 1961.

Sen, Amita, *Ananda Sarvokaje* (Joy in Every Work), Kolkata: Tagore Reserch Institute, Rabindra Charcha Bhavan, March 1983.

Sen, S.P., ed., *Dictionary of National Biographies*, Kolkata: Institute of Historical Studies, 1972.

Sentou (Japanese Public Bath), http://www.japan-101.com/travel/sento.htm (Accessed on 12 December 2012).

Shigemi, Inaga, 'Okakura Kakuzo and India: The Trajectory of Modern National Consciousness and Pan-Asian Ideology Across Borders', tr. Kevin Singleton, *Review of Japanese Culture and Society*, December 2012, pp. 39-57, http://www.jstor.org (Accessed on 23 May 2014).

——, 'Tenshin Okakura Kakuzu and Siter Nivedita: On an Intellectual Exchange in Modernizing Asia', *Japanese Studies Beyond Borders: International Conference on Japanese Studies. Warsaw*, 19-21 May 2006, pp. 1-5, http://*www.jstor.org/stable/42801041*, (Accessed on 24 May 2014).

——, 'The Interaction of Bengali and Japanese Artistic Milieus in the First Half of the Twentieth Century (1901-45): Rabindranath Tagore, Arai Kampo and Nandalal Bose', *Japan Review*, 2009, pp. 149-81, (Accessed on 26 May 2015).

Singh, Babu Gurdit, *Voyage of Komagata Maru, or India's Slavery Abroad,* British Columbia: University of British Columbia, 1989.

Sister, Nivedita, 'India the Mother', *Selected Essays of Sister Nivedita,* Madras: Ganesh,1911, http://archive.or (Accessed on 12 July 2013).

——, 'Japan and Korea', *The Modern Review,* (July-December 1907), rpt. in *The Complete Works of Sister Nivedita,* vol. 5, Kolkata: Advaita Ashram, 1999.

Some, Nagendrachandra, 'Japani Akhanmala' (Narratives of Japan), *Prabasi,* Ashin 1311 BS, 1904, pp. 304-20.

Sutiiste, Elin, 'A Crow on a Bare Branch: A Comparison of Matsuo Basho's Haiku "Kare Eda Ni" and its English Translations', www.researchgate.net/publication (30 June 2016).

Swami,Vivekananda, 'Conversations and Dialogues', *Complete Works,* 4th ed., vol. 5, Kolkata: Advaita Ashrama, 1936, pp. 244-322.

——, 'Letter from Yokohama', Epistles, in *Complete Works,* 4th ed., vol. 5, pp. 3-9, Kolkata: Advaita Ashrama, 1936.

——, 'The Abroad & the Problems at Home (*The Hindu,* Madras, February 1897) in *Complete Works,* 4th ed., vol. 5, pp. 139-47, Kolkata: Advaita Ashrama, 1936.

Tagore, Abanindranath, *Letter to Krishna Deb Burman, Nandan,* December 1986, pp. 22-3.

——, 'E.B. Havell', *Abanindra Rachanaboli,* vol. 9, Kolkata: Prakash Bhavan, 2011.

——, *Jorasankor Dhare* (By the Side of Jorasanko), Kolkata: Visva-Bharati, 1418 BS, 2011.

——, *Letter to Havell, Baishakhi: Abanindra Sankha,* 22, 2012-13, p. 165.

——, 'Obituary of Okakura Tenshin', *Bharati,* Kartick 1320 BS, 1917, pp. 803.

Tagore, Jyotirindranath, 'Adhunik Japan' (Modern Japan), *Bharati,* 1315 BS, 1908, Boishak 18-25, Joistho 84-9, Ashar 133-40, Srabon 175-79, Bhadro 217-20, Ashin, pp. 267 73.

Tagore, Rabindranath, 'Art and Tradition', *Rabindranath Tagore: Philosophy of Education and Painting,* ed. Devi Prasad, New Delhi: National Book Trust, 2008.

——, 'Buddhadeva', *Visva-Bharati Quarterly,* 22.3, 1956-7, pp. 169-76.

——, *Chelebela* (My Chilhood), Kolkata: Visva-Bharati, 1396 BS, 1986.

——, *Gora,* Kolkata: Visva-Bharati, Ashar 1389 BS, 1982.

——, *Gora,* trans., rpt. in *Rabindranath Tagore Omnibus I,* New Delhi: Rupa & Co., 2011.

——, 'India and Japan', rpt. in *Japan Theke Jorasanko,* ed. Satyasri Ukil, Kolkata: New Age, 2005, pp. 265-75.

——, *Japan Jatri* (Voyage to Japan), Kolkata: Visva Bharati, 1417 BS, 2000.

——, *Letter to Abanindranath Tagore, Visva-Bharati Patrika*, Magh-Chotro 1353 BS, 1946, p. 136.

——, *Letter to Gaganendranath Tagore, Visva-Bharati Patrika*, Magh-Chotro 1353 BS, 1946, pp. 134-5.

——, 'Letters to Jagadish Chandra Bose', *Dui Bondhur Chithi Parasparik O Paramparik*, Kolkata: Monfakira, 2008.

——, *Letter to Dr. Takakusu*, dated 31 August 1929, Rabindra Bhavana Archives, FN. Eng. 176/1.

——, 'My School', *Lectures & Addresses by Rabindranath Tagore*, Delhi: Macmillan, 2001.

——, *Nationalism*, rpt. in *Rabindranath Tagore Omnibus III*, New Delhi: Rupa & Co., 2011.

——, *Sfulingo* (Spark), Kolkata: Visva Bharati, 1397 BS, 1992.

——, *Talks in Japan*, ed. Supriya Roy, Kolkata: Shizen, 2007.

——, *The Soul of the East*, April 1925, rpt. in *Japan Jatri*, Rabindranath Tagore. Kolkata: Visva-Bharati, 1417 BS, 2007, pp. 126-33.

——, 'The Message from India to Japan', rpt. in *Japan Theke Jorasanko*, ed. Satyasri Ukil, Kolkata: New Age, 2005, pp. 265-75.

——, 'The Spirit of Japan', 10 July 2010, *Project Gutenberg*, Web. 18 May 2013.

——, ' To the Memory of Mr. K. Okakura', *The Modern Review*, 1916, rpt., in *Japan Jatri* by Rabindranath Tagore, Kolkata: Visva-Bharati, 2007, pp. 160-3.

——, 'To The Indian Community in Japan', April 1925, rpt. in *Japan Jatri*, Rabindranath Tagore, pp. 117-25, Kolkata: Visva Bharati, 1417 BS, 2007.

Tagore, Rathindranath, *On the Edges of Time*, Kolkata: Visva Bharati, 2010.

Tagore, Surendranath, 'Kakuzu Okakura', *Visva-Bharati Quarterly*, 25.3 & 4, 1960, pp. 50-60, http://dspace.wbpublibnet.gov.in:8080/jspui/, (Accessed on 25 December 2013).

Takeda, Hariprobha, 'Japane Santan Palon O Nari Sikha (Child Rearing in Japan and Women's Education), *Bongo Mahilar Japan Jatra O Onnano Rachona*, Kolkata: D.M. Library, 2009.

——, 'Japaner Nari', (Women in Japan), rpt. in *Bongo Mahilar Japan Jatra O Onnano Rachona*, pp. 59-62, Kolkata: D.M. Library, 2009.

——, *Bongo Mahilar Japan Jatra O Onnano Rachona* (A Bengali Woman's Visit to Japan), Kolkata: D.M. Library, 2009.

Tankha, Brij Madhavi Thampi, *Narratives of Asia from India, Japan and China*, Kolkata: Sampark, 2005.

——, 'Writing a Good History on a Modern Plan', in *Shadows of the Past: Of Okakura Tenshin and Pan-Asianism*, ed. Brij Tankha, Kolkata: Sampark, 2007.

'The East India Company in Japan', *Calcutta Review*, 95-96, 1869, pp. 187-92 (Anonymous text).

'Three Bengali Students in Japan', *Prabasi*, Miscellaneous section, Poush 1316 BS, 1909, p. 759 (Anonymous text).

Trivedi, Harish, 'Translating Culture vs. Cultural Translation', *Translation and Culture: Indian Perspective*, ed. G.J.V. Prasad, New Delhi: Pencraft International, 2010.

Valinsigha, Devapriya, 'Mulagandhakuti Vihara: A New Link Binding India to Japan', *The Maha Bodhii* 44, 1936, pp. 273-6.

Visvesvaraya, M., *Reconstructing India*, London: P.S. King & Son, 1920.

——, *Memoirs of My Working Life*, Bombay: G. Claridge & Co., 1951.

Wakakuwa, Midori, 'Japanese Cultural Identity and Nineteenth Century Asian Nationalism: Okakura Tenshin and Swami Vivekananda', in *Shadows of the Past: Of Okakura Tenshin and Pan-Asianism*, ed. Brij Tankha, Kolkata: Sampark, 2007.

Williams, Raymond, *Marxism and Literature*, Oxford: Oxford University Press, 2009.

Yojimbo, Dir. Akira Kurosawa, Perf. Toshiro Mifune, Eijiro Tono, 1961.

Index